BUFFALO
and the
PRESIDENTS

An Account of the American Presidents' Connections

to the Queen City, Including their Visits to the Area

Martin S. Nowak

AMERICAN HISTORY PRESS
STAUNTON VIRGINIA

Copyright © 2017 Martin S. Nowak

All rights reserved. No part of this book may be transmitted in any form by any means electronic, mechanical or otherwise using devices now existing or yet to be invented without prior written permission from the publisher and copyright holder.

American History Press

Staunton, Virginia
(888) 521-1789
Visit us on the Internet at:
www.Americanhistorypress.com

First Printing July 2017

To schedule an event with the author or to inquire about bulk discount sales please contact American History Press.

Library of Congress Cataloging-in-Publication Data

Names: Nowak, Martin S., 1951- author.
Title: Buffalo and the presidents : an account of the American presidents' connections and visits to the Queen City / Martin S. Nowak.
Description: Staunton, Virginia : American History Press, 2017. | Includes bibliographical references and index.
Identifiers: LCCN 2017027816 (print) | LCCN 2017028066 (ebook) | ISBN 9781939995247 (E-book) | ISBN 9781939995230 (pbk. : alk. paper)
Subjects: LCSH: Presidents--Travel--New York (State)--Buffalo--History. | Buffalo (N.Y.)--History. | Presidents--United States--History.
Classification: LCC F129.B857 (ebook) | LCC F129.B857 N69 2017 (print) | DDC 973.09/9--dc23
LC record available at https://lccn.loc.gov/2017027816

Manufactured in the United States of America on acid-free paper. This book exceeds all ANSO standards for archival quality.

To Larry

CONTENTS

Acknowledgments	vi
Preface	vii
1. The Early Years	1
2. Millard Fillmore	25
3. Liberty and Free Soil	44
4. Zachary Taylor	65
5. Lincoln, Johnson and Grant	70
6. Grover Cleveland	101
7. The Late Nineteenth Century	126
8. President McKinley and the Pan-American Exposition	145
9. Into the Twentieth Century	173
10. FDR, Depression, War and Recovery	214
11. The Modern Era	250
12. The Twenty-First Century	275
Epilogue	283
Appendix	285
Notes	290
Bibliography	307
Index	317
About the Author	324

ACKNOWLEDGMENTS

Putting together a book such as this requires the cooperation and help of a host of people. I thank the several institutions, organizations and individuals who rendered assistance and other kindnesses and courtesies. Among them are the staffs of the following: Buffalo and Erie County Library system; State University of New York at Buffalo libraries; Niagara Falls, Ontario Public Library; Butler Library at State University College at Buffalo, especially Linda Webster; and the Buffalo History Museum, especially Cynthia Van Ness.

It was a pleasure corresponding and meeting with Bren T. Price of the Association for a Buffalo Presidential Center, who provided invaluable help with his compilations. Daniel Blachaniec was helpful in solving word processing problems and glitches.

Finally, I want to thank my husband Larry Grabowski for his patience and understanding during the long months that this book was under development. He helped me in more ways than he realizes.

PREFACE

For a city and metropolitan area of its size, Buffalo, New York has had an outsized connection to the presidency of the United States. In a state dominated by one of the largest cities in the world—New York City—the political impact of Buffalo is remarkable. Two Buffalonians, Millard Fillmore and Grover Cleveland, became president of the United States. In addition, William McKinley, our twenty-fifth president, was shot and killed in Buffalo. He was succeeded in office by his vice president, Theodore Roosevelt, who took the oath of office at the home of Ansley Wilcox on Delaware Avenue. It should not be forgotten that Buffalo also produced one vice president, the aforesaid Millard Fillmore, who served in Zachary Taylor's cabinet before the latter's death. Besides Mr. Fillmore, there have been two other area residents who have been major party vice presidential candidates, William E. Miller in 1964 and Jack F. Kemp in 1996. Two women who were trailblazers in presidential politics had ties to Buffalo, Belva Ann Lockwood and Shirley Chisholm. Indeed, although never the site of a major party's national convention, two historically important minor parties held their conventions in Buffalo in the 1840s. At least twenty incumbent presidents have visited the Buffalo area and several others were in the city either before they reached the White House or as former presidents

This book delves into the details of these presidents' visits before, during, and after their presidencies. While presenting the facts, it also provides background context of these events as needed. While the narratives of the lives of Fillmore and Cleveland and the events surrounding the assassination of President McKinley might be considered lengthy, these subjects could hardly be glossed over in any book concerning the Buffalo-presidency connection.

The author has relied extensively on contemporary local newspapers for many of the details of these visits to the Queen City. For many decades multiple papers were published in the city at the same time. These provide contrasting accounts and opinions of the presidential visits, e.g., about the citizens' reactions to a visit, and were often influenced by the political affiliation of the paper. Also, one newspaper may have supplied details that another did not. Since 1982, only one daily newspaper has been published in Buffalo, which naturally restricts the written record of presidential visits to the area.

Of course, for background information and biographies, a number of books proved invaluable. They were also useful for making interesting, if obscure, connections. The internet also proved to be a good source of basic facts, information and clues, which opened the door to further research. Wherever possible, these facts have been cross-checked. In addition, a good bit of old-fashioned serendipity led the author to a few unexpected discoveries.

All available sources have been examined insofar as time has allowed. The conclusions reached are the author's alone and any mistakes of fact or omission are solely his.

Some of the details revealed in this book had remained buried for decades before being brought to light again. But this is not to say that other connections between Buffalo and the presidents, or other visits to the area by distinguished men and women, do not exist. They indeed may.

It is hoped that the pages which follow contribute something of value to the growing number of monographs concerning the history of Buffalo and the Niagara Frontier.

CHAPTER 1

THE EARLY YEARS

George Washington

When George Washington became the first president of the United States in 1789, what would later become the city of Buffalo was a tiny, insignificant settlement on the banks of the Buffalo River. Probably comprised of only two log cabins, if known by any name at all it was called the Buffalo Creek settlement. In the year 1758 the first person of European descent constructed dwellings and settled on the land that would become the port and city of Buffalo, after being ordered to do so by the French government in Quebec.[1] That person was Daniel Joncaire, more formally known as Chabert de Joncaire de Clausanne Daniel-Marie. He was a Quebec-born French citizen, son of the more well known French agent Louis Thomas de Joncaire, and his mother is believed to have been a Native American Indian.

Daniel Joncaire's little settlement on the south bank of Buffalo Creek lasted for a little over a year.[2] Its purpose was to act both as a trading center with the local Seneca tribe and as a communications link between French outposts along the Niagara River and those located farther to the south in present day northwestern Pennsylvania. Joncaire was an interpreter, negotiator, liaison and friendship ambassador between the Seneca and the French. Though he was a French citizen, he had previously lived among the Seneca and was considered an adopted member of the tribe. He also served as a French military officer and as such was involved in countering British influence on the Niagara Frontier and extending

French settlements and influence south to the Allegheny and Ohio Rivers.

The British forced Joncaire off his land at Buffalo Creek when they invaded Fort Niagara and the surrounding area. The contentions between the British and the French along the Niagara Frontier and south of Lake Erie would eventually lead to the French and Indian War in 1754, which would result in the British takeover of French Canada.

It must be noted that Daniel's identity was often confused by his contemporaries, as well as by historians since then, with that of his elder brother Philippe Thomas, as well as their father Louis Thomas. As such, it is sometimes not clear to which man various accounts refer. It is known that Daniel and his brother Philippe were both employed by the French as agents to the Indians and were French military officers familiar with the Niagara Frontier. In late 1753, five years prior to Daniel Joncaire's settlement at Buffalo Creek, either he or his brother, or possibly both, were sent southward from Niagara toward the Ohio River and into western Pennsylvania with others. Their purpose was to establish a French presence on the Ohio and in the surrounding country in opposition to both the native tribes and the British, who were already present in the area. In early December 1753 one of the Joncaires, along with two other officers, arrived at an abandoned English officer's house at Venango, in present day Franklin, Pennsylvania, and set up their quarters there. Most accounts seem to point to Philippe Joncaire as the brother present at Venango,[3] since he is referred to as Captain Joncaire, a rank Philippe achieved, but as far as is known, Daniel did not.

At about the same time a small band of eight white men and four American Indians sent by the British arrived in the area. They were led by Major George Washington of Virginia, whose purpose it was to deliver a message from Governor Dinwiddie of that colony to the French commander in the region demanding that the French should cease incursions into the area. Virginia claimed the territory as its own, and the British had already established a presence there.[4] Only twenty-one years old at the time, Major Washington had learned of Joncaire's presence at Venango and so had led his party to meet the Frenchman at the house they had seized as their headquarters. This occurred on December 5, and according to the record the two parties had a cordial meeting, followed by dinner together. Joncaire advised Washington to present his letter of protest to the French commander at Fort LeBoeuf. The fort, forty miles to the north at the confluence of the Allegheny and LeBoeuf Rivers (now the city of Waterford, Pennsylvania) was just fifteen miles south of Lake Erie.[5] Washington and his group departed for LeBoeuf, and he was invited into the fort where he delivered the letter to the commander. Governor Dinwiddie's protestations were of course dismissed, and a formal letter was given in reply for Major Washington to deliver to his governor.[6] Fort LeBoeuf was the closest that George Washington ever came to what is now the city of Buffalo, a distance of about one hundred miles. Washington recorded these events in his journal, and the entry for November 30, 1753 described the intelligence he had gathered concerning French forces in the area, and detailed the locations of French forts he observed:

> ...the next lies on Lake Erie, where the greatest Part of their Stores are kept about 15 Miles from the other; from that it is 120 Miles from the Carrying Place, at the Fall of Lake Erie where there is a small fort, which they lodge their Goods at, in bringing them from Morail, the Place that all their stores come from; the next fort lies about 20 miles from this, on Oswago Lake; between this Fort & Morail there are three others; the first of which is the English Fort Oswago. From the Fort on Lake Erie to Morail is about 600 Miles....[7]

The "Carrying Place" to which Washington refers is Daniel Joncaire's post above Niagara Falls, later called Schlosser's Landing, where boats were obliged to empty their goods for portage around the Falls to Lewiston, where they could be reloaded onto a small vessel and sail into Lake Ontario. The "Fall of Lake Erie" is meant to be Niagara Falls; "Morail" is Montreal; "the next Fort lies about 20 miles from this" refers to Fort Niagara; Lake Oswago is Lake Ontario; and Fort Oswago is Oswego. The meeting that took place on December 5, 1753 between French Captain Joncaire and British Major George Washington was the first North American meeting of the adversarial nations that would soon clash in the forthcoming French and Indian War.

America Pinckney Peter Williams was the great-granddaughter of Martha Washington, George Washington's wife. America was married to army Captain William G. Williams, who came to Buffalo in 1839 to supervise harbor construction work. Mrs. Williams died in Buffalo in 1842 and is buried in Forest Lawn Cemetery in Buffalo.

Internal Improvements

One of the more contentious points among the politicians of the early American republic was the issue of internal improvements, what we would today call infrastructure. In the late eighteenth and early nineteenth centuries, internal improvements referred almost exclusively to roads and waterways. Under the United States Constitution, which went into effect in 1789, it was not exactly clear what, if any, internal improvements could be funded by the federal government. Article I, Section 8 states that Congress has the power "to regulate commerce with foreign nations, and among the several states, and with the Indian tribes," and also "to establish post offices and post roads." Either of these two clauses could be invoked to justify federal aid to build or improve roads or waterways.

While the need for these internal improvements was generally recognized, the source of finances for them was in dispute. Should such projects be funded by the federal treasury, the individual states, or private enterprise? There was also disagreement as to where these projects should be undertaken, should federal funding be approved. Why should one section of the nation be favored over another for advancement?

Some politicians rejected outright any federal help for internal improvements, saying that such things were exclusively under the purview of the individual states and localities. Others were strong supporters of such federal aid. And still others sought a middle ground, considering each instance on its individual merits. Today, in the twenty-first century, when federal money is awarded to a huge number of state and local government and private projects, it seems almost inconceivable that such a debate even occurred. In those days, however, separation of powers and responsibilities between state and federal governments was considered to be a most serious constitutional matter.

Proposed roads and canals that crossed state lines could more easily win the approval of Congress for federal financing. Those that did not, such as a proposed canal to connect the Hudson River with the Great Lakes, a project wholly within the state of New York, were more debatable. Although this Erie Canal would be located within state borders, supporters of federal aid for the project argued that the benefits of such a waterway would facilitate and encourage increased interstate commerce. Its advantages would spread beyond New York, which supporters of federal aid argued would make such assistance entirely constitutional. The canal would open up the Great Lakes region to settlers and explorers who would ship raw materials to various cities of the eastern seaboard, not just New York City. Finished products would then go west along the canal to supply the expanding western population. A canal would also potentially increase international trade, so it would bring profit to the nation as a whole.

The Federalist Party generally supported federal aid for internal improvements, believing they would strengthen the union among the states. It would also keep the western territories from breaking away and forming their own country if they remained isolated beyond the Appalachian Mountains. Democrat-Republicans were mostly opposed. They feared federal control over states, and the corruption, bureaucracy and self-interest that would naturally result from such federal largesse.

As a private citizen, George Washington favored a network of roads and canals, and even privately helped finance a failed canal project that would have connected the Potomac River to the West, greatly benefitting his landholdings in the bargain. Washington's successor, John Adams, agreed with his views on internal improvements. Whether either man would have supported federal help for the Erie Canal is a matter of speculation, though both were certainly aware of New Yorkers' desire to undertake such an effort. Our third president, Thomas Jefferson, favored construction of canals and roadways, even seeming to promise surplus federal funds for them, but thought that the proposed Erie Canal was "madness," and financially and physically impossible.[8] Although he signed some federal funding of internal improvements into law, he thought that a constitutional amendment was needed for such financing. In the end, President Jefferson rejected the use of federal monies for the proposed canal across New York State.[9]

Jefferson's successor as president was James Madison, and it was he who vetoed the Clay-Calhoun Bonus Bill of 1817, the first and only document to propose federal funds for the building of the Erie Canal. In his veto message, President Madison cited concerns about the constitutionality of such financing. He thought an amendment was necessary, but like Jefferson he did allow some federal monies to be used for certain such purposes. The next president, James Monroe, concurred with Madison, but no bill for funding the Erie Canal was presented to him. His successor, John Quincy Adams, was an ardent supporter of the waterway, but by the time he became president in 1825, the canal was largely complete. In 1817, New York State had decided to fully fund the construction of the Erie Canal with no federal help. An engineering marvel of its time, it was completed in just eight years, and as its supporters had contended, it was a boon to the national economy, as well as to the state and, of course, to the village of Buffalo.

Erastus Granger

A connection between Thomas Jefferson and Buffalo exists in the person of one Erastus Granger. In 1800, both Erastus and his cousin Gideon Granger were important supporters of Jefferson's candidacy for president in the Grangers' home state of Connecticut. When Jefferson became president he rewarded the cousins by making Gideon his Postmaster General and appointing Erastus Superintendent of Indian Affairs for Western New York State. Commissioned in 1804, Erastus Granger moved to the Indian Affairs regional headquarters in Canandaigua and transferred it to Buffalo Creek, as the little settlement on Lake Erie was then known. In short order, he became Postmaster of Buffalo Creek, Collector of Customs of Buffalo Creek, and the first federal judge in the region, holding four federal offices simultaneously, thus becoming the most important citizen on the Niagara Frontier during the first decade of the nineteenth century.

THE EARLY YEARS

William Henry Harrison

Anyone with even a passing interest in the history of the presidency of the United States knows at least two things about William Henry Harrison. He was the first American president to die in office, and he served the shortest time of any president, a mere thirty-two days. But a couple of obscure facts connect our ninth president to Buffalo.

Harrison was born in 1773 at Berkeley Plantation, Virginia, the son of Benjamin Harrison, a signer of the Declaration of Independence and a close friend of George Washington. The elder Harrison was also an acquaintance of Thomas Jefferson, John Adams, Patrick Henry and other Founding Fathers. At age fourteen, young William was sent by his father to take lessons at the small Hampden-Sydney College in Virginia. He eventually decided to pursue a career in medicine, and at age eighteen he was studying at the University of Pennsylvania medical school in Philadelphia.[10] It was there that he received the sad news of his father's death.

Harrison became the ward of Robert Morris of Philadelphia, a friend and confidant of his late father, until he reached twenty-one, the age of majority. Morris is an interesting and underrated figure in American history. Born in England, he immigrated to America and became a successful merchant, importer and financier, eventually accumulating great wealth. Opposed to British rule, he was a member of the Continental Congress during the American Revolution, lending or outright granting money to the fledgling United States government and underwriting various enterprises to help keep the new nation afloat. He developed the first national bank of the United States and became the first U.S. financial agent under the Articles of Confederation, the equivalent of today's secretary of the treasury. He turned down President Washington's offer to become the first secretary of the treasury under the Constitution, but did become a U.S. senator from Pennsylvania. It was his house in Philadelphia that was used as the president's executive mansion by Washington and Adams when that city was our nation's capital from 1790 to 1800.[11]

After he left government service, Robert Morris engaged in land speculation, and it is here that the connection between William Henry Harrison and Buffalo comes about. Morris, as previously noted, was the guardian of young William after Harrison lost his father in 1791. One of Morris' land investments was in Western New York. In 1791 he purchased almost all the land west of the Genesee River in New York State, including what would become the city of Buffalo and Erie County, and held it for about two years before selling it to the Holland Land Company for a third of a million dollars.

But this indirect connection is not the only one between Buffalo and William Henry Harrison. In 1792, against Robert Morris' advice, Harrison left school and sought an officer's commission in the United States Army. He became an on-again, off-again, career soldier. His service was in the Northwest Territory, which comprised the present-day states of Ohio, Indiana, Michigan and Wisconsin, and part of Minnesota. After distinguished service, Harrison temporarily left the army in 1798, entered politics, and was appointed governor of the Indiana Territory in 1800. In 1811 he defeated a confederation of Shawnee Indians led by Tecumseh and his brother The Prophet at the Battle of Tippecanoe, Indiana. This elevated his stature nationally and raised his political profile.

When the War of 1812 broke out Harrison was commissioned a brigadier general in command of the Northwest, that is, the area that had formerly been the Northwest Territory. Although the village of Buffalo was not part of the Northwest, the Niagara Frontier was a strategic location for both sides in the war. General Harrison became involved in the military movements and strategy around the Great Lakes. The British had controlled Lake Erie since the start of the war, and American naval forces, led by Commodore Oliver Hazard Perry, were determined to wrest that control from them. Perry was backed by land forces led by General Harrison, who were gathered along the southern shore of the lake, primarily near the mouth of the Maumee River near the present-day site of the city of Toledo, Ohio.

In the late summer of 1813, Commodore Perry made his move, culminating when he engaged the British naval forces in the Battle of Lake Erie on September 10. At least three ships built on the Niagara

Frontier took part. Perry and his sailors were victorious, and after the battle he composed one of the most famous lines in American naval history in a message which was delivered to General Harrison:

From the U.S. Brig Niagara, on Lake Erie,

Sept. 10, 1813

Dear General:

We have met the enemy and they are ours; two ships, two brigs, one schooner and one sloop.

Yours with great respect and esteem,

O. H. Perry

The message was a signal to Harrison to cross the lake with his troops and engage the British soldiers and their Indian allies encamped on the north shore of Erie at the Thames River, near present day Chatham, Ontario.

The invasion took place on October 5, 1813 and the Americans prevailed in what came to be known as the Battle of the Thames, which resulted in the death of the great Shawnee Chief Tecumseh. This in turn led to the end of most fighting at the western end of Lake Erie and to the dissolution of the British-Native American alliance in the war.

Harrison and his men had crossed Lake Erie on more than ninety vessels of various sizes.[12] The general had been putting together this flotilla during the summer of 1813 while encamped on the Maumee, but the contractor he had engaged to supply him with boats proved to be less than competent. He heard of a trader and boatbuilder plying the waters of the lake and made contact with him. The man was Samuel Wilkeson, who would one day become mayor of the city of Buffalo.

Wilkeson was then living with his family in Portland in Chautauqua County. Most of his trade was carried on between Pittsburgh and Buffalo by way of the Allegheny and Conewango Rivers, Chautauqua Lake, Lake

Erie and the Niagara River, transporting various goods between the two places as well as making forays into various points along Lake Erie. He was one of the few freight forwarders operating on the lake at the time, and he had built his own keelboats. General Harrison sent for him and contracted him to build and supply several boats for his troops. Wilkeson went to the Grand River in Lake County, Ohio, just east of Cleveland, with a group of lumbermen and carpenters, and these workers promptly constructed the necessary vessels which obviously performed admirably in the crossing of the lake.[13]

Late in 1813 Samuel Wilkeson marched to Buffalo with the Chautauqua County militia, arriving on December 29, the day before the British burned the village to the ground. The militia had to retreat in the face of overwhelming British forces. In 1814, he relocated to Buffalo, operated a store at Main and Niagara, became a justice of the peace the following year, and as noted, eventually became mayor of the city of Buffalo in 1836.

Following his victory in the Battle of the Thames, and before the burning of the village of Buffalo, General Harrison and his men were ordered to the Niagara Frontier for duty. Commodore Perry's fleet, which now included British vessels captured during the Battle of Lake Erie, transported the army to Buffalo. The village of 1,500 people was reached on Sunday, October 24, 1813. Included in the fleet, which anchored in the lake off Buffalo Creek, were the brigs *Niagara*, *Caledonia* and *Hunter*, the schooners *Arieland* and *Lady Prevost*, and the sloops *Little Belt* and *Trippe*. The ships were greeted by a gathering of exuberant Buffalonians, and the heroes Perry and Harrison were welcomed by Colonel Cyrenius Chapin of the Buffalo militia. That evening, it was reported that the village was brilliantly illuminated in honor of the fleet.

The following day, at 2 p.m., General Harrison, Commodore Perry and about eighty army and navy officers under their commands were honored at a sumptuous banquet given by the citizens of Buffalo. This was held at Pomeroy's Tavern at the northeast corner of Main and Seneca Streets, an establishment owned and operated by Ralph M. Pomeroy from 1811 to 1822. The site is now occupied by the seventeen-story Main Seneca Building, 283 Main Street, formerly known as the Marine Trust Building. The dinner was hosted by the Buffalo militia and General Peter B. Porter, and was also attended by a number of prominent village residents.[14] At four o'clock a total of thirty-one toasts had been drunk, including the following by General Harrison:

> Our naval supremacy on the lakes – May its importance be felt and our government be always determined to retain it.

Later, this toast was offered in praise of General Harrison by General Porter:

> General Harrison – The accomplished soldier and scholar of the woods.

During that banquet, and into the following day, a fierce gale lashed the lakeshore, during which three vessels of the fleet were severed from their anchors and run ashore.

Soon thereafter Commodore Perry left town by stage for Rhode Island to rejoin his family. General Harrison and his troops left Buffalo, crossed the Niagara River at Black Rock and marched on to Fort George in Newark, Ontario (now Niagara-on-the-Lake), which was then under American control. Thus ended the Buffalo visit of future President William Henry Harrison.[15]

James Monroe Visits Buffalo

On June 1, 1817, less than three months after his inauguration, President James Monroe embarked on a lengthy tour of the northeastern and northwestern sections of the United States. Undertaken less than three years after the end of the hostilities of the War of 1812, the principal reason for the journey was to gauge the adequacy of existing military fortifications and to examine sites for proposed installations. It was also a good will tour, a kind of "meet and greet" with the people of the expanding nation. The president's schedule would take him to Baltimore, Philadelphia, New York City, Connecticut, Rhode Island, Boston, New Hampshire, Maine, Vermont, and then continue westward through northern New York State. Stops included Plattsburgh, Ogdensburg, Watertown, Sackett's Harbor and then on by ship across Lake Ontario to Niagaraland and beyond.[16]

During the duration of the three month trip, President Monroe traveled by land and water through some rough and undeveloped territory. He and his party had to put up with bad roads, the fording of creeks and streams lacking bridges, and various other inconveniences. At times they were required to sleep in primitive Indian huts using their coats and saddles as bedding. Monroe was accompanied by General Joseph G. Swift, a distinguished veteran of the War of 1812, Major General Jacob J. Brown, and Joseph J. Monroe, the president's brother and private secretary.[17] On August 6 the president sailed for Sackett's Harbor across Lake Ontario aboard the U.S. brig *Jones*, landing near Fort Niagara at the mouth of the Niagara River two days later.

President Monroe, as commander-in-chief of the armed forces, was received at the fort with a salute, after which he made a hurried inspection of the facility, which took no more than an hour, since he was anxious to stay on schedule. The presidential party proceeded from Fort Niagara up the Niagara River to the village of Niagara Falls, arriving at the home of Judge Augustus Porter, brother of Peter B. Porter and one of the pre-eminent citizens of that place. The president stayed that night at the judge's home.

Meanwhile, on July 29, the *Buffalo Gazette* had printed this notice:

> A meeting of the citizens of this village is requested at Mr. Kibbe's tavern on Wednesday evening at 7 o'clock for the purpose of making suitable arrangements for the reception of the President of the United States.[18]

On Saturday morning, August 9, 1817, President Monroe and his companions left the Falls and headed south on a road toward Buffalo. After riding through Black Rock they were met at its southern end by the members of the citizens' committee from Buffalo, as well as a group of other Buffalonians, around noon. This group escorted the president down Main Street to Landon's Tavern. Landon's was a log structure which stood at the southwest corner of the present-day Exchange and Washington Streets, now a parking lot under a thruway overpass. Inside the tavern, the committee delivered a welcoming address to President Monroe, to which he gave a short, extemporaneous reply. Several prominent Buffalonians were introduced to the president, after which he dined at Landon's in their company.

That very afternoon the president and his traveling companions boarded the U.S. schooner *Porcupine* and headed for Detroit, at the time located in the Michigan Territory. All in all, he probably spent no more than two or three hours in Buffalo.[19] From Michigan, Monroe traveled through Ohio, Pennsylvania and Maryland, before ending his long journey in Washington, D.C. on September 17, 1817, having been gone for more than three-and-a-half months.

Vice President Van Buren

In 1835, Vice President Martin Van Buren made a visit to the Queen City, fewer than two years before he would become the eighth president of the United States. He had been in Rochester in late August, and then stopped in Niagara Falls. It was not certain that he would also journey to Buffalo, but in the evening of September 1 he arrived in the city and took a room at the Eagle Tavern. This was located on the west side of Main Street south of Court Street, two buildings north of the American Hotel.[20]

The following day, the vice president and his friend Enos Throop, a former judge, congressman and governor of New York, then serving as a naval officer at the Port of New York, took a steamboat excursion on Lake Erie. A light meal was served on board and a few toasts were offered. It is not known how long Van Buren stayed in Buffalo, but it was probably not more than two days.[21]

Peter Buell Porter

One of the most prominent citizens of the Niagara Frontier in the first half of the nineteenth century was Peter Buell Porter. He was born in 1773 in Connecticut and moved to Canandaigua, New York sometime before 1800, where he started a law practice. Here he joined his older brother Augustus, a surveyor, who had previously moved to the Finger Lakes city.

The two men invested in the shipping business and acquired large landholdings. They bought large tracts in Black Rock and Lewiston, and along the brink of Niagara Falls, including all of Goat Island. Their shipping business operated on Lakes Erie and Ontario and they soon were granted a lucrative monopoly by New York State to operate the land portage route used to carry goods from Black Rock to Lewiston around Niagara Falls and the swift currents of the upper and lower Niagara River. They joined with Benjamin Barton and Joseph Annin to operate their firm, Porter, Barton and Company. Peter moved to Black Rock in 1809, Augustus to Niagara Falls in 1816 and Barton settled in Lewiston.[22]

Peter Porter built a house at Black Rock that overlooked the Niagara River. It was burned down by the British during the War of 1812, but rebuilt in 1816. He planned to develop Black Rock to compete with Buffalo, two miles to the south, for the lake shipping trade. He became the first Erie County resident to represent the area in Congress, where he served in the U.S. House of Representatives from 1809 to 1813 and 1815 to 1816. During the War of 1812 he was appointed an army general in command of all American forces on the Niagara Frontier.

Peter Porter was a champion of the Erie Canal and served on the Erie Canal Commission. Despite this, he was unsuccessful in having Black Rock chosen as the western terminus of the waterway, losing out to Buffalo, although the canal would still pass through Black Rock. In 1828 he was chosen to be U.S. secretary of war by President John Quincy Adams, the first Erie County resident to serve in a federal cabinet position. He held that post for a year, until the end of Adams' term in office.

Peter Porter married the widow Letitia (Breckenridge) Grayson in 1818. She was from a prominent Kentucky/Virginia family and was the daughter of John Breckenridge, who was U.S. attorney general under President Thomas Jefferson in 1805-06. Her nephew Joseph Cabell Breckenridge was a U.S. senator, and vice president of the United

States from 1857 to 1861 under President James Buchanan. He was the presidential candidate of the southern wing of the Democratic Party in 1860. After joining the Confederate army during the Civil War, he served with distinction as a major general, and became the Confederacy's last secretary of war in 1865. When Letitia Breckenridge married Peter Porter in 1818, she was a slaveholder, and she brought five or six slaves from Kentucky with her to the Porter home in Black Rock. All but two of them eventually escaped to Canada.[23] Slavery was still legal in New York at that time, and remained so until 1827. Peter Porter sold his house on the Niagara River at 1192 Niagara Street and moved to Niagara Falls in 1837, where his wife Letitia died in 1838. The house on Niagara was bought by Lewis Allen, uncle of Grover Cleveland. When he moved to Buffalo in 1855, it was this house that young Cleveland lived in for several months.

Peter's brother Augustus is largely credited with founding the village of Niagara Falls, New York, due to his and his brother's extensive landholdings there. Augustus built his house in what would later become the village, and then city, and promoted and developed the place as a location for industry. He was also the first county judge of Niagara County.

Earlier in his life Augustus Porter had been a surveyor. He was an assistant to the chief of a party of surveyors hired by the Connecticut Land Company to survey lands along the southern shore of Lake Erie in 1796. Moses Cleaveland, a distant older cousin of future President Grover Cleveland, was the superintendent of the survey team. First coming to Buffalo Creek, he met with Red Jacket, Farmer's Brother, and other Iroquois leaders to convince them that their company owned the land south of the lake.[24] Heading west, Cleaveland chose the spot and laid out the grid for a city on the lakeshore in Ohio. Porter then supervised the survey of the plat. He and his colleagues decided to name the spot after their boss – Cleaveland (the "a" was later dropped).[25] Augustus Porter was also later hired by Robert Morris to survey Morris' landholdings in western New York State. Morris, as previously noted, was the guardian of the young William Henry Harrison from 1791 to 1794. In 1791, Morris had purchased the land in Western New York that would later become Buffalo and Erie County.

In 1885 the state of New York decided to buy the privately-owned land around Niagara Falls, including Goat Island, and establish what is now Niagara Falls State Park. Most of the land comprising the park was owned by the heirs of Augustus and Peter Porter. The bill authorizing the purchase and formation of the park was signed into law by Governor Grover Cleveland, that same Grover Cleveland who had lived in Peter Porter's old house on Niagara Street, and whose distant cousin had worked on the survey team with Augustus Porter to lay out the settlement of Cleaveland, Ohio.

The Patriot War and Buffalo Barracks

For about two hundred years the Niagara Frontier was a place of potential international conflict, from the seventeenth through the nineteenth centuries. First there were disputes between the French Canadians and British Americans. Later, after the French and Indian War and American independence, the aggression was continued by the United States and British Canada. As in many contentious border areas, fortifications were built and maintained.

Fort Niagara was built by the French and British in the seventeenth and eighteenth centuries, depending on which nation controlled the area at the time. It is located on the east bank of the Niagara River near its mouth at Lake Ontario. The river, which connects Lakes Erie and Ontario, was vital in the transportation of men and goods into and out of the interior of the continent. But passage through the Niagara was problematic because of the beautiful but dangerous Niagara Falls and its associated rapids, rocks and whirlpool currents, which blocked the way of an uninterrupted route between the lakes.

The solution was a portage route around the falls and rapids, a road along the river bank on which small vessels and/or goods could be carried or carted for a few miles around the falls area, then put back on the water. This portage route existed along the eastern (today the American) side of the river and went inland for a distance. Its northern or downstream terminus was located at Lewiston Heights, now located in the town of Lewiston, New York. The southern or upstream end was at an area about a mile-and-a-half south of the falls and was protected for a brief period by a French fort called Little Fort Niagara, or Fort du Portage, from 1750 to 1759. The portage road was under control of the French until about 1760.

Following the French and Indian War, the French were finally routed from the Niagara Frontier by the victorious British. The French destroyed the Little Fort Niagara before the approaching British forces could seize it. The Redcoats rebuilt the fort in 1760 and renamed it Fort Schlosser, after one of its commanders. A brick chimney that survived the destruction of the French fort was incorporated into the new one. That chimney still exists today, but not in its original location. It is now along the Niagara Scenic Parkway north of the water intakes and is called the Old Stone Chimney.

The location of Fort Schlosser was at the area presently occupied by the water intake towers of the Niagara Power Authority. The British also built several defensive blockhouses along the portage road that they now controlled, because the route was still subject to lingering French attacks. On Navy Island, near Grand Island in the Niagara River, the British established a naval base directly opposite Fort Schlosser.[26] In 1764, they also built Fort Erie, directly across from what would become the city of Buffalo, to defend the source of the river. The British controlled the Niagara Frontier during the American Revolution and did not vacate the American side until 1796. Fort Schlosser was occupied by the Americans during the War of 1812, but was burned by the British in 1813. The original Fort Erie was rebuilt in 1803 on higher ground, and was contested in a spirited battle in 1814 between the Americans and British.[27]

International troubles along the Niagara River did not cease with the end of the War of 1812. In the late 1830s came the Patriot War.[28] This was essentially a Canadian conflict, but it spilled over into the United States. In the fall of 1837 disaffected Canadians banded together in an attempt to overthrow British rule by armed force. This action occurred in mainly three theaters along the border with America: the Thousand Islands-Lake Champlain region to the east, the Niagara Frontier, and the Detroit area in the west. The ultimate purpose of this insurrection was either complete independence for Canada from Britain or its attachment to the

United States. In the Lower Canada colony of the Thousand Islands area it was led by Louis Jean Papineau of Montreal, and in the Upper Canada colony of the Niagara Peninsula it was led by William Lyon MacKenzie, a Toronto newspaper editor and former mayor of that city. Americans had a great deal of sympathy for the rebels. Some also favored the annexation of Canada into the U.S. as a non-slave state to counter balance the probable annexation of Texas as a slave state.[29] After they lost initial battles to the superior British forces, many of the insurrectionists fled to the U.S., where they found sanctuary and support, and a great number came to Buffalo.

William MacKenzie was one of those who escaped to the Queen City, where he made speeches and successfully amassed military and financial support for the Patriot cause. The Canadians who fled to Buffalo formed armed bands with sympathetic and adventurous Americans. About two hundred of these Patriot "soldiers," most of them Americans, managed to seize British-controlled Navy Island and there, on December 13, 1837, they declared the Republic of Canada. Soon they were joined by hundreds of others. Arms were shipped to the rebels on the island from Schlosser's Landing on the American shore via the American steamship S.S. *Caroline*. But the British, crossing into American waters in the Niagara River in late December, captured the *Caroline* at Schlosser, killed one onboard, set it afire and pushed it toward the falls, where it was eventually swept over after breaking apart.

By this time, the events occurring along the Canadian border had drawn the serious attention of the U.S. government and President Martin Van Buren. The federal government was enjoying peaceful relations with Britain and endeavored to curtail Americans' participation in what it considered to be an internal British Canadian matter. President Van Buren wanted no war with Great Britain, so he sought to enforce the United States' neutrality laws along the northern border. These laws prevented any American from carrying on a hostile activity against any country with which the United States was at peace. First, the Van Buren administration notified the governors of Vermont, Michigan and New York asking them to use their powers and influence to stop violations of the law. It also ordered federal district attorneys and customs officers in the affected areas to enforce the law, but they were almost powerless to do anything.

In Buffalo, Mayor Josiah Trowbridge, General Potter of the New York militia and New York Governor William L. Marcy issued proclamations asking the people to desist from aiding the Patriot rebels, all to no avail. These officials advised that only an armed force could deter the activities. On January 5, 1838, President Van Buren issued a proclamation calling on all Americans to observe the neutrality laws and threatening the arrest of violators. He also conferred with Major General Winfield Scott and dispatched him to the Niagara Frontier, asking him to use diplomacy and restraint, while at the same time gathering a force of some 3,000 New York militiamen under his command. At public meetings in Buffalo, while clothed in an impressive full-dress uniform, General Scott calmed the people's passion. After much coaxing, he soon witnessed the withdrawal of the Patriot forces from Navy Island, and demonstrated to the British that he would tolerate no incursions into American waters.[30] By spring of 1838 the situation along the Niagara Frontier had calmed down, and sporadic flare-ups of Patriot activity had ceased along the entire American-Canadian border by 1841.

The Patriot War troubles in the Buffalo area convinced the federal authorities in Washington that something should be done to prevent such events from occurring in the future. President Van Buren had sent General Scott to the Niagara Frontier to quell the disturbances, but the general had to rely on the state militia, and on militiamen from interior counties. This was because sympathy for the Patriot cause was so strong in border regions that a force composed of men from those areas could not be relied upon to be loyal to the orders of the general. A force of regular army troops was not available to be dispatched here.

The peacetime army of the United States comprised only eight thousand men in 1838. At least half of them were in Florida fighting the Seminole Indians, and most of the rest were stationed in a few dozen forts in the west from Louisiana up through northern Michigan, trying to keep peace between white settlers and Indians, as well as watching the potentially volatile situation in Texas.

The response of the Van Buren administration was to establish an army outpost in Buffalo to be manned by a contingent of soldiers drawn from the regular army. Actually, the military wanted a presence in Black

Rock, which at the time was still a separate political entity from Buffalo. The first troops were stationed there in tents, with a few officers living in distant rented buildings, which proved to be problematic. With additional troops due to arrive, the solution was to build temporary barracks on leased land. The parcel chosen was in the city of Buffalo near its then-northern boundary on the east side of Delaware Avenue. It was called the Rathbun parcel and was owned by Ebenezer Walden, the first lawyer in Erie County and one time mayor of Buffalo. Known commonly as Walden Hill, the army leased an eighteen-acre portion of the lot owned by Walden on October 5, 1839.[31]

In the summer of 1839, President Martin Van Buren had undertaken a trip through the Empire State. Beginning in New York City, he proceeded up the Hudson River valley, stopping in Ossining, Hudson, Albany and his native village of Kinderhook. It was a somewhat disconcerting journey for the president, because at the time he was very unpopular, in no small part due to the lingering negative economic effects of the Panic of 1837. At many places, government officials refused to even give him a formal welcome, let alone meet with him. Van Buren's aides in turn arranged for a contingent of supporters to follow him from town to town, at least part of the way, to ensure that the president received a cheering reception at each stop.[32]

President Van Buren traveled westward across the state. He arrived at Black Rock by steamboat down the Niagara River, disembarking onto the wharf around noon on Monday, September 2. He was met by members of the Committee of Arrangements from the city of Buffalo, a civic group formed to coordinate events for the presidential visit. The committee had arranged for about thirty carriages to transport citizens desiring to travel to Black Rock from Buffalo to greet the president. Also present was a gathering of citizens of Black Rock. When Van Buren stepped onto the deck of the steamer, he was met with a polite but less than enthusiastic welcome from the crowd. The president entered an open barouche along with Secretary of War Joel Poinsett, who had accompanied him on the trip, as well as Judge Nathaniel Bennett, a prominent Democrat, and Albert H. Troy, a former Congressman and prominent Whig.

A squad of federal troops on horseback accompanied the presidential carriage across the city line into Buffalo where they were met on Niagara Street by a large body of soldiers and city guards, in all numbering some four hundred men under the command of Colonel James Bankhead. They escorted the president to the county court house, followed by the other carriages. After Mr. Van Buren climbed down from the barouche, he was formally welcomed to Buffalo by Judge Bennett. In his remarks, Bennett alluded to the only previous presidential visit to the city:

> The propriety and utility of executive tours were exemplified by that of Mr. Monroe, the only president who was heretofore visited this part of the country. He passed through this now flourishing city when it was comparatively but an insignificant village, and the country was almost an entire wilderness. The strong and favorable impressions everywhere made by him, in the intercourse with his fellow citizens, are still fresh in our recollections.[33]

President Van Buren's reply emphasized his recognition of the great potential for Buffalo's future growth and its deserving of the protection of the federal government and the fostering of its commerce.

At the conclusion of the ceremony there was a call for three cheers for the president, which received only a halfhearted response. It should be noted that the Democratic president was not welcomed by the mayor of Buffalo, Hiram Pratt, who was a member of the opposition party, the Whigs. Van Buren was escorted the short distance to the American Hotel on the west side of Main Street, where he would spend the night. After being formally introduced to many Buffalonians, the president sat down to dinner with about a hundred guests, during which toasts were drunk and speeches made, all of an apolitical nature. Later, Van Buren received several well-wishers, and about one hundred fifty uniformed Buffalo firefighters marched outside the hotel in a torchlight parade in his honor.

The next morning President Van Buren and Secretary Poinsett visited the army barracks to review the troops. Suitable maneuvers were carried out and a *feu de joie* rifle salute was performed. It is not clear where the barracks was located. The Poinsett, or Buffalo, Barracks was not yet in existence, and it seems the federal troops were housed at the time in rented buildings in downtown Buffalo.[34] A newspaper reported that the troops were reviewed in an "enclosure filled with the elite of the city."[35] That afternoon the president and his party were escorted by the City Guards to the railroad station, where they continued their trip to Niagara Falls, Lockport and points eastward on their return to Washington, D.C.

Completed in 1840, the brick barracks and outbuildings that made up Buffalo's new military post surrounded a large parade ground, the entire parcel being bounded by Delaware, Main Street, North and Allen. Franklin and Pearl Streets were not yet extant in that area.[36] The post took the name Poinsett Barracks, named after Secretary of War Joel Poinsett, but was popularly called the Buffalo Barracks. The year 1840 proved to be the peak of the troop population, numbering over six hundred men. By 1844 there were only two hundred soldiers left. The reason for the decline was twofold. A new fort at Black Rock was being built, namely Fort Porter, and the apparent end of the threat of hostilities along the Canadian frontier, especially after a treaty with Britain over disputed areas along the Canadian border.

But until 1845 the Barracks was a focal point of Buffalo society. City residents were thrilled at the sights and sounds of flashy military drills. A post military band was maintained and Buffalonians were often invited to "come and take tea," hear the band play, and dance. The colorfully uniformed officers likewise were guests at functions given by prominent city residents. Several army officers married Buffalo girls during their assignments at Buffalo Barracks, with weddings held on the post.[37]

Millard Fillmore, who at the time of the Buffalo Barracks was a U.S. congressman or former congressman, was said to be a visitor to the army post. Military officers stationed there included Colonel William J. Worth. Worth would later become a hero in the Mexican American War, and the cities of Fort Worth, Texas and Lake Worth, Florida would be named for him.

Another probable prominent visitor to the Buffalo Barracks was General Zachary Taylor, the future president of the United States. In May 1840, Taylor took an extended furlough from his army duties. He and his wife traveled to Pensacola, New Orleans, Louisville, Washington, D.C.

and finally to Philadelphia to visit their sixteen-year-old daughter Betty, who was attending boarding school there. The three of them then went to Boston, and then continued westward across New York State to Niagara Falls. It is not certain how they traveled or what route they took, but they may have come through Buffalo. After seeing the Falls, the Taylors headed south through western Pennsylvania and back to Louisville, which they called home.[38] Because Zachary Taylor's daughter Ann was residing at the Buffalo Barracks with her husband, the post surgeon Dr. Robert C. Wood, it is highly likely that the Taylors would have stopped in for a visit to see them. The time frame seems to point to August of 1840. Indeed, the excursion to Niagara Falls may have only been an interesting addition to the itinerary, with the family's real purpose being to see Ann and Robert. In his book *The Man Who Shot McKinley* author A. Wesley Johns writes that Taylor did indeed visit the Buffalo Barracks to see Dr. and Mrs. Wood, but gives no date, and does not cite a specific source for the statement.[39]

Stories that Jefferson Davis, the future president of the Confederate States of America, was stationed at Buffalo Barracks for a time are untrue. Most of Davis' military career spanned the years 1825 to 1835, during which no federal troops were assigned to Buffalo. The Buffalo Barracks existed from 1839 to 1845. Though Davis rejoined the army during the Mexican American War, his service in 1846 and 1847 was exclusively in the southern states and in Mexico. It is highly unlikely that he was ever in Buffalo. At least one source indicates that one of the officers who served at the Buffalo Barracks was one Jefferson C. Davis and references a photograph of Jefferson Columbus Davis. This was a different person from the more famous Confederate president, whose full name was Jefferson Finis Davis.[40] This Jefferson C. Davis, however, was born in 1828, joined the army in Indiana in 1846, with no indication of a detour to Buffalo in the years leading up to his Civil War service. It is remotely possible that he may have been at Fort Porter in Buffalo at some point, the military facility that succeeded the Buffalo Barracks in the mid-1840s, since he served at different posts along the east coast.[41]

Captain William G. Williams, husband of America Williams, the great-granddaughter of Martha Washington, was stationed as an engineer in Buffalo during the time the Buffalo Barracks was active, though there is no indication that he was under the command of the officers there. Still, he may have possibly interacted with them from time to time.

In June of 1843 President John Tyler embarked on a tour of the northern states. The highlight of the trip was his dedication of the Bunker Hill Monument in Boston, Massachusetts on June 17. The president and his entourage, which included cabinet officers, intended to travel westward from there, but his attorney general, Hugh S. Legare, died unexpectedly in Boston on June 20. Deeply saddened by the sudden loss of a trusted adviser, President Tyler canceled planned visits to Albany, Buffalo, Cleveland and Cincinnati and instead accompanied Legare's body to Washington, D.C.[42] He most likely would have visited the Buffalo Barracks if he had been in the city. His expected arrival date had been June 25.

Former President Tyler visited Niagara Falls, New York in September of 1851, accompanied by his sister-in-law Margaret Gardiner Beeckman and his brother-in-law David Lion Gardiner. Their length of stay is not known, but a letter sent from Niagara Falls dated September 21, 1851 from Margaret to her sister in New York City, former First Lady Julia Tyler, places them at the Falls that day. It is also not known if the three travelers came through Buffalo, though if they visited the Falls it is very likely.[43]

CHAPTER 2

MILLARD FILLMORE

Young Millard Fillmore

The most prominent and distinguished citizen in Buffalo's history was not born in the Queen City, but one hundred fifty miles to the east. On the morning of January 7, 1800, in the dead of winter, Nathaniel and Phoebe (Millard) Fillmore celebrated the birth of their second child and first son, Millard. The blessed event took place in a small log cabin in the town of Milton, in a place called Locke (now Summerhill), Cayuga County, New York, then part of Onondaga County. The family later moved to Sempronius (now Niles), New York.

The Fillmores were poor, and young Millard did his fair share of back-breaking work on the family farm. At the age of fifteen he was apprenticed to an area clothmaker for four years. Millard had received only the most basic instructions in reading, writing and figuring. At nineteen, he enrolled at an academy in Kelloggsville, where he soon became a favorite of his teacher Abigail Powers, who was just two years his elder. The teacher and student promptly fell in love. Meanwhile, Fillmore's father Nathaniel moved the family yet again, first to New Hope then to Montville, where he rented a farm from County Judge Walter Wood.

One day, Nathaniel paid a visit to Judge Wood and arranged for his son to read law with the old jurist. But while learning the trade of a lawyer, the young man and Judge Wood had a falling out and Millard returned to the family farm.

At this point Fillmore the elder decided to move yet again, this time over one hundred miles west, to the village of East Aurora. Though discouraged about his future, this move proved to be serendipitous for young Millard, for in the early 1800s the nearby village of Buffalo was on the cusp of a great expansion in its fortunes.

This coming prosperity would be in contrast to the young man's first visit to Buffalo in 1818. That summer, he had walked one hundred forty miles to Buffalo to see the area and visit relatives in the nearby town of Wales. Buffalo did not make a good first impression, as the charred foundations of buildings burned by the British in the war four-and-a- half years earlier still scarred the landscape. Now, however, as the Fillmores settled in East Aurora, Buffalo was busy constructing the western terminus of the Erie Canal and vastly improving its harbor. It was becoming a boomtown, with business opportunities in every trade, including the law.

In 1822, Fillmore accepted a teaching job in Buffalo and relocated there. In a short time he had obtained a clerkship with a law firm, and in 1823 he was admitted to the bar. He chose to return to East Aurora, where he opened a small office and handled small cases. Here he also assumed his first public position as commissioner of deeds. The office was located at 686 Main Street, now the site of Vidler's Five and Ten. Shortly afterward Fillmore traveled to Moravia, New York, where he married his former teacher Abigail Powers and brought her home to East Aurora. First living with his parents south of the village, they soon moved to a newly built house in East Aurora across from Fillmore's law office. That is the National Historic Site on Shearer Avenue, having been moved many years ago. Young Fillmore's status as a lawyer continued to progress, and when he was admitted to practice law before the state courts, his reputation spread and his circle of influential acquaintances grew steadily.

Even then, at his young age, and continuing for the rest of his life, Fillmore impressed all with his hard work, sound judgment and sincerity. He was careful not to make a hasty decision and was a thoughtful speaker. Physically tall and handsome, he was a modest man, always impeccably dressed, and exhibited pleasant manners. He was cool and dignified under pressure, and showed a great deal of respect, even to his adversaries.

The Anti-Masonic Party

When Millard Fillmore entered politics, it is unclear whether his motivations were for the sake of his career, or stemmed from a genuine idealism. Like most politicians, he probably acted from a bit of both. He identified with the National Republican Party, successor to the old Federalist Party, and supported John Quincy Adams for president in 1824 against the Democrat Andrew Jackson. In 1828 he was a delegate to the Erie County National Republican convention, and a couple of months later he attended the state Anti-Masonic Party convention in Leroy. Apparently Anti-Masonism appealed to him, possibly because of this party's ideas of clean government.[1] The movement was also aligned with the National Republican Party. Local Anti-Masons were so pleased with Fillmore that they made him their candidate for state assembly that year. He won this election and served until 1831.

The Anti-Masons were opposed to Masonry, also called Freemasonry. The Masons were a secret fraternal organization whose origins dated back to the stonemason guilds of medieval Europe. Many prominent men of society were members, including Presidents George Washington and Andrew Jackson. Masons were accused of attempting to corrupt and replace democracy and Christianity, and of favoring fellow members in business and government to the point of subverting justice.

The impetus of the Anti-Mason movement was the William Morgan affair. Morgan was a Mason living in Batavia, when in 1826 he decided to write an expose of the secrets of Masonry, a book which he hoped would get him out of debt. When news of this reached his fellow Masons, Morgan and his publisher were threatened and harassed. Arrested on bad debt charges, Morgan was hauled to jail in Canandaigua on September 11, 1826. Released the next evening, he was accosted by four men as he left the jail and shoved into a carriage. His abductors were Masons. Reports say that Morgan was taken by a relay of horse and carriage across Western New York to Fort Niagara where he was incarcerated in a magazine room (ammunition storage area) within the fort.

Many suspected that Morgan was killed, but no charges were proven. A body pulled from the southern shore of Lake Ontario in Niagara

County was rumored to be his, but this claim was later discredited. Morgan was never heard from again. It is presumed that he was murdered, but by whom is uncertain. In 1880, a monument to Morgan was placed in Batavia Cemetery. The disappearance of William Morgan is the outrage that started the Anti-Masonic movement and political party, whose goal it was to destroy or at least emasculate Masonry in the United States.

Millard Fillmore was not a zealous Anti-Mason. But his stance as an anti-Jacksonian meshed with that of the Anti-Masonic Party and was a springboard for him to advance in politics. Significantly, on the national level the Anti-Masonic Party was the first serious national third party. It held the first national political convention in American history in Baltimore in 1831. It nominated William Wirt of Maryland as its first and only presidential candidate. Wirt finished a distant third in the following year's general election.

Fillmore Moves to Buffalo

In 1830 Millard and Abigail Fillmore moved to the village of Buffalo, settling into a clapboard home at 180 Franklin Street (then no. 114). His parents continued to live in East Aurora. He had accepted an offer to join William Clary in a law partnership. From his home, he walked to their office on the west side of Main Street between Court and Eagle Streets, a location that would contain Fillmore's business for the next two decades. As he quickly moved up in the social and business circles of Buffalo his reputation grew. He became a champion for Buffalo's incorporation as a city and sat as a member of the committee that drew up its first city charter in 1831. In 1832, after he was elected to Congress as an Anti-Mason, his partnership with Clary ended. Soon thereafter he formed another partnership with two younger attorneys, Nathan K. Hall and Solomon G. Haven. The firm of Fillmore, Hall and Haven lasted for a dozen years and became a legendary Buffalo law practice that spawned distinguished successor firms.

In 1834 a fusion of anti-Andrew Jackson Democrats, old National Republicans and Anti-Masons joined forces to form the Whig Party in opposition to the Jackson administration. That same year, the Anti-Masonic

Party disbanded. Millard Fillmore was in full agreement with these moves and enthusiastically supported and worked for the establishment of the Whigs. In promoting the new party, he became associated with Lewis F. Allen, the uncle of Grover Cleveland. Fillmore refused to stand for reelection to Congress that year, but two years later he won his seat back as a Whig.

While in Congress, Fillmore was admitted to practice before the Supreme Court. His concerns included reform of the banking system and internal improvements, and he supported a protectionist tariff. In 1838 he was perforce concerned about events in Buffalo in connection with Canada's Patriot War. He urged the federal government to take defensive measures along the Niagara Frontier, but apparently did not communicate with President Van Buren over the crisis. Although they were from opposite political parties, he was concerned about what actions the president would take.[2] By this time, Congressman Fillmore was so well respected by his colleagues that he was a candidate for Speaker of the House. He lost, but his consolation was being appointed chairman of the Ways and Means Committee, one of the most powerful in the House of Representatives, then as now.

In 1840, the Whigs had their first serious shot at winning the presidency. The Whig Party of New York State played the deciding role in who would be the party's nominee for president that year. Henry Clay of Kentucky was the leading contender for the nomination. He visited Buffalo and Western New York in his pursuit of it, since the area was the most crucial part of the most critical state in the selection process. But neither Fillmore, the leading Whig of the region, nor most of Western New York supported Clay. William Henry Harrison became the nominee, and he won the general election. After Harrison died in office just a month after he became president, the nominal Whig John Tyler succeeded him. Because Tyler was really an anti-Jackson Democrat put on the Harrison ticket to draw southern and Democratic votes, his policies soon clashed with those of the Whig Party, and the Whigs disowned him, as did Fillmore.

In 1842 Fillmore retired from Congress, figuring he could do more good back home in Buffalo. Some historians contend that had he stayed in Congress he would have eventually been elected speaker and been one of the greatest members in the history of the House of Representatives. But fate had other plans for Mr. Fillmore. When he returned to Buffalo, he resumed the practice of law and made a good living at it as the most esteemed attorney in the county.

John Quincy Adams In Buffalo

In July of 1843 former President John Quincy Adams of Massachusetts paid a visit to the Niagara Frontier. The venerable seventy-six-year-old was then a most respected member of the United States House of Representatives. Mr. Adams ventured west across Lake Ontario by steamboat, stopped in Toronto for a couple of hours, then traveled across the lake and landed at Lewiston on July 23. He took accommodations at Niagara Falls, and the next day he toured the area and met his old friend Peter B. Porter, who had served as his secretary of war when he was president. Porter accompanied Adams for several hours, during which Adams was persuaded to spend the next two nights at Porter's home in the Falls.

Adams included a trip across the river to Ontario to visit the Lundy's Lane battleground from the War of 1812, Chippawa, Table Rock and the cavern beneath. On July 25, Millard Fillmore arrived at the Falls to formally invite his old house colleague to Buffalo. Adams accepted this, as well as an invitation from the Cincinnati Astronomical Society to visit that city in November to lay the cornerstone for a new observatory. At noon the next day Adams and his party were taken by coach to Schlosser's Landing where they boarded the steamer *Bunker Hill*, and were met by a committee from Buffalo that included Fillmore, Nathan K. Hall and several others. The trip to the Queen City took four hours, since it included a stop at Grand Island to visit the remains of Ararat, a proposed settlement for the world's Jews.[3]

Upon arrival at Buffalo harbor at the foot of Main Street, a group of thousands cheered a welcome to Congressman Adams. He was transported by open barouche to Court House Park, which was crowded with Buffalonians.[4] Adams and Fillmore climbed onto a stage, where the latter extended welcoming remarks to the Congressman, noting that people of all ages had turned out to "feast their eyes by sight of that extraordinary and venerable man of whom they have heard and read and thought so much [,] the man whom they delight to honor."[5]

Mr. Adams replied with high praise for Fillmore, expressing his awe at the beauty of Niagara, and his thanks to the citizens of Buffalo for their hearty welcome. He also praised their moral principles and closed with the wish that "the blessings of heaven be upon you throughout your lives."[6]

At the conclusion of these remarks, Adams and Fillmore left the stand and entered a coach with Buffalo Mayor Joseph G. Masten for a short ride around the city, which ended at the American Hotel on Main Street between Court and Eagle, where the north end of Main Place Mall stands today. That evening Adams received hundreds of well-wishers at the hotel. The fire companies of the city staged a brilliant torch light parade at 8:30 p.m., and the former president attended a "splendid evening party and supper."[7] On the morning of July 27 Adams received a committee from Rochester that formally invited him to that city, and he accepted. He left by rail for points east at 8:30 a.m. Disembarking briefly in Batavia, Adams narrowly escaped injury when the wooden platform between the train and station collapsed from the weight of the people crowded onto it. He had an instant earlier stepped into the station house, but in any event only one man was seriously injured in the accident.[8]

Just three months later, John Quincy Adams was once again in Buffalo, in conjunction with his visit to Cincinnati to lay the cornerstone for the observatory. His train pulled into town early on the morning of Sunday, October 29, and he checked into a room at the American Hotel at 1:30 a.m., a room that he complained "was so small, so cold, so dark, that they gave me another this morning, very comfortable, the same in which I had slept last July."[9] This was not an official visit. After breakfast that morning, Adams accepted an invitation to stop at Erie, Pennsylvania and received Millard Fillmore, who invited him to attend services with him that morning at the First Unitarian Church, which he accepted. The church building, at Franklin and Eagle Streets, still stands today. Adams commented upon the preaching of Reverend George W. Hosmer from the Book of Matthew, calling it "an excellent and eminently preached sermon."

Congressman Adams also attended an evening Episcopal service and went to an evening party at the home of Mr. and Mrs. Fillmore on Franklin. The next morning before eight o'clock he departed on the steamer *General Wayne* for Point Abino, Ontario, then on to Erie.[10]

National Politics

Even though he had left public office, Millard Fillmore was a leader of the local Whig Party, and by the middle of 1843 he was again seriously involved in politics, trying for the vice presidential nomination on the Whigs' 1844 ticket. At the party's national convention in Baltimore he lost the nomination to Theodore Freylinghausen of New Jersey. The presidential nominee was Henry Clay. Eventually, the Clay-Freylinghausen combination lost the general election to Democrat James K. Polk. The Whigs lost New York State by 5,100 votes, one percent of the total cast. Perhaps if New Yorker Fillmore had been nominated for vice president, the state would have gone for the Clay-Freylinghausen ticket, and if that had happened, the state's electoral vote total would have been enough to change the outcome of the election.[11] Thus Fillmore might have been inaugurated as vice president in 1845. Because he was not nominated for vice president, Fillmore was instead drafted to run for governor of New York, and he lost that contest. He blamed his loss on the votes of immigrants, or naturalized citizens, because Whigs were viewed as nativist, i.e., those in favor of restricting the rights of foreign immigrants. Did this stoke an anti-immigrant stance in the heart of Fillmore?[12]

As the Polk administration unfolded, Fillmore, as a Whig, opposed most of its policies, including the Mexican American War. In 1847 he was running for office again, this time for comptroller of New York, and he was easily elected. In 1848, though he was not interested in the vice presidency, the Whigs nominated Fillmore as their vice presidential candidate as a northern balance to their presidential nominee, the southerner Zachary Taylor. The Democrats ran Lewis Cass of Michigan for president and William O. Butler of Kentucky for vice president. The Democrats and Whigs in 1848 also faced a serious third party challenge from the Free Soil Party, an anti-slavery coalition that had held their national convention in Buffalo that summer. Former President Martin Van Buren of New York was the Free Soilers' choice for president.

The selection of Millard Fillmore as Taylor's running mate was said to have healed a split in the Whig Party in New York, assuring Taylor of a victory in the state. The national election resulted in the triumph of the Taylor-Fillmore ticket. The Whigs supposedly would have won the election against the Democrats even if the Free Soil Party had not fielded a candidate. Fillmore rented out his Buffalo home and headed for Washington in February 1849. He took the oath of office to become vice president on March 4, 1849 in the Senate chamber. As the vice president also served as president of the Senate with the power to cast the deciding vote in case of a tie in that body, the position was a very important one at the time. This was because the jousting between northern and southern states often resulted in close votes among the senators on crucial national issues, especially the slavery question.

Political conniving within Fillmore's own Whig Party denied him any influence within the new Taylor administration. He was undercut by his fellow New Yorkers, Thurlow Weed and William Seward, and was denied a say in most political appointments, even in his home state. Fillmore had never even met Taylor until a few days before they took their respective oaths to become vice president and president, so he had almost no personal rapport with Mr. Taylor. As vice president, Fillmore was opposed to some of the stances taken by the president, but he kept his own counsel. This was a very tumultuous time in American history, with the North and South seeming to move rapidly toward the possibility of civil war over the slavery question. Compromise seemed to be the only way to keep things from boiling over, and the result was that Congress devised and eventually proposed what became known as the Compromise of 1850.

This compromise was actually a series of five acts that would allow California to become a free state, provide for self-determination over slavery in the New Mexico Territory, establish the western border of Texas and have the federal government assume the debt of that state, end the slave trade in the District of Columbia, and strengthen the existing Fugitive Slave Law. President Taylor was opposed to the compromise. Although he was a southern slaveholder, he was unalterably opposed to the extension of slavery to the territories. On the other hand, Vice President Fillmore was a northerner who favored the compromise, including its pro-slavery provisions, because he saw it as the way to prevent violence and unite the country. The alternative, he felt, might be the secession of the southern states and a possible civil war.

Both Taylor and Fillmore took time away from Washington politics in the summer of 1849. Fillmore came to Buffalo and was scheduled to formally welcome President Taylor to the Queen City in early September. Taylor was on a multiple-week-long vacation tour of the North. But illness prevented the president from paying a visit, and Vice President Fillmore instead greeted him at Niagara Falls.

President Fillmore

Though Fillmore had no official say over the Compromise of 1850, save a tie-breaking vote in case of a deadlock in the Senate, a tragic turn of events soon changed everything. President Taylor took ill following a celebration on July 4, 1850, and died of gastroenteritis in the White House five days later. The next day Millard Fillmore was sworn in at the House of Representatives as the thirteenth president of the United States by William Cranch, chief judge of the federal court for the District of Columbia.

President Fillmore made known his support of the compromise measures and signed them into law, thereby forestalling civil war and probably dooming his political career. His support for the Compromise of 1850 and enforcement of the Fugitive Slave Law are usually cited by historians as a shameful act on his part, and not an accomplishment. In doing so they ignore the gravity of the situation in the United States at the time, and instead look at the events from the perspective of the modern era. Fillmore's other notable accomplishments as president of the United States included the opening of Japan to trade with the West, a push for increased foreign trade, support for Hawaiian independence, extension of railroads, support for a canal across the Central American isthmus, reduction of postal rates to stimulate commerce, and advocacy of a plan to develop the Washington Mall close to what we know today.

President Fillmore's Buffalo Visit

Early in 1850, the president had accepted an invitation to visit his home state from the directors of the recently founded New York and Erie Railroad. The company had just completed a 465-mile-long rail line from New York City across the state's southern tier of counties to Dunkirk on Lake Erie. Company officials wished to have the president take an excursion on the line, undoubtedly to help publicize it. A visit to Buffalo would also be included as part of this journey.

The president and his entourage arrived in New York City by steamboat, and on May 14 boarded the train for Dunkirk at the station in Manhattan. Accompanying the president were Secretary of State Daniel Webster, Attorney General John J. Crittenden, Secretary of the Navy William A. Graham, and Postmaster General Nathan K. Hall, the president's old Buffalo friend and law partner. Illinois Democratic Senator Stephen A. Douglas, a key supporter of the Compromise of 1850, was also aboard, as was New York Governor Washington Hunt.

The train stopped in Binghamton and then Elmira, where the passengers spent the night. The next morning, they re-boarded and made brief stops in Corning and Hornell. At each stop the president and his cabinet members appeared on the rear platform of the train, where he gave a short speech, working in an appeal for the Compromise. The crowds were large and respectful. On May 15, the president arrived at the end of the line at Dunkirk. Appropriate ceremonies were held there to welcome him, his companions, and the directors of the railroad company. A huge reception was held at the depot with enough food, in one newspaper's opinion, "to feed an army of 5,000 for a whole week."[13]

The Buffalo Common Council, upon learning of President Fillmore's intention to visit the Queen City, had passed resolutions on May 9 formally inviting him and calling for the appointment of a committee to handle the details of the reception. A citizens' meeting the following evening appointed such a committee of about a hundred prominent city residents, and this group met to work out specifics. On May 15 steamboats carried the committeemen, the Common Council, Mayor James Wadsworth and other interested Buffalonians to Dunkirk to meet and escort the president to Buffalo. At noon, the steamers, with President Fillmore and his party on board, headed up the lake for Buffalo.

Meanwhile, preparations began in the early morning for the reception of Mr. Fillmore. Many houses and businesses displayed the American flag, as did most of the ships in the harbor. A large stage had been erected in Court House Park. On Main Street, along the route of the planned procession, several banners with words of welcome were stretched from building to building across the thoroughfare. Well before noon Buffalonians, as well as inhabitants of surrounding towns and villages, began to gather in the city streets in anticipation of the president's scheduled 3 p.m. arrival. The weather was auspiciously good, and it was a beautiful spring day.

As instructed by the citizens' committee, the various military and civic groups scheduled to participate in the welcome formed on Niagara Street near Main at 1 p.m. Grand Marshal of the festivities was General Nelson Randall, leading the 65th Regiment of the New York State Militia. Other prominent groups taking part were the Buffalo Fire Department and officers of the local and state governments. At 2:30 the formations marched south to the docks of the harbor at the foot of Main Street. The scene was impressive. The many vessels in the harbor flew flags and streamers and were filled with onlookers. Crowds of men, women and children occupied the docks and lined both sides of the Buffalo River all the way to the lighthouse, many standing on bales and barrels to get an unobstructed view. Windows of warehouses, stores and saloons in the area were filled with spectators, and throngs of people lined both sides of Main Street running north from the harbor. Banners stretched across that street proclaimed greetings such as, "WELCOME HOME," "OUR MILLARD FILLMORE," "WELCOME TO ONE AND ALL."

About 3:30 the president's boat was spotted approaching the harbor. An artillery salute was discharged by the militia at Washington and Perry Streets, thereby notifying the assembled crowds, which let out a cheer. Upon docking, President Fillmore and his companions were greeted with another artillery salute and formally welcomed to Buffalo. The party was conducted to waiting carriages, a procession was formed and started its march up Main Street as follows: General Randolph and staff on horseback followed by the 65th Regiment; the president and Mayor Wadsworth in an open barouche drawn by four horses; cabinet secretaries Crittenden, Graham and Hall; Governor Hunt and state officials; the 66th Regiment; the mayor and twelve councilmen of New York City; Dunkirk village trustees; directors of the New York and Erie Railroad; Buffalo city officials; the welcoming committee; Post Office officials; the judiciary and attorneys; the fire department; and civic societies carrying their emblems and banners.

The brilliant, bright uniforms of the military and firefighters made an impressive sight as the line moved up Main Street. Most buildings along the way flew flags and banners, and their windows were jammed with spectators. Each side of the street was packed with onlookers who gave a hearty cheer and wave to the president and other members of the entourage. Some even threw flowers into Fillmore's carriage. The parade's full length extended more than a mile. General Randolph reached Court Street before the last marchers had left the harbor area.

When the procession reached Chippewa it made a left, then another left onto Pearl Street, and headed south to Genesee to Niagara Square and then east up Court Street to Court House Park. There, an immense crowd packed the whole area, at its center a large wooden stage. Mayor Wadsworth escorted the president, cabinet officers and other distinguished guests from their carriages to the platform. He welcomed President Fillmore back to his home town in a short speech praising his performance as the nation's chief executive, while also calling attention to the need for federally financed internal improvements in Buffalo:

> Our own peculiar commercial position at the foot of this vast chain of inland seas around whose borders and their tributary streams millions of free men who fell the forest and fertilize the soil, and towards whose harbor the sails of an active fleet are ever set, has, we believe, some humble

claims to the consideration of the general government.

The mayor closed by thanking Fillmore and his guests for their visit and extending "to you and them the hospitalities of the city."[14] He then introduced President Fillmore to the crowd, which promptly greeted him with nine loud cheers. The president, it was reported, was moved to tears.[15] It was then the president's turn to speak, and he did so eloquently. He first profusely thanked Buffalonians for their hearty welcome and expressed his love for his home town citizens:

> I can hardly persuade myself that it is a reality. It seems more like some hallucination of the mind. But no! Here is the reality, in the thousands of this mighty throng. I came among you, not many years ago, a friendless boy. For all that I am, for all that I hope to be, for all that I hope to do for my country, I am indebted to you. And I hope I am permitted to return to you and spend my days with you, and at last to sleep in yonder graveyard and mingle my dust with yours.[16]

He also alluded to his intention to enforce the execution of the laws of the United States, regarding attempts by certain Americans to invade Cuba, as well as the matter of conflict between North and South. He was interrupted by polite applause several times and enthusiastically cheered upon concluding.

Secretary of State Daniel Webster was then called for by many in the crowd, but it was announced that he had remained back in Dunkirk because his son, who had been traveling with him, had taken ill. Attorney General Crittenden was called upon to speak, but he declined owing to a problem with his voice. He attempted to say a few words, stating that it was a moment of pride, pleasure and honor to be present in Buffalo. Navy Secretary Graham then gave a few brief remarks, followed by Postmaster General Hall, like President Fillmore a Buffalonian. Governor Hunt spoke next, then Senator Douglas, whose speech was considered the most eloquent of the day. Once all the remarks were concluded, Mayor Wadsworth thanked the people for their attendance, and that ended the formal ceremony.

President Fillmore and the other guests were then escorted by the military to the Mansion House hotel on Main and Exchange Streets where they would later enjoy a banquet and spend the night.[17]

President Fillmore had been expected to attend the theater that night, but he declined due to time constraints and the need for rest. The next day, Saturday, he left for East Aurora with Postmaster General Hall to visit his father and friends until Monday morning. Crittenden and Graham left for Niagara Falls, also to return to Buffalo on Monday morning. Meanwhile, on Saturday evening, Secretary of State Daniel Webster made it to Buffalo from Dunkirk. On Monday President Fillmore met with old friends and associates at the Mansion House. The following day, May 20, the entire presidential party headed east by train for visits to Batavia, Rochester and Syracuse before eventually returning to Washington, D.C.

The presidential visit of Millard Fillmore was hailed as being the most impressive and largest demonstration ever held in Buffalo up to that time. The newspapers were unanimous in expressing their praise of the citizens for conducting themselves in such a respectable manner in hosting the esteemed guests.

Former President Fillmore

Soon after he became president, Fillmore decided not to run for the office on his own in 1852, but confided this privately to only a few people. However, in the end he did seek the nomination after being convinced that it was he who would best be suited to unite the Whig Party and the country in the face of increasing North-South sectionalism. Fillmore lost the nomination to Winfield Scott, who lost in the general election to Democrat Franklin Pierce.

As a result, on March 4, 1853, the presidency of Millard Fillmore came to an end. For his policies as president he would be vilified and then ignored by history. He signed into law the Fugitive Slave Act because he saw it as an important part of the Compromise of 1850, which he considered to be a critical series of laws to preserve the Union and prevent a civil war. Once the measure became law, he considered it his constitutional duty to enforce it. He realized that he would be severely criticized for it and that it could well ruin his political career, but because he believed it to be for the good of the country, he courageously took the position of defending the complete Compromise of 1850, including the Fugitive Slave Law.

Fillmore personally hated slavery, but he detested the abolitionists, who would defy the Constitution to eliminate it. He also had little tolerance for those in the South, who advocated secession as the answer to their views on slavery. On October 23, 1850, Fillmore had written in a letter to Daniel Webster, "God knows that I detest slavery, but it is an existing evil, for which we are not responsible, and we must endure it, and give such protection as is guaranteed by the Constitution, till we can get rid of it without destroying the last hope for free government in the world."[18]

Almost immediately after he left office, Fillmore's personal life experienced a tragic event. His wife Abigail caught cold at President Pierce's inauguration, which had been held outdoors in inclement weather. Already not in the best of health during her husband's presidency, her illness developed into pneumonia and she died in Willard's Hotel in Washington at 9 a.m. on March 30, 1853, where the Fillmores had gone to stay after the inaugural ceremonies. The couple had intended to take a tour of the South after Fillmore's term, and so had not immediately set forth to return to Buffalo. Now, the former president would come back to his home town under extremely sad circumstances. Instead of a jubilant welcome home, he would return in mourning to receive the sympathy of its citizens.

Immediately upon learning of the death of the former first lady, President Pierce sent a letter to Fillmore expressing his "earnest condolence in this great bereavement." He canceled a cabinet meeting and directed public offices in Washington to close for the remainder of the day. The U.S. Senate, in session that day, adjourned at noon.[19] On April 1 Mr. Fillmore, along with a few friends and family members, accompanied the remains of Mrs. Fillmore by rail from Washington, through New York and Albany, arriving in Buffalo at eleven o'clock that night. On the very next afternoon, Saturday, April 2, the funeral of Mrs. Fillmore took place beginning at 2 p.m. at the First Unitarian Church at Franklin at Eagle. The sermon was preached by the Reverend Hosmer before a large gathering of family, friends and citizens. Afterward, the remains were conveyed to their resting place at Forest Lawn Cemetery, followed by a large procession of mourners.

Fillmore was dealt a second emotional blow in July 1854 when his twenty-two-year-old daughter Mary died. She had lived with him at the house on Franklin Street since they had left the White House and kept him company. Now, saddened and growing ever more restless, the former president toured the country promoting sectional unity. He was itching to get back into politics again. He moved closer to embracing the nativist American Party because he believed it to be a true national, not sectional, party, and it had absorbed many of his Whig friends after the collapse of that political party.

The American Party's origins date back to 1843. Its founding was a reaction to fears that immigrants and Roman Catholics were gaining a foothold in America; this was viewed as a threat to democracy. Its platform advocated restrictions on immigration, a wait of twenty-one years for citizenship and restriction of political offices to native born, non-Catholic Americans. The American Party was also known as the Know-Nothing Party because it was a secretive organization whose members were instructed to reply, "I know nothing," when queried about its activities. How ironic that in 1855 Fillmore became a member, considering that he first entered politics with the Anti-Masonic Party, which was opposed to the secret society of Masonry. The former president also made it known that he was interested in the Know-Nothing nomination for president in 1856, and he seemed almost assured of this.

In June 1855 Fillmore embarked on a year-long tour of Europe. Despite his anti-Catholic stance, he cordially met Pope Pius IX in the Vatican, once he was assured that he would not have to kneel or kiss his ring. While in London, he met his one-time political nemesis, former President Martin Van Buren, who was also on an overseas trip. He also met the American minister to Britain, future President James Buchanan, whom he would oppose in the 1856 election for the presidency. He also bailed out Horace Greeley, the future Democratic presidential candidate and another of his political opponents, who had been jailed in London for bad debts.

In June 1856, while still in Europe, Fillmore was nominated by the Know-Nothing Party as its candidate for president of the United States. He also accepted the Whig nomination for the same office, though it was virtually a dead party by then. Interestingly, the Know-Nothings chose Andrew Jackson Donelson as candidate for vice-president, the nephew and ward of the late Andrew Jackson, who had also been President Jackson's private secretary and adviser in the White House. Being an anti-Jacksonian had probably been Fillmore's main reason to enter politics as an Anti-Mason in 1828. Now, however, the two men agreed that the American Party was the country's best hope against sectionalism and disunion.[20]

The Fillmore-Donelson ticket lost to the Democrat James Buchanan in the general election. The new Republican Party, the apparent successor to the Whigs, finished second. Fillmore won twenty-one percent of the popular vote and the electoral college votes of only one state, Maryland's eight. If Fillmore had had any chance, it was largely dashed by large numbers of his supporters voting instead for Buchanan, seen as a much stronger choice to win and keep the sectional Republicans out of the White House. Fillmore emphasized the danger of a sectional party gaining power in the United States. His utterances and writings during the campaign hardly mentioned anti-Catholic and anti-foreign sentiments at all. They were mostly about the danger of the Republicans gaining power and dividing the country. Without Fillmore in the race, the result likely would have been the same, a Buchanan victory.

After the 1856 election, both Fillmore and the American Party ended their political careers. He permanently retired from politics. Having earlier given up the practice of law, he now had no means of income and was worried about his future well-being. Fate, in the person of one Caroline McIntosh, entered the picture. Mrs. McIntosh was the wealthy widow of a Troy, New York merchant, and after being introduced to Mr. Fillmore, the two soon fell in love and married in 1858. The couple bought the Hollister Mansion at 52 Niagara Square, where the Statler Building now stands at the corner of Delaware Avenue. They lived in the huge Gothic home for the rest of their lives.

Millard Fillmore continued to be Buffalo's number one citizen. He helped start, support and maintain several Buffalo institutions that exist to this day in one form or another: the University of Buffalo, the Buffalo Historical Society, the SPCA Buffalo Chapter, the Buffalo Fine Arts Academy, the Buffalo Club, Buffalo Hospital Association, the Buffalo Society for Natural Sciences, and the Young Men's Association Library.

Though he is usually ignored by historians and often mocked and disrespected by them when he is remembered, this is perhaps due to his being considered by academics through a twenty-first century lens, rather than considering the man in the context of the times in which he lived. Fillmore was a pragmatist, and this attitude to divisive political issues was not unique. Even Abraham Lincoln supported the Fugitive Slave Law, voicing that support in his first inaugural address.[21] Fillmore's views on slavery, foreigners and Catholics were not out of the mainstream at the time. He never liked slavery and did not emphasize the anti-foreign, anti-Catholic doctrine of the Know-Nothing Party during his 1856 run for president. Rather, he seemed to have been attracted to it because he considered it to have been a party that was truly national in scope, an idea in which he deeply believed. Sectionalism was anathema to him.

CHAPTER 3

LIBERTY AND FREE SOIL

New York Anti-Slavery Politics

Like the establishment of the Anti-Masons, another of the most important political movements in American history was organized in Western New York State in the first half of the nineteenth century. As opposition to slavery in America grew in the northern states, various groups promoted the cause. The foundations of this opposition were moral, religious, political and economic.

One of the early influential associations of this kind was the American Anti-Slavery Society, founded by the abolitionist William Lloyd Garrison in Philadelphia in 1833. At this same time, many local churches, whose denominations were nominally anti-slavery, started being more vocal in their opposition to the "peculiar institution." Because the secular anti-slavery societies and these churches shared a hostility toward slavery, the efforts of these groups often melded together. For instance, the leaders of both tended to be one and the same people. These abolition churches took the lead in spreading the anti-slavery message. Interestingly, the center of church-based abolitionism was Central and Western New York. Why was this?

A combination of factors made the area particularly receptive to the movement. Central and Western New York were largely settled by New Englanders who moved westward for fertile land and greater opportunity. There already existed in their old communities a type of Protestant revivalist Christianity. Good economic times in the 1830s gave the people confidence that they could achieve a religious and societal "perfectionism." At first, even the economic downturn in the late 1830s served to reinforce the drive toward the perfect world. Furthermore, Upstate New York was an important stop in the Underground Railroad network of way stations for escaped southern slaves. The region usually provided the last hiding places for the African Americans before they were spirited across the Canadian border, beyond which they would be safe from being returned to bondage under the Fugitive Slave Law.[1] However, some of the escaped slaves felt safe enough in New York that they settled in the area. With a white population overwhelmingly sympathetic to their plight, they had little fear of being turned in to the local authorities, who probably would have balked at enforcing the law anyway. This exposure to the Underground Railroad may have been another reason that Central and Western New York was a hotbed of anti-slavery sentiment.

Church-based abolitionism sprang from and coexisted with the anti-establishment beliefs of church members. They rebelled against church hierarchy and authoritarianism in the greater society. This was a reflection of the tensions in America at large over the scope and meaning of democracy. As democratic principles began to take hold in the churches, congregations wanted local lay control, and hence they turned against the authority of their pastors. This often resulted in a split in the congregation with the formation of separate "perfectionist" churches. Because they believed that the church hierarchy was evil, they also went against other forms of authority, including systems that supported slavery, the most serious form of despotism. They came to support a kind of social radicalism that also favored women's rights and prohibition of alcohol, among other causes. The fire and brimstone preaching of lay pastors in these perfectionist abolitionist churches, as well as the reputation of Central and Western New York as a place whose religious movements were born and flamed out, gained the epithet "burned-over district" for the region. It was only a matter of time before these churches, along with some members of the secular anti-slavery societies, began to advocate for political action to achieve their goals. No longer content with speech making and questioning of candidates about their views on slavery, which had poor results, they decided to meet to determine their political involvement.

The two most important leaders of this shift toward politics were Alvan Stewart of Utica and Myron P. Holley of Rochester. Stewart was a lawyer and founder of the New York State Anti-Slavery Society. Holley was a former state legislator, a driving force behind the construction of the Erie Canal and a canal commissioner. By early 1839, both men were advocating the establishment of an anti-slavery political party. Through correspondence and meetings, they gradually gained increasing support for a third party despite strong opposition within the anti-slavery movement. By late October, Stewart, Holley and their circle of like-minded men called for a convention to determine their nominations for the presidential and vice presidential elections of 1840. They chose to hold this meeting in Warsaw, New York.[2]

Why Warsaw, a little village with a population of only a few hundred? It was home to the congregation of the Warsaw Presbyterian Church, many of whose members espoused anti-authoritarianism and abolition of slavery.[3] Within a year, these members would break away to form their own abolitionist Church of Warsaw. Warsaw was one of those communities of the burned-over district that had a fervent anti-slavery contingent, so it would not be unwelcoming to an anti-slavery convention meeting in its midst, and was no doubt familiar to Holley, Stewart or any number of their supporters. In addition, mob violence against abolitionists had sometimes occurred, and Warsaw had proven to be a safe haven from such attacks.[4]

On November 13, 1839, the convention was called to order at the Presbyterian Church. After much discussion, the delegates nominated James G. Birney for president, and Francis J. LeMoyne for vice president. Birney was a forty-seven year old former slave owner who, by the 1830s, had freed his slaves and moved from Alabama to Cincinnati. LeMoyne was a forty-one year old physician from Pennsylvania. Neither man was present in Warsaw and both summarily declined the nominations. Despite this setback, the anti-slavery movement continued to organize. The dismay of anti-slavery advocates at the nomination for president of William Henry Harrison by the Whigs in December 1839 to oppose Democratic incumbent Martin Van Buren in 1840 kept the drive for an anti-slavery political party alive. Neither Harrison nor Van Buren was trusted to oppose the pro-slavery forces in the country.

Like Warsaw, Arcade, New York was a Western New York village involved in the anti-slavery movement, with church leaders there active in it. On January 29, 1840, the Western New York Anti-Slavery Society met at the Arcade Congregational Church.[5] It nominated a slate of candidates for state offices and approved a call for a national nominating convention. This Arcade convention probably drew many of the same people who had attended the Warsaw meeting two months earlier. Myron Holley was present. Similar meetings held around the same time in Farmington and West Bloomfield, both in Ontario County, were not successful at approving a resolution for a national convention. But through Holley's efforts a National Third Party Anti-Slavery Convention was called to meet in Albany, New York on April 1, 1840 to discuss the matter of political involvement.[6] One hundred twenty-one delegates attended, 104 from New York State, but none from the Midwest. Both supporters and opponents of the third-party movement were present. It nominated Birney for president and Thomas Earle, a fifty-one year-old Philadelphia lawyer, for vice president. This time both men accepted.

This anti-slavery party was disorganized, subject to serious internal disputes, and did not even have a formal name at the time of the 1840 election. It drew only 6,225 votes for president and had no impact on the election, which was won by Harrison. Nevertheless, its leaders regrouped and called for a national convention in New York City in early 1841. On May 12 delegates from every northern state save Michigan met in the city, but the meeting was dominated by New Yorkers and New Englanders. It was at this convention that the organization began to function as a cohesive political party. Calling itself the Liberty Party, in 1844 it nominated James G. Birney for president and for vice president Thomas Morris, a sixty-five-year-old former Democratic U.S. senator from Ohio, who was later replaced by William Jay of New York, son of Founding Father John Jay. It set up a national committee to coordinate activities and adopted a set of basic beliefs. Finally, it agreed to meet again in two years.

The Liberty Party Convention In Buffalo

Pursuant to the resolution passed at the New York convention, the national committee in time decided to hold the Liberty Party's 1843 convention in Buffalo, New York on May 24. Why did the Liberty Party choose Buffalo? Though a growing city, it paled in comparison to New York, Boston or Philadelphia, all of which were important northern centers of politics and business. Though it was close to the burned-over district of ecclesiastical abolition fervor in Central and Western New York, Buffalo sported not one abolition church. The closest were in Collins in Erie County, Lockport in Niagara County, and Perry, Castile, Warsaw and Arcade in Wyoming County.[7]

The reasons for choosing Buffalo were its location and its ability to accommodate overnight guests. The Liberty Party and anti-slavery territory stretched across the northern tier of states, from Iowa and Illinois in the west to Maine and Massachusetts in the east. Buffalo was centrally located in this territory, and had the added advantage of proximity to the burned-over district, which had already held important Liberty Party meetings in Warsaw and Arcade. Also, being at the terminus of the Erie Canal and situated on Lake Erie on a major rail line, it was relatively easy for travelers to reach Buffalo. Delegates to the convention who stayed overnight could be put up at the city's hotels and temperance houses.[8]

However, the May gathering had to be postponed until September 6 due to concerns about ice on Lake Erie, as explained in the *Signal of Liberty*, an anti-slavery weekly published in Ann Arbor, Michigan:

NOTICE

To the Liberty Party Abolitionists throughout the United States:

DEAR FRIENDS -
The providence of God having placed insurmountable obstacles in the way of holding a United States A.S. Convention at Buffalo, on the 24th and 25th days of May next, as appointed,

owing to the thick ice which covers Lake Erie, and as we are credibly informed by friends in Ohio, will not be removed till the middle of June next, in consequence of which, our friends in Ohio, Indiana, Illinois and Michigan could not attend except at great inconvenience and expense – the navigation of said Lake being indispensable, or nearly so, to their attendance - the said convention is therefore postponed until the first Wednesday in September next, and Thursday following at Buffalo, when we shall hope to have returns from the London Convention. It is hoped that each State will send as many delegates as each State is entitled to Representatives in Congress. However, all are invited to attend.[9]

As the September date approached, the convention had to be rescheduled one more time due to conflicts with elections in Maine and Vermont.[10] Finally, on Wednesday, August 30, 1843, the Liberty Convention opened in the Queen City. Most historians consider this to be the Liberty Party's first truly national convention, for it was not run only by New York and Massachusetts men, as in 1841, but with input from a cross-section of states.[11] And because the party membership had increased considerably in the last two years, it drew a more diverse crowd than had been present in New York City.

On the morning of August 30 participants began to gather in Court House Park and in the Court House itself to prepare for the convention. Already a great white tent had been pitched where the meeting would be held. This enormous tent was provided by Oberlin College of Ohio. Oberlin was an institution that trained and educated many of the abolitionist pastors and speakers throughout the North. It routinely lent out the tent to Liberty Party conventions as well as evangelical revivalist meetings. On a mast at the peak of the tent flew a blue banner with the words, "HOLINESS TO THE LORD." It was said to provide enough room for 5,000 people.

The better part of the morning was spent organizing, but in the afternoon the delegates got down to business. Their main focus was to organize the campaign for the 1844 presidential election, to reaffirm the nominations made in 1841, and to debate resolutions. An estimated

1,500 men and women, most of them spectators, not delegates, sat and stood under the tent on a fine summer day to hear the speakers, who included a runaway slave and a woman, rarities for any public mass meeting. In fact, the woman, Abby Kelley, was the first woman to ever address a national political convention. It was also the first national convention to have African American delegates.

This being a political gathering, a great deal of demagoguery and nastiness was spewed forth. Yet with the Liberty Party membership so greatly composed of ecclesiastical abolitionists and revivalist churchmen, religion was a good part of the mixture. Indeed, the convention probably had the air of a Christian revival gathering more than that of a political meeting. The association of religion with politics drew the condemnation of the Buffalo newspapers. So too did the speakers' vituperations against organized religion and advocacy of illegal measures to end slavery, to include an uprising by American slaves.

The resolutions, thirty-eight in all, were introduced by Salmon P. Chase of Ohio, who in due time would become a U.S. senator, secretary of the treasury and chief justice of the United States, and whose brother Edward was a Lockport attorney. The resolutions essentially supported equal rights for all, stated that slavery was contrary to the principles of American liberty and ought to be banned by every state, that slavery should not spread beyond its present limits, and should be banned in the District of Columbia. Also, the Fugitive Slave Law should be repealed, a sound currency should be supported, and freedom of speech, trial by jury and right of petition should be considered inviolable.

The next day, August 31, debate continued on the resolutions, and they were passed. Nominations for the offices of president and vice president of the United States were taken up. James G. Birney and William Jay had been nominated previously at the New York City convention of 1841, but a letter from Birney was read in which he asked his nomination to be reconsidered, as was a letter from Jay in which he declined the vice presidential nomination but urged retention of Birney for president. The delegates unanimously chose Birney for president, and for vice president Thomas Morris of Ohio. A total of 148 delegates cast votes. A raucous evening session followed, which was described as stormy, justifying a potential uprising by the slaves and featuring speakers who heaped abuse on organized Christianity and various politicians. The gathering finally dispersed at 1:30 a.m. when the convention adjourned. Overall, the convention was deemed a success. It avoided any serious rift and managed to fashion a compromise among the different viewpoints presented.

Once again, in 1844, the two major parties nominated presidential candidates who repulsed anti-slavery advocates. They were Henry Clay of Kentucky for the Whigs and James K. Polk of Tennessee for the Democrats, with Clay, the Great Compromiser, slightly less onerous to them. Liberty's Birney won over 62,000 votes for president, 2.3 per cent of the total, but did not win any electoral votes. Polk, the Democrat, was elected President. Many historians say, however, that the Liberty Party decided the election by polling 15,814 votes in New York State, compared to 232,452 for Clay and 237,588 for Polk. They contend that enough of those Liberty votes would have gone to Clay in the state had Birney not been on the ballot, thus giving the Whigs the state's electoral votes instead of Polk. That would have resulted in Clay getting the majority of electoral votes nationally. Because of this, Whigs and moderate anti-slavery Americans strongly condemned the Liberty Party for disrupting the process and "stealing" the presidency for Polk.

After the election, the Liberty Party reassessed itself and contemplated the future. Never having a strong national leadership, most developments took place on local and regional levels, including conventions and participation in elections. There were disagreements over the party's direction, mainly over whether to collaborate with more moderate anti-slavery advocates outside the party. Eventually, the proponents of cooperation and coalition with anti-slavery Whigs and Democrats won the day. By 1847 the party began to de-emphasize total abolition of slavery in favor of adamant opposition to its extension. Religious zeal within the Liberty ranks was giving way to practical politics. This paved the way toward what would eventually come to be known as the Free Soil Party.

The Second Liberty Party Convention In Buffalo

In advance of the 1848 presidential election, a debate ensued within the

Liberty Party as to whether a national convention should be held early or closer to the election. Coalitionists, who favored cooperation with outside politicians, supported a later convention, after the Democrat and Whig conventions, because they believed that would help draw disaffected members of the major parties into the Liberty Party, and that a later meeting would favor selection of a presidential nominee from their faction. The more conservative members wanted an earlier convention so that a candidate from their faction would have a better chance of securing the nomination. The party's national committee decided in favor of an early convention, for October 1847, and once again chose to meet in Buffalo.

The conventioneers converged on Buffalo and a large number of delegates met at the Court House on Washington Street at 9 a.m. on Wednesday, October 20. Most of the prominent Liberty men were in attendance, including, once again, Salmon P. Chase of Cincinnati. Chase had become very influential within the party and was a coalitionist. Most coalitionists were from the Cincinnati area of southern Ohio and by the time of this convention they favored a multi-party anti-slavery union.[12] At the Court House, general preparations were hammered out pursuant to the formal opening of the convention. It was scheduled to meet in the big tent from Oberlin College in a vacant lot at one corner of Eagle and Ellicott Streets, but the tent had not yet arrived, so business opened in the Court House. At 10:30 it was announced that the tent had arrived, but obviously too late for any part of the morning session.

The convention was called to order by the national committee's chairman. It began with various organizing initiatives, including appointment of convention officers. After an opening speech and a song, the convention recessed. It reassembled under the big tent at Eagle and Ellicott at 2 p.m. A hundred forty delegates, fairly proportioned among the states, all of which were represented (albeit northern states), were part of an attendance that totaled five hundred. Not only were the coalitionists and conservatives present, so too were members of the Liberty League, an offshoot of the Liberty Party formed months earlier that believed in the uncompromising permanency of an anti-slavery party, but which for the time being remained within the Liberty Party itself.

The next morning the delegates reconvened at the tent, and then adjourned to a nearby theater. The afternoon session commenced at 2:15, and continued the morning's debates over various resolutions, including arguments over proposals to nominate a presidential candidate. Efforts by Chase to postpone the selection of a nominee failed. Talk of dissolving the party circulated but went nowhere.[13] An evening session assembled at the Court House at 7 p.m. At 8 o'clock voting for a presidential nominee began, following endorsement speeches for several men. Nominated for president was John P. Hale, longtime Democrat and anti-slavery U.S. senator from New Hampshire, with 103 votes to 57 for all others. He was a compromise choice between coalitionists and conservatives. Chosen for vice president was Owen Lovejoy of Illinois, with 76 votes. However, Mr. Lovejoy declined the nomination, and Leicester King of Ohio was then unanimously selected to take his place. In short order the convention adjourned.

There had been serious and spirited debate on certain points, at times acrimonious but never outright hostile. Ten resolutions had been adopted. The majority reaffirmed the party's opposition to slavery and called for its end by constitutional means. An amendment contending that slavery was already unconstitutional in the states was defeated. One resolution, which could be interpreted to address oppression beyond slavery, read as follows:

"That the laws in the several states, designed to oppress and degrade particular classes of individuals, are indefensible in principle, and ought to be repealed."[14]

Though the coalitionists lost the battle over delaying the presidential nomination, the resolutions, which were in effect the party's platform, were decidedly coalitionist, for they appealed to a wider electorate than conservatives would have liked and were more practical than purely moral in tone.[15] This was a directional change for the party, which opened it up to cooperation with Whig and Democrat anti-slavery forces.

The Buffalo newspapers voiced a negative view of the Liberty Party during its convention. They saw it as a threat to the order of the established two party system in America, a one issue party with no specific long term practical purpose save to embarrass the two major parties and be a spoiler.[16]

National Liberty, Barnburners and Free Soil

After the Buffalo convention, the coalitionists continued their efforts to form ties with anti-slavery politicians outside of the Liberty Party. Salmon P. Chase and like-minded Liberty men, most of whom were from Ohio, wanted to form an alliance with anti-slavery dissidents from the Democrat and Whig Parties to form a new, stronger movement. Eventually, the coalitionists began communicating with Barnburner Democrats of New York and Conscience Whigs, whose main base was New England.

The Barnburners, also known as Radical Democrats, were so called after the proverbial farmer who would burn down his barn to rid it of rats. In other words, they were considered to be unreasonable, if not mindless. They were almost exclusively New Yorkers and, while not abolitionists, they were opposed to the extension of slavery beyond where it already existed. They also disagreed with most Democrats over banks and internal improvements. The Conscience Whigs were moralists who believed that slavery should ultimately be abolished, but until then it should be confined to the states in which it was currently legal.

The Democratic and Whig Parties held their national conventions in late May and early June of 1848. They nominated Lewis Cass of Michigan and Zachary Taylor of Louisiana, respectively, for president. These choices did not please the anti-slavery members of either party. Cass was considered to be a friend of the southern slaveholders and Taylor was himself a slaveholder. The disaffected Barnburners walked out of the Democratic convention and met in mid-June in Utica, New York, where they nominated Martin Van Buren as their alternative Democratic presidential candidate. Disappointed Conscience Whigs met in Worcester, Massachusetts, and coalitionist Liberty men held a People's Convention, or Free Territory Convention, in Columbus, Ohio open to all anti-slavery advocates. Neither of the latter two meetings produced nominations for president. All three groups agreed to meet together in Buffalo in August. They had seen the wisdom in uniting their energies to put forth a third national candidate for president in 1848 in a national Free Soil convention.

The term "free soil" was first used in the early nineteenth century as a slogan for a land reform movement, specifically the concept that federal land should be given away to homesteading settlers. It evolved in the 1840s to include the anti-slavery crusade.[17]

A couple of months before the Free Soil convention, for two days Buffalo was the center of political activity with national overtones. On June 13, 1848, Democratic presidential candidate Lewis Cass made an overnight stay in the city on the way to his Michigan home. He was received by 5,000 supporters as he arrived at the railroad station. He made a brief speech as he was welcomed at his hotel that evening.

The next day, John Van Buren, son of the former president and leader of the Barnburner faction of the Democrats, arrived in Buffalo to address a rally, having been invited by the chairman of the Erie County Democratic Party. Cass and Van Buren did not meet, though they were in the city at the same time for a few hours. Also, on June 13, delegates began arriving for a National Liberty Party convention. Its attendees consisted mainly of 104 Liberty League members who rejected any union with Democrats or Whigs. It also drew a few Barnburners who observed the proceedings. There is no indication that John Van Buren attended. The group styled itself the National Liberty Party in contrast to the established Liberty Party that it thought had abandoned true party principles.

This convention started with a preliminary meeting on June 14 at the Court House, during which the suitability of John P. Hale as a presidential candidate was discussed. The Oberlin tent had been pitched at one corner of Ellicott and Eagle Streets for its main activities and the afternoon session was held there. It opened with a lengthy speech by Gerritt Smith of Central New York, a wealthy businessman who was one of the founders and bankrollers of the original Liberty Party. Far from being the one issue party it was supposed to be, his speech not only was anti-slavery in nature, but touched on free trade, a graduated income tax, denunciation of banks, universal suffrage and reform of the Post Office. A series of other speakers followed, including former slave Frederick Douglass. Though opposed to the group, he was allowed to speak due to his status as the most prominent former slave in the United States. Thirteen resolutions were adopted, mainly denouncing betrayal of the Liberty principles, endorsing land reform, and opposing slavery.

The convention continued the next day with morning, afternoon and evening sessions during which many speeches were delivered. At 5 p.m. nominations for president were taken up. Smith was overwhelmingly chosen as the party's 1848 presidential nominee, with Charles C. Foote of Michigan for vice president. One Buffalo newspaper criticized the convention as "a meagre and inefficient one" and called the party "an absurd and impracticable organization."[18] As it was, the National Liberty Party was only a small group constituting a small fraction of the main Liberty Party.

What was described as an immense and enthusiastic gathering streamed into Court House Park late in the afternoon of Thursday, June 15 to attend the 6:30 p.m. Barnburner proceedings. They were there to hear the speech of John Van Buren, even as the National Liberty Party convention was meeting nearby. Crowded with Barnburner supporters, as well as curious regular Democrats and Whigs, officers were appointed and resolutions passed as preliminary speeches denounced the nomination of Lewis Cass for president. When Van Buren came forward to speak, he was greeted with tumultuous and sustained applause. He launched into his talk, which was full of criticism of the Democratic Party and Cass. He rallied the troops for two hours in an entertaining campaign speech that alternated with sarcasm, humor and seriousness.

The *Buffalo Daily Courier*, supporter of Cass, excoriated Van Buren in its pages, accusing him and his faction of attempting to throw the election to the Whig Taylor. The Courier called Van Buren an ingrate, apostate, a shameless unblushing renegade, and a traitor to his father.[19]

The Free Soil Convention In Buffalo

Now it was the Free Soilers' turn. Buffalo was chosen for the Free Soil national convention for the same reasons that the Liberty Party met here – its central location in relation to the anti-slavery movement and the relative ease of getting to the Queen City. Also, the successful Liberty conventions held in the city in 1843 and 1847 gave Buffalo a reputation as an accommodating place to hold similar political gatherings.

In early August, Free Soil delegates, supporters and observers began streaming into the city for the big two-day event, scheduled to open on Wednesday, August 9. They came by rail, horseback, lake steamer and canal boat, and took up rooms in Buffalo's hotels, inns, temperance houses and, most likely, private homes. The Mansion House Hotel at the southwest corner of Main and Exchange Streets was the headquarters for most of the leaders of the convention.[20] It was estimated that there were as many as 20,000 visitors. Prominent attendees included Salmon P. Chase, John Van Buren, the poet Walt Whitman, noted former slave Frederick Douglass, future Democratic presidential nominee Samuel J. Tilden, and Charles Francis Adams, son of the recently deceased John Quincy Adams.

In the evening of August 8 a torchlight parade was conducted through the city streets, featuring a boisterous crowd chanting Free Soil slogans and carrying images of Martin Van Buren, Thomas Jefferson, Liberty Party stalwart John P. Hale and David Wilmot, the author of the (in)famous Wilmot Proviso which would have prohibited slavery in any territory the U.S. had annexed from Mexico in the recent war. Early in the morning of August 9 a huge crowd gathered in and around Court House Park. Already at 5 a.m. a large group had assembled for prayers. An immense tent had been erected on park grounds. At 8:30 the tent opened, followed by a fevered dash for seats on the wooden stands inside. In short order the place was filled to capacity, all seats and standing space taken up by thousands of people.

Eventually the crowd was brought under control. Preliminary speeches were made, offering encouragement to the adherents of anti-slavery, denouncing opponents and extolling the virtues of the Free Soil movement. Speakers freely took to the podium with their remarks as no set agenda prevailed under the tent. The audience cheered, shouted and sweated. The weather both inside and outside the tent was sultry, sweltering and stifling, a typical humid August day in Buffalo. At one point, a platform erected for reporters collapsed, causing some minor injuries. The crowd was asked to leave the tent and return at noon for the formal opening of the convention.

The convention reassembled in the great tent at noon and was called to order. It was resolved to have each state present appoint one man to an organizing committee, and once chosen, the nineteen-member body retired to the Court House across Washington Street. The convention was then recessed until three in the afternoon. At the Court House the organizing committee chose Charles Francis Adams as convention president. A committee of conferees was proposed to set general rules and to choose nominees for president and vice president of the United States, and another committee to draft a set of resolutions, that is, a party platform. The afternoon session convened as scheduled under the tent. After a cacophony of shouts and cries, the crowd was brought to order. Adams was announced as president of the convention and took his seat to thunderous applause. Vice presidents for the convention were chosen, one from each state. An adjournment was called at 6:30, to last until 8 p.m.

The evening session started on time, with a long prayer and a speech by Mr. Adams. Then a report from the Committee on Organization was read out. Per its decision, each state's delegation chose three members each for a Committee on Resolutions. For the Committee of Conferees, six delegates from each state present were chosen as well as three from each Congressional district, selected to give equal representation to the Liberty, Democrat and Whig Parties. It constituted about 500 men. After several lengthy speeches and a song, it was agreed that the Committee of Conferees would meet at the Court House at 7:30 the next morning.

Like the Liberty Party conventions, this one at times was more reminiscent of a religious revival than a political meeting, what with early morning prayer meetings in the park, most sessions opening with a long prayer, and the deep devotion of the multitude to their cause and ideals. Emotional outbursts and appeals to conscience were a common occurrence. Perhaps that is not surprising since a great number of attendees were from the Liberty Party. Convention goers came from every free state in the North, the District of Columbia plus the slave states of Virginia, Maryland and Delaware. As such, a variety of accents could be heard in Buffalo and a diversity of dress could be seen. This was one description of the mass of people that descended on the city:

Among the delegates to the convention in this city are some

of the oddest looking chaps that ever were seen. Some of them are about as verdant as a stripling just escaped from his maternal parent's apron strings, while others look as if they could face a rampant, roaring buffalo without being in the slightest degree intimidated. Hats of all shapes and sizes, from the lofty bell-crown and majestic sugar-loaf to the squatty, rimless, and insignificant tub shape, are sported on this occasion. A few have whiskers and mustachios, but most of them are divested of these appendages. Coats that look as if every tailor in the country had struck out a new and original idea for himself, and which designate the wearer's particular views with more expression than many of the owner's [sic] faces may also be seen. Unmentionables, varying from the liberal bag seat to the scrimpy skin-tight, with legs both short and long without particular reference to the requirements of the wearer, in connection with neat, tidy and fashionable appareled [sic] to make up the variety.[21]

The second day once again began with a prayer gathering at the park at an early hour. Convention delegates began streaming into the tent and the morning session was called to order by Mr. Adams at nine o'clock. The platform of resolutions was read to the crowd. There were fifteen resolutions in all and they were met with great enthusiasm by the delegates. A motion was made for their unanimous adoption and this was done to immense cheering. The convention then adjourned until 3 p.m. The Free Soil convention was mainly concerned with anti-slavery issues, but unlike the Liberty Party, it also emphasized other concerns. The expression, "Free Soil, Free Speech, Free Labor, Free Men," was the motto of the Free Soilers and it could be heard all during the two-day event.

As noted previously, the term Free Soil was originated by advocates for free land grants from the federal government for homesteading settlers on federal lands. Free Speech reiterated support for the basic American liberty to speak freely in opposition to or in support of any issue, and may have referred to the infamous Congressional Gag Rule which forbade debate on slavery in the House of Representatives during the years 1836 to 1844. Free Labor meant that each man should be allowed to freely sell his labor without competition from slaves who were not paid for their work, and who thus lowered the value of such work. As for Free Men, the meaning seems obvious, though the Free Soil Party did not advocate outright abolition of slavery, but mainly a ban on its extension to any U.S. territory in which it did not yet exist. The fifteen points adopted by the Committee on Resolutions and approved by the convention at large emphasized the anti-slavery theme, but also touched on other subjects. The planks largely satisfied the Liberty men, who apparently struck a deal with the dominant Democrats to nominate a Democrat for president in exchange for a platform that underscored opposition to slavery.

The first ten resolutions concerned slavery, including statements that the federal government had no power to institute slavery in any territory where it did not exist, but also an acknowledgment that Congress had no right to interfere with slavery in states wherein it already existed. They also posited that Congress had no power to make a slave of any man and could not deprive anyone of liberty without due legal process,. They also supported anti-slavery efforts in the Oregon, California and New Mexico territories. The remaining five resolutions called for cheap postage, internal improvements of rivers and harbors, a homestead law, early payment of the federal debt, support for a strong tariff, and finally, resolution fifteen stated: We inscribe on our banner "Free Soil, Free Speech, Free Labor, and Free Men," and under it will fight on, and fight ever, until a triumphant victory shall reward our exertions.

The afternoon session of the second day commenced at 3:30. More speeches were made. When Frederick Douglass was called upon to speak, he took the stand but regretfully declined due to a recent throat operation that limited his ability to talk at length. But Henry Bibb, an escaped slave who lived in Michigan, did deliver a short address. During this general session under the tent, the Committee of Conferees met at the Universalist Church at Washington and Clinton Streets, now the site of the Hotel Lafayette. It was this committee that had in its hands the most important decisions of the convention – the choice of nominees for president and vice president of the United States.

Even before the convention had begun, Martin Van Buren of New York was the frontrunner for the presidential nomination. He had already been nominated by the Barnburner Democrats as an alternative Democratic presidential nominee in defiance of the Democratic National Convention that had chosen Lewis Cass. In addition, he had the cachet and nationwide name recognition due to the fact that he was a former president. The Barnburners on the committee obviously wanted Van Buren. The Liberty men favored John P. Hale, whom they had chosen as their candidate the previous October in Buffalo. The weakest candidate was U.S. Associate Justice John McLean of Ohio, the Whigs' man. McLean, however, wanted his name withdrawn from consideration and this was done by Chairman Salmon P. Chase, who, incidentally, was McLean's son-in-law.

The Barnburners were the most politically astute of the conferees, and they made a deal with key Liberty and Whig men to include resolutions in the platform favorable to them in exchange for support for Van Buren's nomination. It did not hurt their cause that Chairman Chase leaned toward the Democrats, though his roots were in the Liberty Party. In the course of the committee proceedings a letter from Martin Van Buren was read. In it, he expressed his respect and support for the Buffalo proceedings and stated his desire to never again be a candidate for president. But Benjamin Butler of New York, to whom Van Buren's letter had been addressed, iterated his belief that Van Buren would nevertheless accept a Free Soil nomination.[22]

A vote was taken for the presidential nomination. Van Buren won with 244 votes to Hale's 183 and 40 for all others.[23] The former president's nomination was made unanimous by acclamation, and this was followed by terrific cheering which filled the church. Charles Francis Adams, the Whig from Massachusetts, was unanimously chosen for vice president. The committee then adjourned to make their report to the general convention. Toward the end of the afternoon's general session in the tent, one gentleman in the audience announced that the Committee of Conferees had selected as the Free Soil candidate for president Martin Van Buren. This was met by a great round of cheering, as unconfirmed as it was. The convention adjourned for tea until evening.

At 8 p.m. the evening session of the great convention began. After opening speeches the Committee of Conferees filed into the tent at 9:30, ready to reveal the convention's nominees for president and vice president of the United States. Chairman Chase announced to the crowd that Martin Van Buren had been unanimously selected as their candidate for president. This announcement set off the most enthusiastic demonstration of cheers and shouts. There was much waving of hats, handkerchiefs, banners and hands. After some semblance of order was restored, Mr. Chase said a letter of support had been received from former President Van Buren. More cheers. He then announced the choice for vice president, Charles Francis Adams. There followed more cheers, after which Chase asked, "What action will the convention take upon these recommendations?" It was moved that they be adopted by acclamation, and it was so done.

A small committee was formed to officially inform Mr. Van Buren and Mr. Adams of their nominations (though Adams was present). More speeches were made by fired up speakers. And a resolution of thanks to the residents of Buffalo for their kindness and attention was passed. This was followed by the reading of Martin Van Buren's letter of support to the crowd. Near midnight the convention adjourned and most attendees formed into a long torchlight procession that marched through Buffalo's principal streets, with drums beating and rallying cries, "Van Buren and Free Soil, Adams and Liberty!" A huge banner was carried by the marchers that spelled out the names of their candidates.

The next morning a huge exodus of conventioneers from Buffalo began. By and large, the convention was deemed a huge success by those who had attended. Martin Van Buren formally accepted the Free Soil nomination for president and the party waged a spirited campaign in the fall of 1848. In the end, Van Buren received 291,263 popular votes, just over ten per cent of the total cast. The Democrat Cass got 1,220,544 (43%) and the Whig Taylor, 1,360,009 (47%). Van Buren did not win a state and so received no electoral votes. Most historians contend that Taylor would have won the election even in a two-man race with Cass. Van Buren probably took enough votes away from Cass in New York to give the state to Taylor, but the opposite most likely occurred in Ohio and other Midwestern states. It is difficult to extrapolate what would have, could have, should have happened. Whatever the possibilities, Taylor went to the White House and events were set in motion to propel his vice president, Millard Fillmore of

Buffalo, into the presidency less than two years later.

It is not known whether Fillmore was in Buffalo during the Free Soil convention. He most certainly did not attend it, since he was the Whig Party's vice presidential nominee. There is no record of him making any comment about it during its two day run. At one point, a speaker at the convention referred to Fillmore, saying no one in the South would vote for him, and that he would only be vice president as a Free Soil man, and that he should come to the convention and ask for a nomination.[24]

After the election of 1848 many Free Soilers were disappointed by the party's showing. Others were satisfied with its performance, if only on philosophical grounds. They had no choice but to reject the major party nominees, they believed. Nevertheless, the Free Soil Party quickly deteriorated. Barnburner Democrats and Conscience Whigs drifted back to their old parties. Indeed, many Barnburners never considered themselves to have left the Democratic Party, only to have joined with Whigs and Liberty men in Buffalo in a grand coalition to elect an alternate Democrat to the presidency. As to the Liberty Party, orthodox members had never acquiesced in joining the Free Soil movement, and the remnants of that Liberty Party attempted to revive, with only minor success, their party of old.

The Compromise of 1850 dealt a brief setback to anti-slavery politics because it seemed to have settled the sectional crisis for the time being. But in a few short years the anti-slavery movement would heat up considerably and lead to the formation of the Republican Party, which would be composed mainly of old Liberty and Free Soil members, including Conscience Whigs and some Democrats. The Liberty and Free Soil Parties actually ran candidates in the 1852 presidential election but received only a small number of votes that had no bearing on the overall results. In fact, the Liberty Party held what was called a national convention in Buffalo in September 1851 that chose Gerritt Smith as its presidential nominee. What remained of the Free Soil Party renamed itself the Free Democracy and held national conventions in Cleveland and Pittsburgh that year. The Whigs were greatly weakened after losing the presidency in 1852, and were supplanted by the new Republican Party within a couple of years.

Though often ignored in the present day, the Buffalo Free Soil convention was one of the most important events ever held in the city, the largest political assembly that had ever met in the U.S. up to that time, and was a landmark in the nation's history. It was a meeting that demonstrated the union of anti-slavery activists and politicians from the two major political parties — the Democrats and the Whigs — with the insurgent Liberty Party. In Court House Park in central Buffalo were sown the seeds of another major political party, even as the Free Soil Party itself was being born. That new organization would be the Republican Party, as the anti-slavery men regrouped in the early 1850s.

Though the slavery question would not be settled until a terrible civil war was fought, the Buffalo convention, held in the heart of the city, was one of the more significant events that took place in the long struggle to resolve the slavery question in America. It had demonstrated just how powerful the anti-slavery sentiment was in the country.

CHAPTER 4

ZACHARY TAYLOR

In the nineteenth century it was the common practice of federal officials to escape the oppressive heat and swampy humidity of Washington, D.C. during the summer months. President Zachary Taylor was no less desirous of leaving the place for a while, and so on August 19, 1849 he began a weeks long tour through the Middle Atlantic states and New England, to include a visit to Buffalo. Not only would he be enjoying cooler weather, he would also get out to meet the people, something that politicians have always been inclined to do.

As Taylor made his way through Baltimore and westward across Pennsylvania to Erie, he was greeted by enthusiastic crowds. Unfortunately, during his sojourn he was seized by illness. It is uncertain which disease he suffered from, perhaps cholera. By the time the president reached Erie he was wracked with fever, and was suffering from a combination of vomiting and severe diarrhea. He was so weak that doctors feared for his life. But Old Rough and Ready recovered during the course of a week, and by Saturday, September 1 he felt well enough to leave Erie by lake steamer for Niagara Falls and Buffalo. The president tolerated the voyage well. The boat left Erie at 9 a.m. and by five in the afternoon it had arrived off Buffalo harbor. During the trip Taylor was "attentively observing the different ports, as they were passed late in the afternoon. He made careful inquiries about the necessities of Erie and Buffalo harbor – asking and receiving information from General Reed [businessman Charles M. Reed of Erie] and other gentlemen as to the precise localities where breakwaters and other defences were needed."[1]

It was hoped that the president would stop at Buffalo, but his steamer proceeded to Black Rock (still a separate village from Buffalo) where it pulled into the harbor, discharged a few passengers and took on a pilot. President Taylor appeared on the deck of the boat after it docked and said a few words to the cheering people who had gathered there, expressing his hope to visit Buffalo after the Falls, if his health permitted it. From Black Rock the boat proceeded down the Niagara River to Schlosser's Landing just upstream from the Falls, and it was here that the president and his party disembarked at 7 p.m. On hand to greet him were Vice President Millard Fillmore, several officials of both Buffalo and Niagara Falls, and a group of citizens.

Mr. Fillmore stepped aboard the steamer and in a few minutes he emerged arm-in-arm with President Taylor. It was a crisp, cool early evening with the full moon shimmering on the river water as the president and his fellow travelers entered a rail coach that carried them to the village of Niagara Falls. Upon his arrival the president was taken to the Eagle Tavern Hotel where he was put up in a comfortable room for a four day stay. The next day, Sunday, September 2, he remained secluded in his room, his only visitors being the two physicians traveling with him, who were his son-in-law Dr. Robert C. Wood of the army and Dr. William M. Wood of the navy, no relation.

Over the next three days Taylor received a few callers and did some sightseeing, but his schedule was restricted so that he could get plenty of rest since he was still not fully recovered from his illness. James Bruce, Lord Elgin, who was the governor general of British Canada, the queen of England's top representative in Canada, headed west from Montreal on September 5 with the intention of meeting President Taylor in Niagara. But no prior arrangements had been made, and the president left the area before any meeting could take place.[2]

Though President Taylor hoped to continue with his tour, including a visit to Buffalo, he followed his doctors' advice and the entreaties of his cabinet back in Washington and cut short the journey. On September 6, he left by steamer from Lewiston and went east across Lake Ontario. He made brief stops in Albany and New York

City and by the eighth he was back at the White House.

But a certain little ride that the president took in Niagara on Monday, September 3, deserves attention. At the time he was feeling better and it was a pleasant day, so he decided to go out for a carriage ride with his son-in-law, Dr. Wood, and Alexander C. Bullitt, editor of the *Washington Republic* newspaper. One of the men's destinations was the new suspension bridge over the Niagara River Gorge that connected the United States and British Canada. It had been completed by Charles Ellet, a premier civil engineer of the time, and was opened for carriage traffic on August 1, 1848. It was located just above (south of) the Whirlpool, at the narrowest point of the Niagara Gorge. It consisted of two black towers on each bank and a white oak plank road supported by red painted cables.[3]

It was not enough to just ride up to the bridge and gawk at this marvel of modern engineering. One had to actually cross over the span to get the full experience. And so President Taylor's carriage crossed the bridge. At first glance it simply seems like a case of a president acting the part of a tourist, but as soon as Taylor crossed the mid-point of the Niagara River, he left the United States and entered Canada.[4] As inconsequential as this act appears, it nevertheless has a significance, however slight, in American history.

For over a hundred years we have been told that the first American president to leave the country while he was president was Theodore Roosevelt, who made a 1906 trip to Panama. But that is not correct. President Taylor was first. What evidence is there to support the fact that Zachary Taylor beat out TR by fifty-seven years? It comes in the form of newspaper reports of the time, but a clue is contained in a 1985 biography of Mr. Taylor by author K. Jack Bauer, who wrote, "He rallied rapidly on the third and visited Goat Island and drove across the newly constructed bridge of Charles Ellet to Canada."[5]

And from the newspapers, the *Buffalo Daily Republic* of Monday, September 3, 1849 carried this entry:

LATEST NEWS!
(By Telegraph for the Republic.)
[BY THE CANADA LINE.]

NIAGARA FALLS, Sept. 3 – 11 A.M.
The President is better this morning. He was able to cross the Suspension Bridge during the morning.

The *Daily Union* of Washington, D.C. reported this in its edition of September 6, 1849:

> TELEGRAPHIC REPORTS FOR THE UNION.
> Gen. Taylor at Niagara Falls.
> BUFFALO, Sept. 3 – The President arrived at the Falls on Saturday evening. He is quite well, but weak. He rode over the suspension bridge this afternoon. It is his intention to visit Buffalo on Thursday, and leave that city by the 3 o'clock train.

The *Republic* of Washington, D.C., in its September 8, 1849 edition, definitely puts Taylor in Canada. First, a column reprinted from the *New York Courier and Enquirer*, with the dateline NIAGARA FALLS, Monday, Sept. 3, 1849, says:

> This morning the pure air invited to out-door exercise, and he [Taylor] visited the suspension bridge, and points of interest adjacent to the falls, in company with Dr. Wood, of the army, and Mr. Bullitt, of the Republic.

In another column from the same newspaper of September 8, 1849, again a reprint from the *New York Courier and Enquirer*, with the dateline NIAGARA FALLS, Sept. 4, 1849, we read this:

> The President's journey into Canada West yesterday extended no further than the end of the Suspension Bridge – a very brief visit, indeed, to a "foreign power."

There is no evidence that President Taylor left his carriage to set foot on Canadian soil. Indeed, the vehicle's wheels may never have left the wooden planks of the suspension bridge. Yet he did leave the United

States and was, for a few minutes at least, under the jurisdiction of a foreign power, that being England, which at the time still claimed Canada as its possession.

This was not a momentous event in American history. It apparently drew scant attention at the time and caused no sense of consternation in Washington, D.C. After all, it was a leisurely, touristy foray into Canada by President Taylor. It was not an official visit and it is doubtful that the president even met a Canadian at the other end of the bridge.

Perhaps it has no significance other than to prompt a change of a few words in history and biography books. But the correct answer to the trivia question, "Who was the first president of the United States to visit a foreign country while in office?" is Zachary Taylor, not Theodore Roosevelt.

CHAPTER 5

LINCOLN, JOHNSON AND GRANT

For more than a century Abraham Lincoln has been one of our country's favorite and most well respected presidents. He is part of American folklore. Lincoln visited the Niagara Frontier three times, each time before he became president. His ties to Buffalo can be considered tenuous, but he is as honored and revered in the area as in the nation at large.

Lincoln's first trip to Buffalo occurred in late September of 1848. At the time, he was serving in the U.S. House of Representatives and was returning home to Springfield, Illinois after the first session of the thirtieth Congress. Lincoln was traveling with his wife, Mary, and sons Robert and Edward. They first went to New York City and New England where Whig Congressman Lincoln did some campaigning for Zachary Taylor for president. They then headed westward by rail, stopping at Albany, New York where Lincoln met Taylor's vice presidential running mate, Buffalonian Millard Fillmore. From there the Lincolns continued westward, arriving at Buffalo's Exchange Street Station on Monday, September 25.[1] The family would have spent the night at a Buffalo hotel, though which one is not known. The next morning, they boarded the lake steamer Globe, which carried them on a ten-day voyage to the Chicago harbor.

In 1857, Mr. and Mrs. Lincoln and their children, this time three sons, took a vacation trip to Niagara Falls. They traveled by train from Chicago to Buffalo. Once in Buffalo, the Lincolns would have had to transfer from the Exchange Street Station east of Main Street to the Erie Street depot west of Main where they would have boarded a train to Niagara Falls. The two stations were not connected by rail tracks at the time. On July 24, 1857, the Lincolns checked into the Cataract House hotel in Niagara Falls.[2] During their stay they viewed the falls from the American side, including Goat Island, and crossed over into Canada via the suspension bridge near the Whirlpool. They probably stayed at the Cataract House on July 25 also. From Niagara Falls the family most likely took the train the next morning back to Buffalo and transferred to a connecting train that carried them eastward as they continued their vacation in New York City.

In February of 1860 Lincoln went to New York City and New England on a speaking tour. He was a rising star in American politics. He traveled from Springfield to New York via Philadelphia, which indicates that he did not go through Buffalo. Lincoln returned from New York on the Erie Railroad to Dunkirk, and later said he was unable to honor a request to speak in Buffalo at that time due to time constraints.[3]

Abraham Lincoln was elected president in 1860. The following February he embarked on his famous pre-inaugural journey from his Springfield home to Washington, D.C. This trip would take him through Indiana, Ohio, across New York and south to the nation's capital, and would include a stop in Buffalo. Lincoln took this lengthy and rather roundabout twelve day journey to Washington to see the people and let them see him. He was a politician who no doubt welcomed the publicity of such a tour, which might help him gain support for his policies in a most difficult time in our nation's history. To Indianapolis to Columbus, Pittsburgh and Cleveland the train passed, with stops at smaller cities and towns along the route, where Lincoln would appear on the train's rear platform and give a short speech. His last overnight stay before Buffalo was at Cleveland. With him were Mrs. Lincoln and sons Robert, William and Thomas.

The inaugural train's first stop in New York State was at the village of Westfield in Chautauqua County on the afternoon of Saturday, February 16. A few months earlier a young village girl had written to Lincoln suggesting he grow a beard to improve his appearance. He did so, and now, after a few remarks form the train, he wished to thank the girl. He asked the crowd of some two thousand if Grace Bedell were present. Indeed she was, and Lincoln called for her to come forward. The eleven-year-old girl did so, and was given a handshake and a kiss from the president-elect, who told her that he had grown the whiskers for her.[4]

The train stopped at Silver Creek for a few minutes, then it was on to Buffalo where it chugged into the Exchange Street Station at 4:30 in the afternoon. Buffalonians' support and enthusiasm for Lincoln expressed itself only too much, at times manifesting itself in a dangerous lack of control. The authorities tried to keep people out of the depot, but were unsuccessful. An estimated 10,000 citizens were sardined into the building and on the platform. Thousands more were massed in the surrounding streets, some of whom had been there for hours in the cold. When Lincoln stepped off the train he was welcomed to Buffalo by noisy cheers and its most prominent citizen, former President Millard Fillmore. Fillmore was not exactly a Lincoln supporter, but was gracious enough to show his respects to the president-elect, his one-time Whig compatriot.

As Fillmore, Lincoln and his party made their way through the station to waiting carriages, they were jostled and pushed by the surging crowd. One newspaper compared the depot to a sausage stuffer.[5] A company of militia soldiers present to clear the way and offer protection was for a time useless, as they too were swarmed and overwhelmed by the crush of humanity, their bayonets dangerously flailing around. Finally, they were able to escort the guests to the carriages. Lincoln and Fillmore entered an open carriage, despite the near-freezing temperature. The others followed in several other carriages, including city officials. Some guests had to walk to their Main Street hotel.

The carriages went west on Exchange then north on Main. The streets were snow-free but wet and muddy. The entire route was thronged with cheering, waving spectators, not only at street level, but in windows and on roofs. The procession stopped north of Eagle Street at the American Hotel.[6]

Soldiers cleared the way for Messrs. Lincoln and Fillmore to enter the building, where the president-elect was reunited with his family, who had been escorted off the train and taken to the hotel before the mass of humanity had overwhelmed the station.

After several minutes, Lincoln, Fillmore and Asaph Bemis, city councilman acting for ill Mayor Franklin Alberger, stepped out onto the outdoor second story balcony of the hotel to great applause from the crowded street below.

Mr. Bemis made short welcoming remarks and introduced the president-elect. Mr. Lincoln promised adherence to the Constitution and thanked the citizens for their "magnificent reception." He then retired to his room.

At 6:30 p.m. a grand reception was held at the hotel. Lincoln stood at the top of the first flight of stairs above the lobby and shook hands and exchanged pleasantries for three hours with the thousands of guests who had gained admittance. Meanwhile, Mrs. Lincoln and son Robert greeted Buffalonians in one of the parlors of the hotel. At 9:30 a delegation of German Americans addressed the president-elect, after which the Lincolns retired to their suite of rooms.

The next morning, Sunday, Mr. Lincoln was driven to the First Unitarian Church at Franklin and Eagle Streets.[7] He sat in a pew with former President and Mrs. Fillmore, who had invited him to attend the service. Afterwards, they were driven to the American Hotel where they called on Mrs. Lincoln. The four of them then went to the Fillmore home on Niagara Square for lunch and conversation until about two o'clock. In the evening, Councilman Bemis and Mr. Fillmore escorted the president-elect to St. James Hall at Washington and Eagle Streets.[8] There they attended a 7:30 lecture by the Reverend John Beeson, who spoke about the wrongs perpetrated upon American Indians by settlers and government agents. Lincoln and a sizeable audience listened politely. At the end of the speech the president-elect stood at the door and shook hands with many of the attendees.

The Lincolns' train was scheduled to leave the Exchange Street Station at 6 a.m. the next day, but an earlier departure time was quietly arranged to prevent another occurrence like the one that accompanied the party's arrival two days earlier. An escort of soldiers took the visitors to the station at 4:30 a.m. and by 5:45 they were safely aboard their train. Though the depot was crowded with onlookers, it was not nearly as thronged as it had been on Saturday. As the locomotive steamed out, "Old Abe bowed his farewell to Buffalo, its committees, its military and its crowds," and headed east to Batavia.[9]

John Wilkes Booth

Another famous, or rather infamous, visitor to Buffalo in the early 1860s was none other than John Wilkes Booth. Booth was one of three actor brothers, sons of the famous Shakespearean actor Junius Brutus Booth. Junius Jr., Edwin and John Wilkes followed in their father's footsteps. Young John was considered a performer worthy of the Booth name, but one who did not quite measure up to the stature of his father or elder brother Edwin. Yet with his charm, handsome looks and fiery eyes, he became very popular.

He began his professional career in 1855, playing in Philadelphia and cities in the South, from Baltimore in his native Maryland to Richmond and Montgomery. By 1860 things were going so well for Booth that his manager persuaded him to expand his horizons. If he truly wanted to be a first-tier star he would have to perform in the North. So, in early 1861, J. Wilkes Booth, as he was billed, embarked on an ambitious tour that took him to Rochester, Albany and Portland, Maine.

Later that year he came to Buffalo, among a host of other cities including Chicago and Detroit, and in coming years he would play Boston and New York. The Civil War had begun in April of 1861, so John Wilkes could not travel freely to the South, which he loved, and where he enjoyed his greatest fame. This added to Booth's already considerable anger at the North and the federal government. Though the slave state of Maryland had remained within the Union, many of its residents, including Booth, were strong supporters of the Confederacy.

J. Wilkes Booth made his Buffalo debut at 8 p.m. Monday, October 28, 1861, beginning a run of twelve performances in as many nights at the Metropolitan Theater. His appearances had been duly advertised in advance, and theatergoers looked forward to the performance of another Booth, since his brother Edwin had played Buffalo two years earlier.

In 1861 the Metropolitan Theater was Buffalo's premier playhouse, drawing top talent to its stage. It was located at 193 Main Street, now 249 Main, a site occupied by small office buildings. In 1868 it was renamed the Academy of Music, but burned to the ground in a fire in 1895.[10] In the mid-nineteenth century the usual practice was for a touring star, such as Booth, to appear in a variety of lead roles during his booking in a particular venue, supported by a cast of local actors. The day after his debut, as Pescara in *The Apostate*, the Buffalo Daily Courier praised the actor's performance:

> [His] acting has much of the strange power and effect of the Booth [his father], and the living Booth [brother Edwin]; and all of the greatest passional command of feature and gesture, the quiet intense by-play of eye and nerve, yet with more of the grotesqueness of person and style then any of the family that we have ever seen. We do the present star no discredit in ranking him much below his brother…and those who know the elder Booth, and that inheritor of a priceless heirloom, the brother of the present star, will find in J. Wilkes Booth a worthy son of an incomparable sire.[11]

This reflected a theme which haunted the younger Booth his entire career, the constant comparison to his more accomplished father and brother Edwin. While a star in his own right, he would always be measured against the other Booths, and often politely critiqued as a great actor worthy of the name Booth, but not at the same level as the rest of his family.

The young actor's subsequent performances during the run in Buffalo included Hamlet, Othello, Richard III and Romeo. While he was praised as a fine actor, the critics opined that his performances would have been enhanced if he had been able to draw on the encouragement of a more crowded house, reflecting the fact that the Metropolitan failed to sell out on many of the nights. Booth again played the Metropolitan from July 6 through 11, 1863. He performed in seven plays, including two shows on the tenth. He must have been terribly distraught at this time, for his beloved South had only days before suffered serious defeats at the Battles of Vicksburg and Gettysburg.

The newspaper reviews of Booth's acting were very favorable. The July 7 *Buffalo Commercial Advertiser* noted about his performance in Richard III:

> ...a crudeness, so to speak, is sometimes apparent in his rendition, yet this is counterbalanced by the frequent flashes in which the true genius, inherent in him, manifests itself.[12]

After his appearance in the Lady of Lyons, the paper said:

> We believe Mr. Booth is destined to occupy a rank in his profession second to none in the country.[13]

Of the same play, the *Buffalo Daily Courier* made this ironic comment about Booth:

> Although his acting lacks tone, we are impressed with the immense original power lying back of all he attempts. Wilkes Booth is just the man for our citizens to admire, and we shall look to our dramatic people for a recognition of his claims.[14]

Besides acting in the plays, there is no record of any other activities in which Booth was engaged during his stays in Buffalo. Undoubtedly he stayed and took his meals in a downtown hotel. It is known that Booth traveled to Montreal at least once to meet with Confederate agents in 1864, long after his Buffalo appearances. The Niagara Frontier was a prime entry point into southern Ontario, though whether the actor ever crossed the border here is not known.

J. Wilkes Booth played his greatest role at Ford's Theater in Washington, D.C. on the night of April 14, 1865 when he shot and killed Abraham Lincoln. He fled to Front Royal in Caroline County, Virginia, where a posse of federal troops and agents caught up to him in a barn. He was mortally wounded in the neck and died on April 26. One of the soldiers who had chased down Booth was Buffalonian John Winter (1843-1922), whose share of the reward money paid for the assassin's capture was $1,600.00.[15]

Lincoln's Funeral

President Lincoln's funeral was a long, drawn-out affair, taking place over the course of seventeen days. With Mrs. Lincoln's approval, it was decided that, after obsequies in Washington, D.C., the late president's body would be taken back to Springfield, Illinois via railroad. The route it would follow was to be essentially the same one as that of Lincoln's pre-inaugural journey of 1861, but in reverse. At several cities the body would lay in state for viewing in an open casket. Buffalo was one of those cities.

On Thursday, April 27, 1865 at 7 a.m. President Lincoln's funeral train pulled into the Exchange Street Station. On board were many dignitaries, but the only family member among them was the late president's son, Robert. Former President Millard Fillmore was aboard, as head of a Buffalo citizens' committee that had boarded the train in Batavia. Unlike the rambunctious scene of 1861, this time the depot was kept clear of people. Lincoln's casket was carried and placed upon an elaborate horse-drawn funeral car, draped and canopied in black.

The body was conveyed several blocks through mobbed streets of subdued, rather well-behaved Buffalonians. From Exchange Street, up Main to Niagara to Delaware, Tupper and back down Main Street to St. James Hall at Washington and Eagle, the six white horses pulled the hearse. This was the same hall in which Lincoln had attended a lecture during his 1861 stop in the city. At St. James, the casket was carried inside, its upper lid removed, and the public was allowed to file by the coffin to view Lincoln's face. From 10 a.m. till eight at night about 100,000 went through. They included former President Fillmore, Buffalo Mayor William Fargo and the city council, and a twenty-eight year old young man named Grover Cleveland, who would twenty years hence rival Honest Abe's reputation for morality in the White House.[16] Shortly after the doors to St. James Hall closed, Lincoln's coffin was carried out to the hearse, transported back to the Exchange Street Station and placed back aboard the train. By 10 p.m. it was on its way west toward Cleveland.

Buffalo's pomp and circumstance and emotional outpouring for the funeral had not been as great as in other cities, but it received compliments for the tasteful conduct of its citizens and its overall decorum. The reason for this subdued behavior was twofold. On the day of the Washington funeral a few days earlier, the Queen City had held an emotional grand funeral pageant, minus the body of the late president, complete with canopied funeral car and every manner of civic and military pomp. Perhaps suffering from "mourning fatigue," Buffalo decided not to repeat the scene. Also, officials correctly surmised that a shorter ceremony would let more people view Lincoln's remains.[17]

President Johnson and General Grant in Buffalo

Andrew Johnson became president of the United States after the murder of Abraham Lincoln. Lincoln and Johnson had been elected president and vice president, respectively, on the Union Party ticket in 1864, which the Republican Party had temporarily renamed itself for that campaign. But Lincoln was a northern Republican and Johnson a southern Democrat. Johnson, a Tennessee native who had remained loyal to the Union for the duration of the Civil War, was chosen as Lincoln's running mate to demonstrate sectional unity across the United States at a time of violent political discord. No one dreamed that the president would be shot and killed, thereby elevating the Democrat Johnson into the White House.

Johnson was in the most unenviable position of any person to take office as president. First of all, neither he nor any man or woman could measure up to the status of the martyred Lincoln. Secondly, as a Democrat who had run for office allied with a Republican, he was not trusted by either northern or southern Democrats. And as for the Republicans, after a short honeymoon period, Johnson came to be vilified by them.

While historians at first denigrated his performance as president, his reputation was somewhat restored in the early twentieth century. By the late 1900s, however, Johnson was again being defamed and belittled by a new crop of historians, eager to judge him by modern sensibilities, rather than in the context of his own time.

The most popular person in America following the Civil War was

Ulysses S. Grant. Having led the Union to victory as general-in-chief of the Union armies, he retained that position after the conflict. His main post-war concern was with the army's occupation of the southern states. But a problematic situation erupted along the United States' northern border with British Canada in 1866. That was the Fenian Invasion, which echoed the Patriot War agitations of the 1830s. This new problem was an armed invasion of Canada by Catholic Irish Americans who had formed themselves into a military organization called the Fenian Brotherhood. They were the American branch of the radical Irish Revolutionary Brotherhood of Ireland.

The Fenians had met in Chicago in 1863 to formulate their plans, which were to invade and wrest control of Canada from the hated British, who also occupied Ireland at that time. Once that was accomplished, they planned to negotiate a British withdrawal from their ancestral homeland. The Fenians raised money and recruited an army of some 10,000 men, most of them Civil War veterans from both North and South who were experienced in battle. Most of the arms they acquired came from U.S. Army arsenals which were selling their surpluses that were no longer needed after the war. Though the Fenians' plan to take control of Canada from the British seemed far-fetched, they assumed they would be tolerated by the U.S. government, since the British had favored the South during the recent Civil War. The Fenians were also counting on help from Irish Canadians.[18]

During the spring of 1866 Fenian forces began to gather at strategic places along the Canadian border, from the shores of Maine in the east to Buffalo in the west. In Washington, the Johnson administration had gotten wind of the Fenian machinations and warnings were issued that the federal government would not tolerate any violations of the Neutrality Act of 1838. That law authorized use of the U.S. military to prevent American citizens from taking up arms against countries with which the United States was not at war.

Troubles started in Maine in April, and American troops under George G. Meade of Civil War fame were sent by General Grant to patrol the Canadian border in that area and seize ammunition from the troublemakers. The Fenians fled westward. Meanwhile, in Buffalo, Fenians had been gathering ammunition and almost a thousand recruits in the city in anticipation of a raid on Canada. Many of the men unabashedly walked about the streets dressed in the organization's green uniforms and black hats.[19] This aroused concern within the city, and Mayor Henry Wells put the police on alert and notified Federal authorities. The navy sent two steamers to patrol in the lake. The army at Fort Porter on the Niagara River was ill-equipped with only fifty soldiers and in no position to stop the activities of the better-equipped and experienced Irishmen.

The Fenians launched their foray into Canada from Buffalo on June 1, 1866. Several vessels carrying several hundred of their soldiers crossed the Niagara River from Black Rock, and six hundred men made their landing at Bowen Road in Fort Erie. Led by a former Union colonel, they proceeded to take Fort Erie and advanced toward Ridgeway before being repulsed by a superior Canadian force.

The Buffalo newspapers reported extensively on the Fenian invasion. During the conflict across the Niagara, the city received a distinguished visitor. It was none other than General Ulysses S. Grant himself. Grant had gone to West Point for the funeral of General Winfield Scott, which took place on June 1. Scott had been stationed in Buffalo for a time during the War of 1812 and had been in the Queen City in 1838 to quell the disturbances of the Patriot War. He was the unsuccessful presidential candidate of the Whig Party in 1852, which had denied the candidacy to incumbent President Millard Fillmore of Buffalo. General Grant was scheduled to go from West Point to St. Louis, and a bit of serendipity brought him through Buffalo en route to that city. The visit happened on June 2, in the midst of the Fenian incursion into the Niagara peninsula of Canada.

Grant arrived, probably at the Exchange Street Station, at about 1 p.m., accompanied by his wife and a staff member. He probably never left the depot, issuing an order assigning General W. F. Barry of Buffalo to command American forces on the frontier, with authority to stop the Fenians. Grant spent only a half an hour in Buffalo before departing for the west on the Lake Shore train.[20]

By late in the day of June 2, the Fenians were in full retreat from Canada, going back across the Niagara to Buffalo, and several hundred men were seized by the navy's lake steamers during the night. Most were eventually released and sent home.[21] Attempted Fenian invasions of Canada elsewhere along the border were also unsuccessful and the Irish Americans dispersed within a short period of time. But the dream died hard, and other Fenian raids occurred sporadically along the border until 1871, albeit not in the Buffalo area.[22]

Some of the arrested Fenians were defended in court *pro bono* by the young Buffalo lawyer Grover Cleveland. In 1871 several stood trial at Canandaigua, and he arranged for their defense there. They were convicted, but Cleveland successfully petitioned now-President Ulysses S. Grant for commutation of their sentences.[23]

By 1866 relations between President Andrew Johnson and the Radical Republicans who controlled Congress had become very strained. In an attempt to sway public opinion in his favor and help elect a Congress that fall that would be more agreeable to his policies, the president decided to take a late summer rail tour of the northern states.[24]

Though presidents had been making goodwill tours since the days of Washington, this was the most blatant political sojourn undertaken by a chief executive up to that time. A practice so common today, in 1866 it was considered to be an affront to the dignity of the office. Officially, it was a trip to Illinois to dedicate the cornerstone of a memorial to the late Senator Stephen A. Douglas.

President Johnson's eighteen-day excursion began on August 27 and took him to Baltimore, Philadelphia, New York, Albany, Niagara Falls, Buffalo, Cleveland, Toledo, Detroit, Chicago, St. Louis, Indianapolis, Louisville, Cincinnati, Pittsburgh and lastly Harrisburg. Many brief stops were also made along the way at smaller cities and towns. It came to be called the Swing Around the Circle.

The first part of the trip went well, with the president receiving favorable press reviews and friendly receptions from the crowds. But at times his fellow travelers received an even warmer welcome, for they included the Civil War heroes General Grant, General George Armstrong Custer and Admiral David Farragut. Also touring with the president were Secretary of State William Seward, Secretary of the Navy Gideon Welles, and numerous other government officials. Mrs. Johnson did not make the trip with her husband, but daughter Martha, along with her husband, did.

Johnson delivered essentially the same speech at each city, the message that the North and South needed to be reconciled, and therefore the Radical Republicans had to be rejected by the voters for the sake of unity. By early September the presidential train, consisting of only two coaches and one baggage car, was moving across Western New York. On the first it went through Albion, Medina and Lockport, and the president duly made brief remarks at each station. That afternoon at 4:30 the train reached the depot at Niagara Falls. The visitors were greeted with hearty cheers from a large crowd, then they were driven to the International Hotel. There they were welcomed by Augustus Porter, nephew of the late Peter B. Porter who had served as secretary of war under President John Quincy Adams.

President Johnson gave a speech from the balcony of the hotel, as did Secretary Seward, and General Grant and the others were introduced to those gathered below. Later a grand reception ball was held in their honor in the dining hall, attended by all except Johnson and Seward, who were too fatigued to attend. During the dances, the elegant movements of General George Armstrong Custer were noted, which were far more smooth than those of Grant or Farragut.[25]

The next day was Sunday, and the president, Secretaries Seward and Welles, General Grant and some others were driven around the village and onto Goat Island where they took in the spectacular views of the cataracts and the gorge below. That afternoon General Grant went across the suspension bridge onto the Canadian side and traveled as far as Table Rock.[26]

On Monday, September 3 at about 8 a.m. a reception committee from Buffalo arrived at Niagara Falls, led by former President Millard Fillmore. At around 8:30 the members marched to the International Hotel, where they met President Johnson and his entourage and accompanied them by carriage to the railroad station. All entered a special train for Buffalo, which left promptly at 9 a.m.

After a brief stop in Tonawanda, during which the president was welcomed and gave brief remarks from the rear platform, the train headed into Buffalo. As it passed by Fort Porter, a twenty-one-gun salute was fired.

Right around 10 a.m. the locomotive chugged into the Erie Street Depot. The large concourse of people assembled there gave the presidential party a cheering welcome amid the booming of cannons. The inside of the station was festively decorated with American flags and evergreens, and portraits of Lincoln, Grant and Stephen Douglas. Over one entrance was a picture of the taking of Mobile, Alabama by Admiral Farragut. Over another, a banner proclaimed, "Glory to God in the Highest and on Earth, Peace, Good Will to Men." Beneath it were portraits of Lincoln and Johnson.

The president and his party were escorted off the train by Mayor Chandler J. Wells through the station and into waiting open coaches. A brief circuit through the streets of Buffalo followed. Leading the procession was a formation of hundreds of military men including bands and drummer boys. Then followed a total of thirty-six carriages, the first being the mayor's, drawn by six horses and containing President Johnson, Secretary Seward and former President Fillmore. In the others were Grant, Custer and other generals, Admiral Farragut, Secretary Welles and scores of dignitaries.

The route of the grand procession was up Erie Street to the Terrace then to Main Street north to Tupper, a left turn onto Tupper westward to Delaware, then south on Delaware to Niagara Square. The streets were packed with people, as were the windows of buildings along the route. Many of the structures were decorated with American flags. Onlookers also occupied soap boxes, lamp posts and stairways to get a good look at the distinguished visitors.

The strains of the approaching bands led to sustained cheering, which became loudest when the carriages containing President Johnson and General Grant rode by. Buffalo men, women and children waved and shouted friendly greetings and the president, standing with hat in hand in his open coach, acknowledged the cheers.

When the parade reached Niagara Square, it found that space filled by about 20,000 cheering people. The police cleared a path for the president and his retinue from their carriages as they made their way onto a white canopied stage, handsomely decorated in flags, which had been erected at the south end of the square. However, the carriage in which General

Grant was seated turned out of the procession and was driven to the nearby home of former Buffalo Mayor William G. Fargo on Niagara Street at the northeast corner of Franklin.[27] The reason proffered for the general's not attending the ceremony was that he was ill. Given that Grant was reportedly drunk in Cleveland, the presidential party's next major stop on the tour,[28] it is not too far-fetched to surmise that he was either ill from a hangover or too intoxicated to appear with the others at the square. Niagara Square in every direction was filled with an intermingling of people, horses and carriages indiscriminately disarranged. Some onlookers stood in their coaches in order to get a better view, and many clambered up the railings of the stage itself, obstructing the view of others.

Once the crowd was quieted down, former President Fillmore came to the front of the platform with President Johnson and Secretary Seward to make some welcoming remarks:

> Mr. President. The pleasing duty had been assigned to me of welcoming you and your distinguished ministers and the gallant officers of the army and navy accompanying you to the hospitalities of the City of Buffalo…. All have cordially united in this testimony of respect to the chief magistrate of the nation. They know and appreciate your patriotic devotion to the Union, during the darkest days of the rebellion…. I repeat the cordial welcome to our city and regret that your stay is necessarily so brief. Allow me the honor to present you to our citizens.[29]

President Johnson then strode forward, bowed, and delivered his address. It was not a lengthy one, and in it he thanked Mr. Fillmore for his past words of encouragement, defended his own actions regarding Reconstruction and appealed to the people's sense of justice regarding the country's reunification, and to put nation before party:

> The North cannot do without the South, nor the South without the North…. I have pardoned rebels when I was governor of Tennessee. I have pardoned more since I have been president of the United States. I believe a man may sin, do wrong, and

afterward repent and do right and become a good citizen... Thank God the people love the Constitution above party. Rally around the altar of the Constitution without any regard to party.[30]

The president was applauded following his speech, after which Secretary Seward stepped up. Initial cries for General Grant were answered by Seward with the explanation that the general was ill. The secretary basically echoed Johnson's remarks in his talk.

There were shouts for the others, and in acknowledgment Admiral Farragut and General Custer each uttered a sentence or two. Mr. Fillmore made brief closing remarks, and then a path was cleared by police through the crowd so that the presidential party could walk to the nearby residence of Mayor Wells, which was located on Washington Street at Court House Park. There, they enjoyed a lunch, and at half-past twelve the procession was reformed and the carriages moved down Mohawk to Main to the Exchange Street Station. Once again, the streets were thronged with cheering Buffalonians, who were acknowledged by President Johnson, standing in his carriage, bowing with hat in hand.

At the depot, the departing guests were met by an immense crowd and were escorted to their waiting special train, the engine trimmed with flags, flowers and evergreens. Loud calls were made for Grant and Farragut, and they appeared on the rear platform just before the train moved out at 1:10 p.m. on the Lake Shore road toward Erie and Cleveland.

The Buffalo newspapers gave generally positive reviews of President Johnson's visit, with the main exception being the *Buffalo Express*, obviously a supporter of the Congressional Radical Republicans, who were opposed to the chief executive. That paper continually belittled President Johnson in its coverage. It said that the "popular reception which Mr. Johnson met during the ride throughout the streets of the city, was certainly the most frigid, the most studiously and significantly cold, that any high dignitary of a nation ever experienced." The publication called the crowds "grimly silent," reporting that the cheers and applause that broke out at any time during the visit were directed at General Grant and Admiral Farragut, and not intended for the president.[31]

Historians throughout the years have said that the Swing Around the Circle enjoyed great support from the people until Cleveland, where Republicans began to plant hecklers in the crowds to goad President Johnson into making intemperate remarks. That he did, using increasingly belligerent language seen as very undignified for his office. By the end of the tour on September 15, 1866, even his supporters saw it as disastrous for him.

The Death of Millard Fillmore

In 1874, Buffalo lost its most prestigious citizen, Millard Fillmore. At home on the morning of February 13, 1874, just after shaving, Fillmore's left arm dropped to his side. He lost feeling and movement in the limb. This stroke extended to affect the left side of his face and caused him to lose his voice and ability to swallow. His friend Dr. James P. White was called, and under his care the paralysis subsided after a few days and Fillmore was able to speak again.

Thirteen days later, on February 26, he experienced a second attack after which he was not able to walk. Dr. White, assisted by a Dr. Gray of Utica, tended to Fillmore, but the patient was unable to rise from his sickbed. Rumors of his death spread about the city, but he was still alive, said to be resting calmly with retention of his mental faculties. On March 7, he spent a restless night and took a turn for the worse that afternoon. On Sunday, March 8, he continued to sink, but was able to take some liquid food, after which he remarked, "The nourishment is palatable." He never spoke again and after an hour lost consciousness. Buffalo's first citizen died peacefully that night at ten minutes after eleven at the age of seventy-four. Present at his bedside were his wife Caroline, brother Cyrus, son Millard Powers, Dr. White and a few attendants.

For the next few days the Buffalo newspapers were filled with eulogies to Fillmore, as well as reports on his death and funeral. Naturally, on the local level he was praised effusively. On March 9, Mayor Lewis P. Dayton formally announced the death to the Common Council, which passed resolutions in respect to his memory and to form a committee of five to confer with a committee of citizens to render the honors to the city's illustrious citizen. The Superior Court adjourned for the remainder of the week and the Court of Sessions for the day. A committee of citizens was that day appointed by the mayor and met to coordinate funeral arrangements. The funeral date had been set as March 12.

In Washington, D.C. on March 9 the U.S. House of Representatives adjourned at 1:54 p.m. in honor of Mr. Fillmore, who had served in that body. Eulogies for the deceased were spoken and a committee of seven was chosen to attend the funeral in Buffalo: Lyman K. Bass, Buffalo's representative in Congress and a former law partner of Grover Cleveland; Thomas A. Swann of Maryland; Henry B. Sayler of Indiana; C.D. McDougall of New York; Horace Maynard of Tennessee; Erastus Wells of Missouri; and Mark H. Dunnell of Minnesota.

President Ulysses S. Grant telegrammed his regrets that he would not be able to leave Washington to attend the funeral. He ordered federal offices to be closed for the day of Fillmore's funeral, and that the usual military honors for a former president be observed. He issued the following proclamation through the state department:

> It is with deep regret that the President announces to the people of the United States the death of Millard Fillmore, one of his honored predecessors, who died at Buffalo, N.Y., last evening.
>
> The long continued public services and eminent purity of character of the deceased ex-President will be remembered beyond the days of mourning in which the nation will be thrown by the event which is thus announced.
>
> As a mark of respect to his memory it is ordered that the Executive Mansion and the several departments at Washington be draped in mourning until the close of the day on which the funeral shall take place, and that all business shall be suspended on the day of the funeral.
>
> It is furthermore ordered that the War and Navy Departments cause suitable military and naval honors to be paid on the occasion to the memory of the eminent citizen whose life is now closed.[32]

Former President Andrew Johnson was invited by the Buffalo

committee, but sent a telegram that said, "It is deeply regretted that I cannot be present and join in the formal ceremonies...of one of the nation's most distinguished sons...a pure, upright citizen, a wise and patriotic statesman."[33]

On March 11, the U.S. Senate passed a resolution honoring Fillmore, and appointed three members to attend the funeral: Reuben Fenton of New York, Hannibal Hamlin of Maine, and Thomas F. Bayard of Delaware. Senator Roscoe Conkling of New York paid a tribute to him on the Senate floor. New York Governor John A. Dix cited pressing business in Albany in sending his regrets, but two members of his staff would be in Buffalo to represent him. The State Senate and Assembly appointed committees to came to Buffalo.

The newspapers in other cities throughout the United States took note of former President Fillmore's passing, though many of them downplayed his accomplishments, no doubt owing to a lingering prejudice over his support of the Compromise of 1850. One thing they all agreed on was Fillmore's spotless integrity.

Typical of the comments in the press was this from the Troy, N.Y. *Times*:

> Mr. Fillmore was not a great man, but he was essentially a good man, honest in his intentions and thoroughly devoted, we believe, to the good of the country.

And from the *Chicago Tribune*:

> Mr. Fillmore, though not a man of genius, owed his success to no less desirable qualities. He was from the earliest day distinguished for his personal integrity, which was never impeached or questioned...History will not forgive him for lending his influence to the slave power; but, having said this, it remains to be said that he ranks among the able, competent and dignified Chief Magistrates of his country.[34]

The citizens' committee and its various subcommittees methodically put in place plans for the Thursday funeral. Various civic associations met, expressed their interest in attending the ceremonies as a body, and were invited. The bar association met to eulogize its former member. Oscar Folsom, Grover Cleveland's friend and one-time law partner, called the meeting to order. It is not known if the future president himself was present or attended any of the ceremonies. The bar passed resolutions requesting all members to attend Fillmore's funeral. The Brewers' Association of Buffalo resolved that its members would not make beer deliveries on the day of the funeral. The military was given a prominent role in the funeral obsequies.

Most out of town guests arrived on the day before the funeral and were put up at various hotels. On the next day the Buffalo schools and all places of business in the city were closed, save for a few that were open in the morning hours. The embalmed remains of former President Fillmore lay in repose in the front west room of his Niagara Square mansion. The casket was of an oval shape, of dark red rosewood, with eight silver handles. A solid silver plate on the lid bore the following inscription:

MILLARD FILLMORE
Born January 7th 1800
Died March 8th 1874

The inside of the open coffin was lined with white silk. The deceased was dressed in a black suit. Though his face appeared emaciated, he was said to be wearing a "calm and natural expression." Beautiful floral pieces were arranged around the casket. Undertaker Henry D. Farwell's firm on Niagara Street downtown handled the body preparation and supplied the coffin. Henry F. Meacham of that company was directly involved.

At 9 a.m. on Thursday, March 12, about fifty family members and friends were gathered in the room, including Mrs. Fillmore, Millard Powers, and Mr. and Mrs. Cyrus Fillmore. A brief religious service was conducted by Reverend Dr. V. R. Hotchkiss of the Washington Street Baptist Church, assisted by Reverend Dr. John C. Lord of the Central Presbyterian Church. It began with a Bible Scripture reading followed by a eulogy of Mr. Fillmore, a prayer and a benediction.

Outside the mansion in the bitter cold, some fifty members of

Company D of the Buffalo City Guard, a New York State National Guard unit, waited in formation on Delaware Avenue. At 9:30 eight soldiers were led by an officer and they entered the house and carried the coffin to a waiting hearse. The vehicle was decorated with black and white crepe as well as the American flag. The soldiers formed on either side of the hearse and escorted the body of the late president through Niagara Square onto Niagara Street to Pearl, then to Erie where they halted before St. Paul's Episcopal Cathedral. Neither music nor drumbeat had accompanied the small procession. The carriers lifted the body from the hearse and bore it through the Erie Street doors into the church, and placed it on a platform in the vestibule.

This catafalque was covered in black velvet trimmed with white cloth and rosettes. Black and white drapes were suspended from the ceiling of the room and at the head and foot of the casket were placed bouquets of flowers. A crown lay at the head and on the lid rested two crosses and a star, while at the foot stood a cross of white flowers. With a contingent of Company D standing as an honor guard around the body, at 10 o'clock the public was allowed to pass into the Erie Street entrance, through the vestibule to view the remains, and out the Pearl Street door.

At eleven the doors were closed for a few minutes to allow the Congressmen, the city committee and a few other dignitaries to pay their respects. After that, the stream of citizens was allowed to resume. At 12:30 Company D was relieved by U.S. infantry regulars from Fort Porter. At one the church's bells began a funeral toll, and thirty minutes later the line to view the late president was halted. About 25,000 of his fellow Buffalonians had passed by Fillmore's coffin.

Distinguished guests began arriving at the cathedral for the 2 p.m. service, until the place was filled. Present were the dignitaries from Washington and Albany, the Buffalo Common Council, the city's Board of Trade, the judiciary, members of the bar, the Council of the University of Buffalo, of which Mr. Fillmore was chancellor, representatives of the Buffalo Historical Society, and many others. The rector of St. Paul's, Reverend Dr. William Shelton, as well as several other clergymen, approached the casket at the vestibule door inside the cathedral. The ministers led the coffin, carried by six soldiers, up the main aisle to the chancel.

"I am the resurrection and the life," intoned Reverend Shelton. The coffin was followed up the aisle by eight honorary pallbearers, who were George Babcock, William Bird, Elam Jewett, Noah Sprague, Oliver Steele, O.H. Marshall, George Clinton and Henry Martin. The casket was placed on a raised platform covered with black cloth in front of the chancel. Several floral arrangements surrounded it. The service began with a hymn, a prayer was read, then Reverend Shelton climbed to the pulpit and delivered a lengthy sermon and eulogy. Upon its conclusion, the choir of fifty voices sang another hymn, and the coffin was carried out of the church and placed back in the hearse to the strains of "Nearer, My God, To Thee."

A crowd of thousands had gathered around St. Paul's before and during the service, and they observed the proceedings as the mourners passed out of the cathedral. Also formed around the building were various military detachments. When all was ready the procession to Forest Lawn Cemetery moved out, heading north on Pearl Street. A formation of Buffalo policemen came first, then a contingent of army officers, a cornet band, the 74th Regiment of the New York State National Guard, Company D of the City Guard, another band, the 65th Regiment, the clergymen, a third band, and army infantry regulars. Then came the hearse followed by many carriages carrying the family, friends, distinguished guests, the mayor, common council, city officers, judges, members of the bar, board of trade and other citizens.

From Pearl Street, the marchers turned east on Eagle to Main, which was a change in the earlier publicized route. Both sides of the streets were lined with people who solemnly watched the sad procession go by. The buildings were profusely draped in mourning. The marchers made a left turn onto Chippewa and then headed north up Delaware to the cemetery. All along the way there was no let-up in the mourners standing along the streets. The bands played dirges. On Delaware near Ferry Street a mounted officer was thrown from his horse but was not seriously injured. And also at Ferry, Company D split off to the right and left while the rest of the cortege passed through to Forest Lawn.

The procession marched through the cemetery till it reached the Fillmore family plot. A gray granite shaft marked the resting places of the former president's first wife Abigail and daughter Mary. Close by were the graves of Fillmore's friends and former law partners, Solomon G. Haven and Nathan K. Hall. Hall's grave was mounded with fresh dirt and covered with flowers. He had died just six days before Fillmore.

An open grave lined with sandstone was ready to receive the former president's body. A military guard of honor stood at the entrance to the family enclosure as the bearers carried the coffin in to the sound of a dirge. The family, Reverends Shelton, Hotchkiss and Lord, and family physician James P. White gathered around the grave. As the casket was lowered, Reverend Lord recited a brief prayer and benediction. Then all turned from the gravesite and reentered their carriages, and those gathered in the cemetery returned to the city.

The Death of Caroline Fillmore

The death of the second Mrs. Millard Fillmore, Caroline (Carmichael) McIntosh Fillmore, occurred on Thursday, August 11, 1881, some seven and one half years after her late husband's passing. She had continued to live in the Fillmore Mansion on Niagara Square in Buffalo, and it was there that she died.

In mid-October of 1880 Mrs. Fillmore had suffered a stroke that affected her speech and caused weakness on her left side. She did, however, recover strength enough to walk about and take almost daily carriage rides. On Sunday, August 7, 1881, she suffered a second stroke that left her in grave condition, and a third attack four days later resulted in her death at age sixty-seven.

On Saturday, August 13 at 3 p.m. a brief service was held at the mansion, officiated by the Reverend John Gordon of the Washington Street Baptist Church, who had been at Mrs. Fillmore's bedside when she died. She was then buried at Forest Lawn Cemetery next to the late president.

An obituary that took up a few column inches appeared in the Buffalo newspapers with only a couple of sentences reporting the funeral service, not unusual for a prominent widow's demise. Perhaps more space would have been devoted to her, but her death occurred in the midst of national attention to the condition of President James A. Garfield, who was struggling to survive a fatal bullet wound delivered by an assassin on July 2, 1881 at the railroad station in Washington, D.C.[35]

President Grant in Chautauqua and Buffalo

Ulysses S. Grant had visited Buffalo twice as the ranking military man in the country. In 1875 he came to Western New York as commander-in-chief, that is, as president of the United States. In that year, Dr. John Heyl Vincent and Lewis Miller (whose daughter married Thomas Edison), the co-founders of a yearly Methodist camp meeting on church land on Lake Chautauqua, decided they needed some publicity for their summer gatherings. What better way, they thought, than to invite the president to stop in for a visit? Grant accepted their invitation, perhaps in part because Dr. Vincent was an old acquaintance from when both men had lived in Galena, Illinois.

On Saturday, August 14, 1875 President Grant arrived by rail at Jamestown on the eastern end of Lake Chautauqua, and was greeted by a cheering crowd and cannon salute. After lunch at the home of a local merchant he was driven to the dock on the lake and boarded the steamer *Jane Bell*. It was decked out in red, white and blue bunting, evergreens, flowers and a portrait of the president. Six other boats accompanied the president's to its 3:30 p.m. landing at Fair Point. Fair Point was the name of the place where the meeting was being held, before being legally changed to Chautauqua two years later.

President Grant was escorted off the steamer to the cheers of 20,000 people and a band playing "Hail To The Chief." The police and workers then cleared a path for the presidential party—which consisted only of the president, his son Ulysses Jr., and his private secretary General O. E. Babcock—to the outdoor amphitheater, which had long been filled to capacity by an eager audience of about three thousand people. This was not the historic amphitheater, which was unforgivably demolished in 2016 and replaced by an inauthentic replica, but it may have been located at the same site.

The president and other dignitaries took seats on the stage and he was introduced to the audience, which responded with rousing applause. General Grant seldom gave speeches and he did not at this appearance. He stepped forward and spoke only a few words of thanks:

> Ladies and Gentlemen, it gives me great pleasure to meet you here at this beautiful place, but as I am not much of a speech maker myself will leave it to Dr. Vincent to express to you my gratification and pleasure.[36]

After a couple of speeches and songs, the president stood up, came forward and bowed to yet more cheers. He shook hands with some members of the audience then was escorted to his quarters for some rest. This consisted of a large striped tent, divided into two compartments, furnished and carpeted, with a veranda out front. It was a far cry from the general's war time tents, in which he had spent many a day. This was one of the attractions of Fair Point, the concept of connecting to nature, and very few permanent structures existed at the time.

President Grant made a brief appearance at a prayer service that evening. Afterward the campground was illuminated with Chinese lanterns, hanging from trees, and calcium lights. There were paper balloons sent aloft and a firework display. The next morning was Sunday and at 9 a.m. the president attended a Sunday school meeting. This encampment at Fair Point was, indeed, officially called the Sunday School Assembly, featuring speeches and discussions on the importance of teaching the children Christian values. After an 11 a.m. service, also attended by the president, he was presented with two Bibles as a gift from his hosts. In the evening, President Grant had dinner at the nearby home of Lewis Miller. He and his traveling companions then left by lake steamer at 9 o'clock for Mayville, where they boarded a train. The ultimate destination of the president was Rhode Island, where he had a Tuesday engagement.

The train left the Mayville station at 9:40 p.m. and went through Brocton to Buffalo, arriving at the Exchange Street Station at 11:38. A committee of escort that had occupied the private presidential car since Mayville alighted, leaving the president, his son and his secretary as the car's sole occupants.

Those three gentlemen remained in the car and retired to their beds for a few hours of sleep. At 4:35 a.m. the next morning, Monday, August 16, the car was attached to a New York Central train and was soon headed eastward out of the depot.

Known by only a handful of people, with no one to greet him or see him off, President Grant had made the most secretive visit of any chief executive to the city of Buffalo. As for the camp meeting at Fair Point, the president's visit proved invaluable. Within a couple of years its name was changed to the Chautauqua Institution and its agenda expanded beyond the religious realm. The publicity generated by Grant's visit drew more visitors and national attention and it soon became a thriving establishment, an iconic piece of Americana copied by "Chautauquas" throughout the country, even as far west as Ashland, Oregon. It today remains relevant and draws nationally known speakers and entertainers to its summertime programs.

Former President Grant In Buffalo

Ulysses S. Grant made two visits to Buffalo as a former president. After retiring from the presidency in 1877, he attempted to capture the Republican nomination for president for another term in 1880, but lost out to James A. Garfield. However, he made several campaign appearances in support of the Republican ticket during that fall's presidential campaign, one of which was in Buffalo.

General Grant arrived in Buffalo on Thursday, October 28, 1880 to make an appearance with Senator Roscoe Conkling of New York. His train pulled in at 1 p.m., stopping just short of the Exchange Street Station so that the former president could alight from his car at Michigan Street. He was met by Sherman S. Jewett, who was a Buffalo industrialist and civic leader, and several other people.

Climbing into an open barouche, Grant, Conkling and Jewett rode through old Wells Street between ranks of the Buffalo chapter of the

Mystic Order of 306, a national organization in favor of a third term for the general. The "306" referred to the number of delegates at the recent Republican National Convention who voted for Grant for president. West on Seneca Street, up Main, west on Chippewa to Mr. Jewett's home the little parade went, led by a military band.[37] The "306" men followed the general's carriage. The streets along the way were packed with immense crowds who shouted out their hurrahs and cheers as the distinguished hero passed by, doffing his hat to acknowledge the welcome.

At the Jewett house, General Grant rested for awhile. At three o'clock Grant and Conkling appeared on Main Street at the Central Wigwam. Wigwams were a late nineteenth century political phenomenon, temporary structures built for political meetings. They did not resemble Indian wigwams, despite the name. Buffalo's Republican Central Wigwam was supposedly capable of holding 10,000 people, although that was probably an exaggeration. The wigwam was so packed with people that they could not move. Ladies fainted, there was pushing and shoving, and order could not be maintained. The entrance of Grant, Conkling and Sherman Rogers only added to the chaos as shouting and cheering broke out. The building's interior was decorated with flowers and flags and bunting and a huge "306" banner. Grant, Conkling and Rogers sat at a table on a stage.

A Republican glee club and the 74th Regiment band played a few numbers. Mr. Rogers introduced General Grant over the din of the crowd. Grant came forward and shouted, "Fellow citizens! As I cannot possibly make myself heard I shall not say anything to you, but introduce you at once to Senator Conkling."[38]

Those who could not see were not satisfied until Grant stood on one of the tables. Senator Conkling then spoke for two hours, till 6 o'clock. Immediately afterward the general was driven to the home of James N. Matthews on Delaware Avenue for dinner. Matthews was the owner of the *Buffalo Express* newspaper. Next was a torchlight parade scheduled for 8 o'clock that night. At least a couple of hours prior the downtown streets were filled with marching, uniformed groups of torchbearers, Grant enthusiasts and Republicans. Music and fireworks filled the air and hordes of revelers took over Main Street from Exchange to Allen.

The focal point of all this was the Tifft House hotel on Main, in front of which a reviewing stand had been set up for the guest of honor, former President Grant.[39] He appeared on the stand at 8 p.m. to the accompaniment of tumultuous cheers. Fully 30,000 men and women were packed into that block of Main Street. At 8:35 the parade moved out from lower Main. As the various marchers passed Tifft House, Grant tipped his hat. He was not alone on the reviewing stand, since more than a score of other dignitaries stood with him. Around the top of the stand gas jets burned and a limelight shone on it.

The streets were absolutely packed with cheering, boisterous crowds as fireworks exploded from the buildings on Main Street, mixing with the blare of marching bands. The marchers became disorganized as they passed Tifft House due to the jam of onlookers. Many left the parade ranks by the time it reached Allen Street, with only fragments continuing to Porter, Niagara and back to Main. Practically all the buildings and homes along the way were decorated in flags, banners and balloons. Once the parade had passed the reviewing stand in its entirety, General Grant was driven to the Jewett house where he held a reception and shook the hands of two thousand well-wishers.

The day's events probably made for the noisiest, lengthiest political demonstration ever held in the city of Buffalo. Even before the arrival of General Grant, the city had held a huge industrial parade that morning. Workers marched and various Buffalo companies showed off their wares in wagons. It was largely in support of the high import tariffs favored by the Republicans.

Though ostensibly a campaign rally for the Republican Garfield-Arthur ticket, the festive atmosphere of the day was more of a celebration of the visit of a war hero, a "Ulysses S. Grant Day." And as many critics were quick to point out, it seemed to be an advertisement for a third presidential term for Grant in the future. However, during the day the former president did manage a few remarks in favor of the Republican presidential candidates, saying, "The Democratic Party organized as it is now is under the control of the rebel brigadiers....We want to be ruled by northern people while we are alive."[40] A unifying message, indeed.

Former President Grant was in Buffalo again three years later. But it was a quieter, more subdued and private visit. At around 8:30 p.m. on Friday, November 16, 1883, the general's train pulled into Buffalo. Accompanying him were his son Fred, Mayor Franklin Edson of New York, and Grant's business partner Fernando Ward. Mr. Charles F. Bingham of Bingham and Morgan iron foundry served as their host and escort, and at whose request, it was said, they stopped in Buffalo. Ostensibly this was a pleasure trip, but rumors persisted that it was a business excursion by Messrs. Grant and Ward through Pennsylvania and New York in search of investments.

General Grant and the others were driven directly from the railroad depot to the Genesee Hotel at the northwest corner of Main and Genesee Streets and promptly served an exquisite dinner.[41] After exchanging pleasantries, the former president retired to a hotel room. Following breakfast the next morning, the entire party boarded a train for Rochester.

Ely S. Parker

Another Ulysses S. Grant connection to the Buffalo area is through his acquaintance with a Native American. One of the most accomplished, yet too often ignored, American Indians in United States history had his roots in the Buffalo vicinity.

Ely S. Parker was three-fourths Native American, one of his grandmothers being white, but he was a full member of the Seneca Nation.[42] He was born in 1828 in what is now the hamlet of Indian Falls within the town of Pembroke in Genesee County, on the Tonawanda Creek Reservation. The reservation is still in existence, though much smaller, in Genesee, Erie and Niagara Counties. It is not legally part of the current entity known as the Seneca Nation of Indians.

Parker was also given the Seneca name Ha-sa-no-an-da, which means Leading Name. As was increasingly common at the time, he went by the two names, a practicality for someone with one foot in the Seneca world and the other in the white man's realm. In addition to learning tribal traditions, Parker received a white child's education at a missionary school and was an excellent student, becoming fluent in both Seneca and English. Already at a young age, he realized that he and his tribe had to learn to live and prosper in the dominant white man's world.

Young Ely's education was furthered at Yates Academy in Orleans County and Cayuga Academy in Aurora. Because of confusion and conflict in tribal relations with the government, it was necessary for representatives of the Seneca to make trips to Washington, D.C. to advocate and explain their concerns. At age fifteen Ely Parker accompanied tribal elders to the nation's capital to interpret for them because of his mastery of English, his intelligence, his manners, and knowledge of the white man's ways.

On one trip he actually met President James K. Polk and dined with him and First Lady Sarah Polk in the White House. Parker was a great admirer of Mrs. Polk and proudly told the story of how she had once stopped her carriage on the streets of Washington when she saw him walking along and invited him to take a ride with her.[43] He also met with that immortal trio of U.S. senators, Daniel Webster, Henry Clay and John C. Calhoun.

Parker was interested in becoming an attorney, so he read law in Ellicottville. But he was refused admittance to the bar because he was an American Indian. He then attended Rensselaer Polytechnic Institute in Troy, New York where he studied engineering and secured work on the Erie Canal. In 1851 he was named Grand Sachem (leader) of the Six Nations of the Iroquois and took the name Do-ne-ho-ga-wa, meaning Keeper of the Western Door. At this time, he came into possession of a medal which had been awarded to Red Jacket by President George Washington for his commitment to peacemaking. Red Jacket, a great Seneca chief, was Ely Parker's great-grand uncle.

By 1835 Parker was chief engineer of the Chesapeake and Albemarle Canal in Virginia. He was then given an engineering position working on lighthouses on the Great Lakes, a federal military position for which he was awarded the rank of major. He also worked on Mississippi levees. By 1857 he was assigned to engineering duties in Galena, Illinois. While there he became friendly with a local clerk and war veteran named Ulysses S. Grant, and the two men became friendly.

When the Civil War broke out in 1861, Parker wanted to enlist but was refused because he was an Indian and thus not technically an American citizen.[44] But in 1863, his old friend Grant secured his entry into the U.S. Army. Colonel Parker became General Grant's aide-de-camp and secretary, serving with him from the Battle of Vicksburg onward.

Parker accompanied Grant to Appomattox Court House, Virginia and was present when Confederate General Robert E. Lee surrendered his forces to General Grant there on April 9, 1865. Grant had penciled out a draft of the surrender terms, and when Lee finished reading it, Grant wanted the agreement written out in ink. He asked Colonel Theodore Bowers to do it, but Bowers was so nervous that he could not write. Bowers passed the notebook and had Colonel Parker transcribe the terms in ink. When finished, Parker brought it to General Grant, who signed and sealed it and passed it on to General Lee.

At one point, Lee was introduced to all the Union men in the room. When introduced to Parker, he stared at him for a moment, extended his hand and said, "I am glad to see one real American here."

Parker replied, "We are all Americans."

Colonel Parker then wrote out directions for carrying out the surrender terms, in his own words.[45]

Parker was promoted to brigadier general and stayed on as General Grant's aide after the war. When Parker married in 1867, General Grant was his best man. When Grant became president of the United States in 1869, he appointed Parker as the Commissioner of Indian Affairs, the first Native American to hold the position. He remained at that post until 1871, when he resigned after being wrongfully accused of crimes by corrupt federal officials who became rich from cheating the Indians, practices that he had tried to end. Parker then became a Wall Street investor, made a fortune, lost it in the Panic of 1873, and then became a New York City Police Department clerk. He died on August 31, 1895 in Fairfield, Connecticut. Initially buried there, his body was exhumed and moved in 1897 to Forest Lawn Cemetery in Buffalo. He rests there today near his great ancestor, Red Jacket.

CHAPTER 6

GROVER CLEVELAND

Young Stephen Grover Cleveland

On March 18, 1837 in Caldwell, New Jersey, the Reverend Richard Falley Cleveland and his wife Anne welcomed into the world the fifth of their nine children. They named him Stephen Grover after Reverend Cleveland's immediate predecessor at the Presbyterian Church in Caldwell, where little Stephen's father was pastor at the time. Richard Cleveland was a modest man of the cloth. Every few years the Presbyterian Church reassigned him to another location. It was not long before he was moving his family to Fayetteville in Central New York, and then nearby Clinton and Holland Patent.

The career of a small town minister did not make for an extravagant lifestyle, but the Clevelands maintained a modest lifestyle. The boys of the family were compelled to find work to contribute to the support of the family. When he was sixteen, Stephen's father died in Holland Patent. This meant that the Cleveland boys would have to work even harder to support their widowed mother and their younger siblings. Young Cleveland took a job as an assistant to his older brother William, who was a teacher at New York City's Institute for the Blind. He left this position after a year, realizing that he was not cut out for such a vocation.

At eighteen, Cleveland decided that he would go west to find his calling. He headed for the city of Cleveland, named for a distant cousin, because he felt that it was as a good a place as any to start. Perhaps he would pursue a career in law. He headed west on the Erie Canal and when he reached Buffalo he decided to visit his Uncle Lewis Allen and his wife Margaret, who was his late father's sister.

This was not the first time Cleveland had visited his uncle and aunt. Five years earlier as a young teen he had made the journey to the Queen City, and in a later interview Mr. Allen said that his nephew had made several trips to see him during the boy's childhood.[1] On this return visit, the young man explained his intentions to his Uncle Lewis. Allen reasoned with Stephen about his plans, reminding him that he knew no one in Cleveland and had no employment prospects there. But in Buffalo, a growing city with plenty of opportunities for ambitious young men, he could count on his Uncle Lewis for support.

Allen needed immediate help writing and editing a book about shorthorn cattle, and he promised that he would help young Cleveland secure a position reading law at a Buffalo firm, which could lead to a comfortable career as an attorney. Duly convinced by his uncle, Stephen decided to take his chances with Buffalo and remain with him.

Lewis F. Allen

Lewis F. Allen (1800-1890) had moved to Buffalo from Massachusetts as a young businessman and prospered from various investments and real estate transactions. Eventually he purchased acreage on Grand Island. He made a fortune selling timber from the land and later established an experimental farm there. He also grazed cattle on his Buffalo property clear up to Main Street. Allen Street, named for him, is a former cowpath.

At this time, in 1855, Allen was one of the most influential citizens of Buffalo, perhaps second only to former President Millard Fillmore. He was a president and one of the founders of the Buffalo Historical Society, served on the first board of health in Erie County, was a state legislator for a time, founded the first city cemetery association, was a founder of the New York State Agricultural Society and the Erie County Agricultural Society.

In 1837 Allen had purchased the property of Peter B. Porter of Black Rock after Porter moved to Niagara Falls. This included Porter's house at 1192 Niagara Street near Ferry Street overlooking the Niagara River, and this is the home in which Grover Cleveland was welcomed by his uncle. Porter had been President John Quincy Adams' secretary of war. The house was demolished in 1911 and the site today is occupied by a brick building and parking lot owned by Rich Products Corporation. Prominent visitors to Allen's house were Millard Fillmore, William Seward, Horace Greeley and Henry Clay.

Grover Cleveland's Early Career

Cleveland helped his uncle finish the cattle book, and Allen got the young man a position reading law at one of Buffalo's prestigious law firms, Rogers, Bowen and Rogers, a successor partnership to Millard Fillmore's old practice. Though not considered brilliant, Cleveland's intellect, character and hard work eventually earned him recognition and his career began to take off. He moved from his Uncle Lewis' house after several months to be closer to his place of employment, which was on the top floor of the five story Spaulding's Exchange Building on the west side of lower Main Street. This was a large office and retail structure, later the site of the old Memorial Auditorium and now part of the Canalside area.

Cleveland himself was now living at the Southern Hotel at the corner of Seneca and Michigan with an old Fayetteville friend as his roommate. He then took a room at 11 Oak Street. In short order the law firm moved to offices on the south side of Erie Street, which stood on a triangular patch of land between Main and Pearl. Cleveland was admitted to the bar in 1859 and remained as a clerk with Rogers, Bowen and Rogers until 1863. In the years 1862-63 he lived at 29 Swan Street.

During these years, Cleveland saw less and less of his Uncle Lewis Allen and eventually became estranged from him. The fact that the young man began to associate with a rough crowd, that is, young bachelors like himself who liked to hang out at beer halls and saloons, did not stand well in the opinion of the Allens. An even bigger reason for the split was over political differences. Lewis Allen was a devout Republican, having chaired the first Republican convention in Erie County. Cleveland gravitated to the Democrats, perhaps because his employers at the law firm were Democrats and he would have been exposed to their ideas in the office.

Cleveland started to dabble in politics at ward meetings and gained connections. He was appointed assistant district attorney of Erie County in 1863, a position he held until 1865. When in 1864 his boss, the district attorney, decided to retire, Cleveland made up his mind to run for his seat. He secured the Democratic nomination but lost to Republican Lyman K. Bass, his friend and future law partner.

In 1866 Cleveland took a position with the legal firm of Vandepoel and Company, which had their offices over the old post office at the northwest corner of Washington and Seneca Streets, a site now occupied by the Main Seneca Building. In 1867 he had a law office in the Hollister Block at the southeast corner of Main and Seneca, a site now occupied by the One Seneca Tower's plaza. His name now appeared on his firm's shingle: Laning, Cleveland and Folsom. The year 1868 found him rooming at the United States Hotel at Pearl and Terrace, in 1869 at a rooming house at the corner of Pearl and Swan, in 1870 at 22 W. Seneca Street, and then at a boarding house at 47-51 Niagara Street in 1871-72. That was the former mansion of William Fargo of Wells Fargo fame.

In 1870 Cleveland won election as sheriff of Erie County and served in that capacity from the beginning of 1871 until the end of 1873. His tenure in that office is best remembered for his role in springing the trap door in two hangings of convicted criminals, but he proved his mettle as an excellent, honest, no-nonsense administrator. By this time, Cleveland was assuming his familiar appearance. Years of eating rich food and drinking tankards of hearty beer at German saloons packed on the pounds. He became known to his friends as "Big Steve" and to his nephews as "Uncle Jumbo."

Upon leaving the sheriff's office, he was a partner in three variously named firms: Bass, Cleveland and Bissell; Cleveland and Bissell; and Cleveland, Bissell and Sicard. The offices of these successive firms were located at a building at 284 Main Street Street at the northwest corner of Swan, called the Weed Block after the Weed and Company hardware store on the ground floor. It was a squarish five story white brick building. The Weed Company retail display windows fronted Main Street. On the

Swan Street side was an open air, outdoor flight of stairs leading up to a second-floor entrance for the offices upstairs. One imagines that climbing the stairs could be quite hazardous during a Buffalo winter.

Cleveland's utilitarian offices were on the second floor overlooking Swan. A brick addition in the back provided apartments, and Cleveland took one on the third floor, its windows also overlooking Swan Street. His living quarters were well appointed, with comfortable furniture and a small personal library.[2]

Cleveland's law firms were among the most highly respected in the fast growing city. As an attorney, he preferred working behind the scenes and seldom made a court appearance. He was tenacious in his reasoning and worked exceedingly long hours in service to his clients. He had a great memory and intense powers of concentration. Without fail he was honest and ethical.

In his personal life, Cleveland preferred a rather simple existence, living in run-of-the-mill boarding houses and apartments close to work. He did not put on airs. He took his meals in restaurants and beer halls and preferred the company of other males, usually bachelors as he was. He was almost always unaccompanied by females and expressed an aversion to marriage. For the most part he did not attend social events. Yet he also enjoyed poetry, literature and history. His demeanor was friendly, but he could be stern and gruff. He was thrifty, yet did not seem to care much for pursuing great wealth, only to be comfortably secure.[3]

Despite the intense dedication to his profession, Cleveland made time for leisure pursuits. He frequently made visits to see his mother in Holland Patent, but apparently had no desire to do extensive traveling.[4] From at least the time he was a young lad visiting his Uncle Lewis' home and his farm on Grand Island, Cleveland enjoyed fishing and duck hunting on the Buffalo area waterways and marshes. He and several friends even bought Beaver Island, off Grand Island in the Niagara River, and formed the Beaver Island Club. He and his buddies used the place for fishing, boating, swimming and hunting. And he found time to spend an evening in the back room of a saloon playing cards and raising a glass of brew with his friends and associates.

One man with whom Cleveland supposedly had no relationship at all was Buffalo's most prominent citizen, Millard Fillmore. He often saw the former president riding by in his coach, but never personally knew the man, according to most sources.[5, 6] Indeed, their circles of acquaintance were quite different; Cleveland's was down to earth and rather coarse for genteel society, Fillmore's refined and quite cultured. And yet Cleveland became a friend of Millard Powers Fillmore, the elder Fillmore's only son. Called Powers by those close to him, he was, like Cleveland, a lawyer, only slightly older, a bachelor, and lived in the same apartment building back of the Weed Block.[7] This is undoubtedly how the two men met. Not a great deal is known about their relationship. Cleveland wrote about Powers in reply to James G. Wilson, a biographer seeking information:

> Powers Fillmore was a man of the kindliest impulses and disposition, but very odd in many ways. I do not know of anybody with whom he was at all confidential regarding personal or family affairs. It was plain to see that he loved his father and fondly cherished his memory – though even that could not be gathered from any frequent conversation he indulged in concerning him. But he was exceedingly shy, and above all things, seemed to desire to avoid notice or publicity. You may not see that anything I have written accounts for his conduct in relation to his father's papers; but knowing him as well as I did, I can imagine a connection. And still I am bound to say he has acted strangely in the matter.[8]

Another friend and close acquaintance of Grover Cleveland was John G. Milburn. Born in England, Milburn had come to America at age eighteen and settled in Batavia, studied law, then moved to Buffalo where he set up the law firm Sprague, Milburn and Sprague in 1879. He became acquainted with Cleveland and in 1882 formed a partnership with a member of Cleveland's first law firm, Sherman Rogers. The practice was known as Rogers, Locke and Milburn.

As Milburn became a good friend of Cleveland, he urged him to accept the Democratic Party's nomination for mayor of Buffalo in 1881. When in 1884 Cleveland was running for president and a scandal erupted in Buffalo over an illegitimate child, Milburn was one of his Buffalo friends who defended his reputation, and was a defense lawyer in a related court case in the Queen City in 1890. When Cleveland became president Milburn visited him at the White House at least twice, in the spring of 1885 and in January of 1896.[9] Milburn's Delaware Avenue home was to become a place of national tragedy in 1901 when President William McKinley died there.

Cleveland's most fateful, if not closest, friendship was with his law partner, Oscar Folsom. Like Cleveland, Folsom was a young up-and-coming attorney, of the same generation. The two men became acquainted and by 1869 had formed the firm Laning, Cleveland and Folsom. The Folsom family lived at 168 Edward Street in Buffalo, and daughter Frances was born in it. The house which still stands and is privately owned. Cleveland often visited the Folsom home. In 1875, in a bit of reckless carriage driving, Folsom was thrown from his rig and killed on Amherst near Niagara Street in Buffalo at age thirty-seven. Cleveland delivered his eulogy and was appointed administrator of his friend's estate. In its settlement, a substantial sum of money was awarded to his widow Emma and their eleven-year-old daughter Frances. Cleveland felt a special obligation toward them in the ensuing years, and to Frances he became the strong male presence in her life.

After the death of her father, young Frances moved to the village of Medina, New York and with her mother, and lived with Mrs. Ruth Harmon at 300 North Main Street for three years. That house still stands. The girl attended Medina High School. John Bent, an uncle of Frances, also lived in Medina, and Cleveland made frequent visits to see him, Mrs. Folsom, and Frances. A story which has circulated for decades in Medina claims that a local police constable once apprehended Grover Cleveland under suspicion of stealing Mr. Bent's carriage, but that matter was cleared up once it was realized that Cleveland was using the carriage with Bent's permission.[10]

As she grew into young womanhood, Cleveland's interest in Frances grew more romantic in nature and the two were married in 1886. By that time he was president, and a simple wedding ceremony was held in the White House on June 2. It was the only time in history that a president had been married in the Executive Mansion.

Cleveland Moves Up The Political Ladder

Grover Cleveland had been involved in Democratic Party politics since the late 1850s, had been assistant district attorney of Erie County in the 1860s, and Erie County Sheriff in the 1870s. But his real rise into political prominence began in 1881 when he consented to become his party's nominee for mayor of Buffalo. He was elected on a promise to clean up the blatant corruption that was prominent in the city.

And clean it up he did. He became known as Buffalo's Reform Mayor. He ended the long practice of the city council whereby members received kickbacks for awarding contracts to crooked companies while the mayor looked the other way. "It is a good thing for the people now and then to rise up and let the officeholders know that they are responsible to the masses," he was quoted during the campaign.[11] As mayor, Cleveland's office was located in City and County Hall, now the Old County Hall on Franklin Street. The office was on the second floor just to the left of the entrance portal.

Cleveland's popularity and reputation gained the attention of state Democrats, who nominated him for governor in 1882. After just one year as mayor of Buffalo, he became governor of New York. He repeated his performance in Albany, becoming the Reform Governor, and in the summer of 1884 the Democratic National Convention meeting in Chicago nominated him for president of the United States. He had first been proposed for president at an 1883 meeting of Buffalo luminaries, including Cleveland, at the home of George Urban at 280 Pine Ridge Road in Cheektowaga, a house which still stands today. Cleveland won the election to become the second Buffalonian to become our nation's chief executive.

The presidential contest of 1884 was probably the dirtiest on record. It was during that campaign that the *Buffalo Evening Telegraph* revealed that years earlier Cleveland had admitted fathering a child out of wedlock with a woman named Maria Halpin. Such a rumor had circulated in Buffalo for years. Halpin had named the boy Oscar Folsom Cleveland, combining the two good friends' names. It has been speculated that Grover Cleveland had accepted responsibility for the child because of all the men who could have fathered him, only Cleveland was a bachelor.

His campaign and his Buffalo friends and supporters began damage control, and it was said that Cleveland, above all, wanted everyone to tell the truth. But the truth was hard to discern. The sordid affair involved accusations of rape, kidnapping, alcoholism and promiscuity. Cleveland was portrayed as either sexual predator or honorable citizen, and Halpin as either an innocent victim or a "loose" woman.

In the end, Cleveland won the election against Republican James G. Blaine, who had issues of his own that affected his campaign. Cleveland's first term as president was one of the most accomplished in the history of the presidency. Honest to a tee, he became known as the Veto President for his hundreds of vetoes of outrageous pension and relief bills. He was a fiscal conservative and was opposed to high tariffs, which he believed hurt the working man. But the highlight of his presidency was his White House wedding to Buffalonian Frances Folsom, twenty-seven years his junior and at age twenty-one the youngest first lady in American history.

Cleveland Rejects Buffalo and Again Becomes President

Despite his success and his apparent popularity, Cleveland lost his bid for reelection in 1888 to Republican Benjamin Harrison. Cleveland had maintained his residence back of the Weed Block in Buffalo during the tenure of his mayoralty and governorship and into his presidency. But now that it came time to vacate the White House, he refused to consider moving back to Buffalo with his wife.

There are two reasons why Grover Cleveland turned his back on Buffalo. First, he harbored a deep resentment over the way he had been treated by some of the Buffalo press and some Buffalonians over the Halpin affair. And while he was grateful for the support of many of his Buffalo friends, he also was bitter about those who remained silent rather than defend him. Such a sentiment is expressed in two letters he wrote from Albany to his good friend and Buffalo law partner Wilson S. Bissell shortly after the 1884 election:

> I am busy all day long receiving congratulations of friends in person while through the mail and by telegram they are counted by the thousands. It's quite amusing to see how profuse are the expressions of some who stood aloof when most needed. I intend to cultivate the Christian duty of charity toward all men except the dirty class that defiled themselves with filthy scandal and Ballism.[12] I don't believe God will ever forgive them and I am determined not to do so.[13]

A few days later he wrote to Bissell again concerning tying up loose ends in Buffalo before vacating the governor's mansion in Albany:

> I shall not come to Buffalo – just yet, at all events. As I feel at this moment, I would never go there again if I could avoid it. Elected President of the United States, I feel I have no home at my home.... I want to make some financial arrangements. Perhaps it would be safe for me to arrive there some morning and leave at night.... [N]othing is so annoying to me as my thoughts connected with Buffalo.[14]

Cleveland retained his governorship until January 6, 1885, then moved to a rented house in Albany for the interim until he took up his duties in Washington, D.C. But he did come to Buffalo to take care of business in early January, ending his law partnership and attending a charity ball.[15] Again, he had expressed his feelings about Buffalo to Bissell a few days earlier:

> I do hope that in such circumstances I may be protected from any unnecessary annoyance which might be caused by contact with the dirty and contemptible portion of the Buffalo population. I am glad that there will be no reception in either club.[16]

If that wasn't enough, the second reason that Grover Cleveland's attitude toward his home city soured had to do with the spoils system and office seekers. Just as with his many predecessors, the newly elected president was besieged by a chronic stream of men anxious to be appointed to positions in the new administration – thousands of them, from cabinet positions to the smallest postmastership.

In addition, Buffalonians joined the queue for federal jobs. One interesting anecdote concerns George Gruener, who ran a hotel where Mr. Cleveland often enjoyed a social hour of "refreshment" at the hotel restaurant/bar. Because of that, Gruener thought he had an inside track for an appointment to an oh-not-so-important position – just postmaster or collector of customs in Buffalo. So Gruener went to Washington and was promptly rebuffed by the president.[17]

Cleveland was an advocate of civil service reform. He was a Democrat but believed that Republicans doing a competent job in non-political federal positions should not be removed simply for party affiliation. He also believed in appointing men to office based on merit and qualifications, not on personal or political affiliation. In following such policy, Cleveland disappointed Democrats not only nationally but particularly in Buffalo. Not one of his friends or associates from back home received any significant federal position during his first term. The new president expressed his consternation at Buffalonians for apparently snubbing him because of this. To his Queen City friend Charles W. Goodyear:

> Bissell sent me a clipping from a newspaper in which it was made to appear that my Buffalo friends accused me of having the big head. If I have anything of that kind I will try very hard to get the better of it. One thing I know; neither that nor anything my Buffalo friends may say or do can lessen my affection for them.[18]

And in another letter to Goodyear:

> I feel sick at heart. I don't want to let these friends go.... Of course I thought it a little strange that with the hundreds of invitations, to visit hundreds of places during my vacation, my friends in Buffalo did not care to see me; but I am going to say that I can get along without Buffalo or Buffalo friends. I care much – very

much – for the latter. But by God! I have something on hand here that cannot be interfered with; and if my Buffalo friends or any other friends cannot appreciate that, I can't help it.[19]

Perhaps there were other factors helping to sway Cleveland to settle elsewhere after his presidency. His wife had a somewhat strained relationship with her mother, who was then living in Buffalo. There is also some indication that the "anonymity" of living in a large, crowded city appealed to him. In 1889 he chose to take an apartment with his family in New York City and work for a prestigious law firm there, a move that would have better positioned him for a political comeback. Though Buffalo was a thriving city, New York was even more dynamic and offered stronger political contacts. Still, his estrangement from Buffalo continued. Writing to William F. Vilas on May 20, 1889 regarding the remarriage of his mother-in-law Emma Folsom, Cleveland said, "And she [Emma] will live in Buffalo – the place I hate above all others."[20]

Cleveland was successful in returning to the presidency. He defeated President Benjamin Harrison in the 1892 election to become the twenty-fourth president, the only person in American history to serve two non-consecutive terms as president. This second stint in the White House was more troubling than the first, mainly tainted by a financial panic and Cleveland's actions in the Pullman strike. But finally, a Buffalonian was appointed to a high-ranking federal position. President Cleveland's old Buffalo colleague Wilson S. Bissell served as postmaster general during this second presidency.

Once again leaving the White House, this time for good, the Clevelands moved to Princeton, New Jersey. The former president had accepted a position with the vaunted Princeton University in an idyllic small city setting, a perfect place for a semi-retirement away from politics. Buffalo seems to not even have been remotely considered as a place for the family to settle.

President Cleveland Visits Buffalo

After Cleveland was first inaugurated as president on March 4, 1885, he returned to Buffalo only three times during the rest of his life. All of these visits were brief.

Cleveland's first trip to Buffalo after he became president was in late 1885, his only trip to the city as chief executive. His purpose for returning to the Queen City was to vote, as Buffalo was still his legal residence at the time. His plans were publicized in late October and he specifically requested that no formalities take place during his short visit. It was to be a strictly personal, informal affair. The president left the nation's capital at 7:15 a.m. on November 2 aboard the private car *Minerva*, owned by President J. P. Wilbur of the Lehigh Valley Railroad. Accompanying Cleveland was Wilson S. Bissell, the president's former law partner from Buffalo, who had arrived in Washington a few days before to escort him back to his home town. Also on board were John M. Jester, doorkeeper of the White House, and railway representatives, to see to it that the president's wishes were carried out.

The train followed a route through Philadelphia, Wilkes-Barre, Elmira, Hornell, Warsaw and Attica. At each station a small crowd gathered, despite the lack of publicity, and Cleveland scarcely acknowledged them. In fact, he did not alight from his car at any time before Buffalo. The president's time of arrival in Buffalo was not announced and the train slowed considerably during its last segments so that it would come in late at night to avoid a crowd. Still, word leaked out, and when the *Minerva* pulled in to the Exchange Street Station and stopped between Michigan and Chicago Streets at 12:20 a.m. on Election Day, November 3, as many as 250 people were on hand to greet him. Reporters were anxious for news about the journey, but received only a short reply from Mr. Bissell that the trip had been a quiet one.

After shaking hands with several old friends, Cleveland was escorted to a waiting carriage and he and Bissell were driven to the latter's residence, where the president would be a guest during his short stay in town. That home was at 268 Franklin Street, now the parking lot of WGRZ-TV studios. After getting some rest, President Cleveland was out and about at around 7:30 a.m. In a dark suit, black silk hat and polished boots, he walked, apparently unescorted, straight south down Franklin Street from Bissell's house to his assigned polling place, first district, ninth ward of the city of Buffalo. The ballot was in the office of M.V. Smith, 93 Franklin Street between Niagara and Church Streets, now the site of the Rath County Office Building.

About a hundred of his fellow citizens were there to greet him and shout words of encouragement. As the president stepped up to the ballot box to vote the following exchange between him and a poll worker was recorded:

> "Name, please," said the inspector, covering the whole ballot box with hand.
> "Cleveland," said the President, tumbling to the racket.
> "Full name," bellowed the inspector, covering up the other ballot boxes with his other hand.
> "Grover Cleveland!" answered the man of destiny.
> "Live where?" continued the guardian of the suffrage box.
> "Over Weed's hardware store, corner of Main and Swan Streets."
> "Got it?" said the inspector to the gentlemen at the polling lists.
> "Correct." answered the clerks in chorus.[21]

After marking his ballot and turning it in, Cleveland turned around and cordially shook hands with the admirers crowded about him. Then he was out the door for a short walk in the cold, cloudy and somewhat windy morning air, to Gerot's Restaurant where he took breakfast with an old colleague, Franklin D. Locke of Cleveland's old law firm. Gerot's was a fine dining establishment located at 285 Washington Street, on the east side between Swan and Church Streets. The site is now a parking lot.

From there, the president went to his old law office upstairs at Main and Swan where he received friends and old acquaintances for a few hours. At about 5 p.m. he was driven back to his rail car at the station, accompanied by Charles W. Goodyear and Wilson Bissell. While waiting for the signal to go, the president received several people on board, including the Bishop of Buffalo, the Rt. Reverend Stephen V. Ryan. In short order the train pulled out, with three railroad officials and Goodyear riding with Cleveland at least as far as Hornell. The president arrived back in Washington the next morning at 10:50.

Cleveland did not return to Buffalo to vote during the remainder of his first term as president, in 1886, 1887 or 1888, though he would still have technically been a legal resident of the city. Absentee ballots did not exist during those years, so it could be that he did not vote at all, though it is hard to imagine a president of the United States shirking his citizens' duty to vote.

Former President Cleveland's 1891 Visit To Buffalo

Cleveland's second visit to Buffalo after becoming president took place in 1891 between his first and second terms in the White House. The former president stopped in the city as part of a cross country tour from his New York City home, probably undertaken to gauge interest in his running for president again the following year. It also served to keep his name in the newspapers, and a little publicity could only help a potential candidacy. At the very same time, incumbent President Benjamin Harrison was making his own journey across the continent.

Mr. Cleveland had been formally invited to Buffalo by the city's German Young Men's Association (GYMA) to speak at the organization's fiftieth anniversary observances, and he also accepted an invitation from Buffalo's Cleveland Democracy club to formally dedicate its new meeting place. The former president's train pulled in from the west at the Exchange Street Station at 10:18 a.m. on Monday, May 11, 1891. About a hundred prominent Buffalonians were there to greet it, headed by Buffalo Mayor Charles F. Bishop and Cleveland's old friend Wilson Bissell. Cleveland alighted from the last coach of the five car train, dressed in silk hat and black Prince Albert suit. A hearty cheer went up and enthusiastic handshakes were exchanged, to the apparent pleasure of the honored guest. The ex-president's two traveling companions, Dr. Joseph D. Bryant, surgeon general of New York, and Dr. Joseph H. Senner, a prominent German American, also exited the coach. Cleveland had an especially warm greeting for Henry E. Perrine, the stepfather of his wife Frances, although the former first lady did not accompany Cleveland on this trip.

Mr. Cleveland and his guests were guided to waiting carriages and were driven to the Eagle Street entrance of the grand Iroquois Hotel. Demolished long ago, the Iroquois stood at the southeast corner of Main and Eagle and extended to Washington Street. The site is now occupied by the M&T Bank building, and is known as One M&T Plaza. Once ensconced in his room at the hotel, the former president had a private breakfast with Drs. Bryant and Senner and then received a steady stream of visitors calling to pay their respects. In the afternoon Cleveland was driven out to make a few calls along with Bissell and Perrine. Among those he visited was Mrs. Perrine, who was the former Mrs. Oscar Folsom and the mother of his wife. He also visited Mrs. Bissell, and the family of the late Lewis F. Allen, Cleveland's uncle. The visit to the Allens at the old family homestead on Niagara Street surely brought forth some poignant memories for Cleveland.

After this the gentlemen took a drive through Delaware Park, at the time simply known as The Park. Cleveland was pleasantly surprised at the development of the city even since his last visit six years prior. He stopped at the Bissells' home for lunch. They were then living at 295 Delaware Avenue, now the site of the 285 Delaware Building. That evening Cleveland attended the anniversary celebration of the German Young Men's Association. It was held at the Music Hall at 760 Main Street, which had been built by the GYMA, and it was the home of Buffalo's first symphony orchestra. Many years later the building was remodeled and converted into the Teck movie theater, but was demolished in the late twentieth century. Today it is a vacant lot.

Mr. Cleveland and Dr. Senner were escorted in a carriage by members of the GYMA from the Iroquois Hotel to the Music Hall, arriving at the main entrance at 8:15 p.m. Greeted with polite applause, they were quickly escorted to a box nearest the stage. Seated with the two men were Mr. and Mrs. Perrine and Mr. and Mrs. Bissell. The hall, filled to capacity, was decorated with flowers and greenery. Over the stage hung a banner with portraits of two of the founding members of the GYMA, the years 1841 and 1891, and German and American flags.

At 8:30 the orchestra began playing from a platform before the stage, and the curtain rose to reveal dozens of GYMA members, singers and other guests. Addresses were made in German and English and then Mr. Cleveland sauntered onstage to a standing ovation. To an orchestral fanfare, the audience waved hats and handkerchiefs as the former president smiled and bowed in acknowledgment of the hearty welcome. Once formally introduced, Cleveland gave a speech in which he emphasized the virtues of German culture and the contributions of German Americans:

> On behalf of the American people, I am inclined also to claim tonight that the German character which the Association undertakes to cultivate, is so interwoven with all the growth and progress of our country, that we have a right to include it among the factors which make up a sturdy and thrifty Americanism.[22]

After Cleveland's speech, Dr. Senner spoke, and afterwards a choral selection brought the program to a close. The former president was then driven back to his hotel to attend a late-night banquet in his honor. One of the Iroquois' dining halls was brightly lit by electric chandeliers. A picture of Cleveland hung from one wall. Long tables were set up for the 160 guests, who had paid ten dollars apiece to attend. The tables were decorated with flowers and place settings. Attendees included Mayor Bishop, Buffalo Congressman Daniel Lockwood and Wilson Bissell. This was strictly a male affair, with no ladies present.

A ten-course meal was served beginning at 10 p.m. as a small orchestra provided background music. It was almost 12:30 before John Milburn, Cleveland's old colleague, rose to make post-dinner remarks. The atmosphere was akin to a polite fraternity gathering with humor, laughter and whooping punctuating the festivities.

The former president rose to speak. He talked with a sense of both melancholy and humor, as well as a heartfelt appreciation of his Buffalo roots:

> My mind at this moment is full of the recollection of experiences connected with my early life in Buffalo. Some of these experiences were rugged, but they were healthful; and they appear to me now robbed of everything save the features that make them welcome memories. I recall, too, hosts of good friends who were about me in those days. The living attachments of many of them I still cherish as priceless possessions; and many others I loved until

inexorable death decreed our separation.... As I turn from these saddening reflections and glance over this company, I am still further and more cheerfully reminded of the years which have passed since my life in Buffalo began.

Speaking of himself in the third person, he continued:

> He did a great deal of hard work and was much perplexed and troubled, but I know that his greatest trial was his alienation of many personal and political friends in making appointments to office. It was impossible to avoid this, and it will continue to be impossible in all like cases so long as the applicant for office and the man who is charged with the responsibility of appointment occupy such entirely different points of observation – and just so long as public duty may stand in the way of personal friendship.

And in conclusion:

> I cannot forbear saying to you before I conclude that I have never forgotten the assurance I gave in the presence of thousands of my Buffalo friends during the Presidential campaign of 1884, to the effect that whatever the future might have in store for me I should endeavor so to perform my duty as to merit their approval and friendship. As I visit these friends again self-examination brings home to me no reproaches. I know that I have done no violence to the sentiments and resolutions, which, when I lived among you, received your approval and endorsement. I feel that I can but feebly express my appreciation of the courtesy of this occasion – because language is weak. You must know how I have enjoyed the kindly greeting of my old friends; and I hope I need not tell you how it delights me to witness the growth and increased beauty of my old home. I assure you that from the fullness of a grateful heart I wish for the City of Buffalo boundless prosperity and advancement and for the people of Buffalo Heaven's choicest blessings and contentment which find their abiding place in generous and unselfish hearts.[23]

Following three more brief speeches, the banquet broke up at 2:35 a.m. with final cheers for Mr. Cleveland. He got a few hours of sleep, took breakfast at ten the next morning, then walked two blocks to City Hall on Franklin with his old law partner Franklin D. Locke, arriving at the second-floor mayor's office just before 11 a.m.

He was there at the old office he had occupied as mayor to hold a public reception. More than a hundred men of all political persuasions had been invited to specially greet him, and they spilled out into the corridor and stood at the building's entrance and cheered his arrival. Cleveland exchanged greetings with Mayor Bishop, Congressman Lockwood and a bi-partisan roster of politicians. He positioned himself in front of a desk with Bishop on one side and Lockwood on the other. The doors were opened and a stream of men, women and children came through and exchanged greetings. The former president received all with a pleasant smile and hearty handshake. Many well-wishers uttered more than a simple greeting, but Cleveland had little time to carry on a conversation.

Some interesting comments were directed to him: "Remember your old plumber?" "Hello Grover. Be our candidate in '92?" "You are looking well." One boy in a wheelchair exclaimed, "Glad to see you, Mr. Cleveland!" and the former president stooped to give him a kind greeting. By one o'clock the line had thinned and the doors were closed. About 2,000 people had passed through. Cleveland was then driven to the Buffalo Club at 388 Delaware Avenue for a luncheon with about twenty of his colleagues, including Ansley Wilcox.[24]

At 7:30 that evening, Cleveland left the hotel for yet another engagement. He was escorted to the new Cleveland Democracy club house, located in an elegant leased brick mansion at 351 Washington Street. Long gone, it is now the site of the Robert B. Adam parking ramp behind One M&T Plaza. Founded by Buffalo Democrats following Cleveland's 1884 election to boost support for his upcoming presidency, it still functioned in 1891 as a men's club to support the former president's brand of party principles. It was richly furnished and decorated, and chandeliers brilliantly lit each room. Cleveland appeared in the upstairs assembly room which could seat only 400 of the club's 1,700 members.

People were crammed in the corridors and along the stairway in an effort to hear the proceedings.

At 7:45 the program began. When Cleveland rose to speak he received a loud standing ovation. He lauded the club's accomplishments and rallied the troops to continue the good fight. He especially warned about government overspending:

> I believe the most threatening figure which today stands in the way of the safety of our government and the happiness of our people is reckless and wicked extravagance in our public expenditures. It is the most fatal of all the deadly brood of governmental perversion.... Our Democratic faith teaches us that the useless exaction of money from the people upon the false pretext of public necessity is the worst of all government perversions, and involves the greatest of all dangers to our guarantees of justice and equity.

Cleveland closed his remarks by exhorting his listeners "that those who prefer to serve their fellow citizens in public place must be faithful to their trust."[25] After an ovation, he was escorted downstairs for a reception, during which he shook the hands of 2,000 persons in the space of an hour. After a short rest, he was driven to the Music Hall for the GYMA ball. He stopped on the way for a few glasses of beer and Swiss cheese with his German friends.[26] Mr. Cleveland joined the roomful of 500 exquisitely dressed guests and held an impromptu reception. He did not join those on the dance floor, begged forgiveness due to fatigue. He left before the midnight banquet began.

The next morning Cleveland took an early breakfast at the Iroquois with Dr. Bryant and had a brief chat with two reporters from the *New York Times*. Then he thanked the hotel's proprietors for their hospitality and praised the accommodations. "It is a great thing for Buffalo. I'll have to put up here again some time," he said. When asked about his general impression of his visit, he said, "It was all that I could have wished and more pleasurable even than I had anticipated. I shall not be likely to forget my visit soon."[27]

He then took his leave and with Dr. Bryant was driven to the Exchange Street Station where the two men boarded a train for New York, which pulled out at 8:50 a.m. A few days later Cleveland wrote to his friend Wilson Bissell a letter in which he conveyed pleasant thoughts about the visit:

> My thoughts tonight are very completely filled with the incidents of my recent visit to Buffalo and all that was done for me by my very good friends while there. You will not think it strange, I am sure, that I am constrained to write to you before I go to bed, as chief of them all, to thank you for your kindness and attention. The reception at the Democracy was very pleasant and the speech of President Buell was in exceeding good taste and in all respects very fine. I am glad I went to the ball; we came away before the banquet there began, but I had an opportunity to meet some good friends among the Germans.... Remember me very affectionately to Mrs. Bissell. Give my regards to all the friends who were so kind to me.[28]

Cleveland's Final Visit To Buffalo

Grover Cleveland's last visit to the Queen City came on October 9, 1903 to attend the funeral of his old friend, law partner, and postmaster general Wilson S. Bissell, who had died three days earlier at the age of fifty-six. The former president arrived at the Erie Station in a private rail car with his former treasury secretary, John G. Carlisle, at 7 a.m. The car was pushed onto a sidetrack and guarded by police while John Milburn of Buffalo entered the car and breakfasted and chatted with the two men.

At 9:30 Cleveland sent word to reporters waiting at the station for a brief interview. He gave out a written statement to them:

> I was exceedingly shocked to receive the unexpected news of the death of Mr. Bissell. It is indeed a sad errand that calls me to my old home after a long absence. I knew Mr. Bissell for more than thirty years and have been associated with him in many vocations in life - as an intimate friend, as an associate in professional business, as a co-worker with him in high and

important public duty. With this full opportunity to know him, I have no mental reservations when I say that I regard Mr. Bissell as preeminently an affectionate, sincere, useful and able man. Such men cannot be well spared.[29]

The former president chatted off the record with the newsmen for a few minutes but said nothing for publication about any other matter. Mr. Milburn said the two men would rest until the afternoon funeral, then depart in the evening.

Cleveland and Carlisle were Milburn's guests during their brief stay, and the three of them were driven to Milburn's home at 1168 Delaware Avenue. This, indeed, was the same house in which President William McKinley had died in an upstairs bedroom just two years earlier, and in whose downstairs parlor lay that martyred president's remains for a brief service. It was never said whether Mr. Cleveland visited the death chamber during his short stay at the residence or whether the subject of President McKinley was even broached. It was also the home visited by Vice President Theodore Roosevelt in May 1901 when he was in town to open the Pan American Exposition, and in September 1901 to call upon the wounded President McKinley.

At 11 a.m. Cleveland, Carlisle and Milburn went to the Bissell home at 1069 Delaware, currently the site of the Catholic Academy of West Buffalo, to express their condolences to the widow, then took lunch at the Milburn home. In the early afternoon, Cleveland, before attending the Bissell funeral, went to the Castle Inn on Niagara Square at Delaware Avenue. This had been the last home of President Millard Fillmore, the house in which he had died, but had since been converted into a hotel. First, after the second Mrs. Fillmore died in 1881, it became the Hotel Fillmore, but was expanded and renovated for the 1901 Pan American Exposition and renamed. The reason for Mr. Cleveland's visit was to call on Mrs. Jefferson Davis, widow of the late Confederate president, who was staying there but was very ill. She was too sick to receive visitors, but Cleveland left his card and wishes for a speedy recovery.

Varina (Howell) Davis was the second wife of Jefferson Davis and had been the first lady of the Confederacy. Mr. Davis had been captured by

Union forces at the end of the Civil War and spent two years in prison before being released in May of 1867. He was then later pardoned by President Andrew Johnson as part of a general amnesty. The Davises moved to Canada after his release, joining many ex-Confederates who sought refuge abroad from persecution and prosecution in post-war America. The family first settled in Montreal, and later in nearby Lennoxville.

Just a few days after he had reached Montreal, Mr. Davis traveled to Toronto, then on to Niagara-on-the-Lake to visit old Confederate colleagues. In Niagara he was the guest of James M. Mason, the old Confederate ambassador to Britain. Walking up a hill from the wharf where Davis' boat had docked, they could see Fort Niagara in New York across the river, a large American flag fluttering in the breeze above it. Gesturing toward that banner, Davis commented to his friend, "Look there, Mason. There is the gridiron we have been fried on."[30]

The Davises and most of the other Confederates eventually moved back to the United States, but maintained close ties to Canada, the land that had welcomed them in their time of fear and need. Many often returned to Canada for summer vacations, and Varina Davis was among them. In the summer of 1903 she spent a few weeks in Port Colborne, Ontario, twenty miles west of Buffalo on the Lake Erie shore. She was a guest of the Humberstone Club, which was composed of wealthy summer residents from the southern states. Returning from her stay there, she and her party of twenty detrained at Buffalo for a visit of a few days. Mrs. Davis had apparently been to the Queen City before and enjoyed taking rides around the city.

But this time was different. The seventy-seven year-old widow had arrived in Buffalo on September 21, 1903. Three days later she became critically ill with an intestinal obstruction. For a few days, it was feared that she would die in her ground floor suite at the Castle Inn, but she slowly recovered and on October 17 she was well enough to depart by train for her New York City home.

Grover Cleveland arrived at the Bissell home for the start of the funeral services at 3:30 p.m. He served as an honorary pallbearer. The home was filled with distinguished mourners, including several men who had served in Cleveland's late presidential administration. The closed casket covered in flowers rested in the home's library. A brief fifteen minute service was conducted by the pastor of Trinity Episcopal Church of Delaware Avenue.

Mr. Cleveland and the other mourners were then conveyed by carriage to the church, an edifice that still stands today. The building was filled to overflowing as the casket was carried in and a thirty-minute funeral mass was conducted. Afterwards the coffin was taken by hearse to a crematory near Forest Lawn Cemetery. Only the men attended a short prayer service there, and that marked the end of the mourning rituals. Cleveland and Carlisle returned to the Milburn home, where they remained until evening. They were driven back to the Erie Station and left Buffalo in their private car at 8:10 p.m.

Grover Cleveland, at sixty-six years old, seemed to be vigorous and healthy, though thinner and grayer than during his visit to Buffalo twelve years earlier. He visited Buffalo only three times for a total of less than four days, from the time he first became president in 1885 to the end of his life twenty-three years later. Some historians cite his 1891 visit as proof that he had no enmity toward Buffalo or Buffalonians. His own grandson has said that Grover Cleveland loved Buffalo, though for a time there may have been some animosity.[31] But whether it was the Halpin affair or pushy office seekers or something else, something kept the former president away from his former home of thirty years, a place that admired him and where he had many friends. It could just be that better opportunities for him lay elsewhere. In the end, it must be concluded that Cleveland did, at least for a time, turn his back on Buffalo, but that he retained some fondness for the place and the people he knew there.

In response to notification of a meeting of his old friends in Buffalo held to celebrate his sixty-ninth birthday on March 18, 1906, Cleveland sent a return letter to them dated March 30 in which he said:

> I assure you that I fully appreciate this kindly remembrance. If the advance of age needs consolation, nothing can supply it more completely than the continued attachment and good wishes of the associates of former days. I am happy in the belief that among my treasures of friendship and retrospection the most valuable still remains in the keeping of my Buffalo friends.[32]

Grover Cleveland died on June 24, 1908 at his home in Princeton. He was buried two days later in Princeton Cemetery in a ceremony free of pomp and display. Only close friends, associates and family members were invited, with the exception of President Theodore Roosevelt, Vice President Charles Fairbanks and the governors of New York, New Jersey and Georgia. Mrs. Cleveland did not invite any of her husband's old Buffalo friends. She herself had not maintained a relationship with anyone from the Buffalo area and had not visited the Queen City after her marriage to President Cleveland in 1886.

As with the death of any former president, Cleveland's passing was front page news, but in the Buffalo newspapers the headlines were especially prominent. As soon as news of the death was received, Buffalo City Hall and local courts suspended business for the day and flags were placed at half-staff. The Common Council issued resolutions in respect of the late former mayor, governor and president. Mayor James N. Adam ordered all city offices closed on June 26, the day of the funeral. Many of Cleveland's old friends in the city expressed their tributes and shared reminiscences of him.

CHAPTER 7

THE LATE NINETEENTH CENTURY

While Grover Cleveland dominates the history of the Buffalo-presidency connection of the late nineteenth century, several other men who served as chief executive during that time were in and out of the Queen City before and after their White House years.

Rutherford B. Hayes in Buffalo

From 1877 to 1881, Rutherford B. Hayes served as the nineteenth president of the United States. He did not visit Buffalo during that time, although it is possible that his train may have passed through the city on its way to or from his Fremont home in northern Ohio to the east coast or Washington, D.C.

Hayes definitely made a few stops in Buffalo before his presidency and also came through the city as former president. Rail connections between Buffalo and Cleveland to Chicago were not completed until 1852, which compelled travelers to the eastern cities from points west of Buffalo to use lake boats to the Queen City, then transfer to canal boats, trains eastward, or trains northward to take a boat eastward on Lake Ontario.

For periods of his life, Hayes kept a diary. Though the entries are sporadic, based on these as well as letters that he wrote, he can be placed in Buffalo at various times. At the tender age of eleven, young Rutherford traveled with his sister and mother from their Delaware, Ohio home to New England to visit maternal relatives. The June 1834 journey was made by stagecoach, river boat, lake steamer, canal boat and railroad. From a diary entry we can see that the Hayeses took a steamboat from Sandusky, Ohio to Buffalo:

Monday evening [June 9, 1834] went on board the Henry Clay. Had a pleasant passage down Lake Erie to Buffalo. We went on board a canal boat Wednesday [June 11] morning.[1]

There is no specific indication that they stayed overnight in Buffalo, but it is almost certain. There is no diary entry recording a return trip, except that the family left Vermont for Ohio on October 8, so it is assumed that they probably passed through Buffalo on the way home a few days after that time.

Young Hayes attended Webb Preparatory School in Middletown, Connecticut during 1837-38, and it can be assumed that he came through Buffalo on his way there and back, before and after the school year. He attended Harvard Law School in Massachusetts from 1843 to 1845, so he undoubtedly came through Buffalo at the beginning and end of his school sessions. There is only one definite indication of time spent in Buffalo during his Harvard years, recorded in a letter Hayes wrote from the school dated August 27, 1843. He was describing his journey from Ohio to the school:

At Buffalo I gallanted Mrs. Pease [Mary, the second wife of his cousin John Pease; they did not live in Buffalo] on her first shopping excursion to the fancy stores, gave her what little instruction I could in that most important accomplishment of city ladies - shopping... At Buffalo I left the wedding couple on account of my anxiety to reach here by Commencement, which learned was to take place in a few days. I stopped at Niagara. I spent three hours rambling about the falls.[2]

Hayes was on his way to Harvard through Niagara Falls to Lake Ontario, then eastward by lake steamer. In a letter to his mother from Brattleboro, Vermont, dated July 29, 1847 while on a trip to visit relatives, Hayes wrote:

> Pease and myself arrived here Saturday [July 24] evening after a trip of five days, including about thirty-six hours' stoppages at Buffalo and Troy.[3]

In a diary entry from September 1853, he wrote:

> Visited Cleveland about the 3rd of August; thence to Niagara - three days; returned to Fremont the 8th.[4]

He would have had to change trains in Buffalo both to and from the Falls, or if traveling by lake boat, probably still disembarked at Buffalo. Hayes had entered the political world and was serving as governor of Ohio when he wrote the following diary entry in Albany, New York on July 11, 1871:

> Left Fremont yesterday morning with Uncle Sardis and Miss Sarah Jane Grant; spent the night at Buffalo, and reached here early this evening.[5]

They were going to visit relatives in Vermont and to search for ancestral homes in Connecticut. By July 23 they were back in Cleveland, so probably traveled through Buffalo the previous day on the way back home.

As former president, Rutherford B. Hayes traveled through Buffalo on at least three occasions, as noted in his diary. From an entry dated September 12, 1884:

> Wednesday evening [probably September 17], 10 p.m., left Saratoga...via Schenectady and Buffalo.[6]

He was traveling from a prison reform conference back home to

Fremont. He may not have had to transfer trains in Buffalo, in which case his train would have stopped only to take on and discharge other passengers. From an undated entry of September 1887:

> Friday 9th via Buffalo, Lewiston and steamer on Lake Ontario to Toronto.[7]

Hayes was attending a prison reform congress in Toronto. He most likely would have had to change trains in Buffalo.

From another undated entry of the same month:

> Wednesday morning with Mr. Alfred H. Lore of Philadelphia, left for Philadelphia via Buffalo.[8]

Former President Hayes was on his way to attend an industrial parade and to meet President and Mrs. Cleveland in the City of Brotherly Love.

The accounts of Mr. Hayes' travels through Buffalo demonstrate the importance of the Queen City for most of the nineteenth and early twentieth centuries as a transportation center in the movement of people between the northeast and the northern Midwest. Almost every president from Abraham Lincoln through those of the early 1900s at least passed through Buffalo's train station at some time during his lifetime.

James A. Garfield in Buffalo

Rutherford B. Hayes was succeeded as president of the United States by another Republican from northern Ohio, Congressman James A. Garfield. He was born and lived most of his life in the area southeast of Cleveland.

Even more so than Hayes, Garfield traveled from Ohio to the east and back many times during his life. As a congressman and former Civil War general, he went on many speaking tours, which no doubt were a lucrative source of additional income for him. We know from his diary that he was in Buffalo several times, and perhaps even more often than he wrote, at least to pass through the city. In a letter to his friend Corydon E. Fuller, dated November 17, 1853, twenty-one year old Garfield wrote from Niagara Falls:

> I am now leaning against the trunk of an evergreen tree on a beautiful island in the midst of Niagara's foaming waters.

He may have been on Goat Island, Green Island or one of the Three Sisters Islands. He continued:

> I have been here since yesterday morning and shall take the cars for Buffalo at 2 p.m., and then proceed to Hiram [Ohio].

He took the steamer *Ohio* from Buffalo, probably that evening, for Cleveland.[9]

Young Garfield attended Williams College in Williamstown, Massachusetts from 1854 to 1856. Diary entries from late June of 1854 show that he took a steamboat from Cleveland to Buffalo, arriving in Buffalo harbor at 6 a.m. on June 30. His diary records his adventures for that day, starting with an interesting anecdote about his transfer from boat to train in the Queen City:

> Not knowing the distance nor direction to the R.R. Depot, I entered a cab, and was driven 30 rods [165 yards] when the Jehu [cab driver] stopped at the Depot and demanded half a dollar for his prolonged services. I paid it, but entered it on my memorandum "Fooled for the last time by an American cabman, $.50." In an hour more I was on the cars, and in a short space of time was listening to the roar of Niagara's thundering cataract…. I spent that day and night in the vicinity, staying with a Mrs. Stephen Dunnell. I visited several hours at the Suspension Bridge [near the Whirlpool]…. All the devices and adornments of man can never add to nor subtract from the matchless and eternal glories of the world's Niagara.[10]

He left by train for Rochester the next morning, passing through "the beautiful Grain lands of Western New York."[11]

In the summer of 1856 Garfield graduated from Williams College. He left Massachusetts for his Ohio home on August 7. A September 8 letter from Hiram, Ohio to his friend Fuller explains that "we left Troy the

Tuesday [August 12] after you left us and spent Wednesday [August 13] at the Falls. Took the Buffalo boat that evening...to Cleveland."[12] By 1858 Garfield was president of Hiram College in Ohio. Early in the year he traveled to visit his ill sister Mary near Troy, New York. A diary entry for January 8 puts him in Buffalo that morning, and on his way back to Ohio, he was again in Buffalo. It is not clear whether he left the trains or not, or if they were merely stops to pick up and discharge passengers.[13]

After his Civil War service, General Garfield became a Congressman. In the House of Representatives, he was one of the leaders of the Radical Republicans, so called because the faction favored severe punishment of the South and its citizens for the late rebellion. It was at this time that Garfield became an in-demand speaker and campaigner. Campaigning for Republican Congressional candidates, he stopped in Buffalo in late 1866.

At 1 p.m. on October 31 Garfield arrived by train and took a room at Tifft House. That evening he and two other gentlemen addressed an audience at St. James Hall. It is not clear whether he knew that in that same building had lain the body of President Lincoln the previous year during the funeral journey, but we must surmise that it was pointed out to him at some time. A street band played outside the hall during the day and at night the members of the crowd were permitted to set off fireworks and light a small bonfire at Main and Eagle Streets. The party faithful filed into the auditorium to hear the political oratory, almost filling the place to capacity.

General Garfield left Buffalo at 8:25 the next morning for Niagara Falls with his companions, where they stopped for two hours, "strolling about and playing one unsuccessful game of chess." From there they rode to Albion where Garfield spoke for an hour and a half in a lecture hall.[14]

The future president was on another campaign speaking tour two years later when he stopped at Buffalo to spend the night at the Mansion House on October 20, 1868. He apparently did not speak here on that visit and took an early morning train eastward the next morning.[15]

In a letter to his friend Fuller, dated October 25, 1871, Garfield wrote that he had gone with family from Ohio to the east to visit relatives earlier that month, and that they had stopped for a day at Niagara Falls. This indicates a change of trains in Buffalo.

Near the end of the 1876 presidential campaign Congressman Garfield was once more in Buffalo, speaking on behalf of the Republican candidate for president, Rutherford B. Hayes. Garfield arrived at the Exchange Street Station at 1 p.m. on Friday, November 3, 1876 from Erie, Pennsylvania, only four days before the general election. He was greeted at the depot by Elbridge G. Spaulding, former Congressman and then mayor of Buffalo, who took Garfield to his residence at the southeast corner of Main and Goodell Streets.[16] "After dinner, I went to bed for two hours and then bathed, to sleep and wash away my weariness," Garfield recounted in his diary.[17] At 8 p.m. he was at St. James Hall where he was to address a campaign rally. He was preceded by one other speaker and two musical selections by the Republican Glee Club. After being introduced, he was greeted with thunderous applause.

Garfield proceeded to harangue the audience with stories of how the South would rise again if Democrats controlled the White House. "The success of the Democratic Party means nothing but the triumph of the rebellion," he exclaimed.[18] He said Republicans would continue to "wave the bloody shirt," that is, remind Americans that the Republican Party faithful had sacrificed to save the Union and therefore they had earned the right to stay in power to keep it. Garfield was applauded with loud cheers at the conclusion of his address. By 11:30 p.m. he was back at the station, where he boarded a sleeping car and was shortly thereafter off to his next stop.

The following summer Garfield and his wife Lucretia went on a vacation trip to Canada and came through Western New York on their way there. His diary entry for August 9, 1877 reads:

> Busy with preparations for leaving home until noon…and we took the 3 p.m. train east en route to Quebec. Reached Buffalo in the evening and spent the night at the Clift [porbably Tifft] House.

On the next day:

> Took morning train from Buffalo to Lewiston, thence by steamer to Toronto, and Toronto Boat for Montreal.[19]

On Sunday, July 28, 1878 Congressman Garfield was returning home to Ohio from Washington:

> Awoke at Hornellsville [Hornell, New York] where I took breakfast. Reached Buffalo at 11:15 a.m. At 12:30 took Lake Shore train for the West.[20]

In mid-summer 1878 Garfield and his sons Harry, age fourteen, and James, age twelve, took a vacation trip to Buffalo and Niagara Falls. Included in the group were Harry's fourteen-year-old friend Bentley Warren, son of William W. Warren, a former U.S. representative from Massachusetts, plus Burke A. Hinsdale, a close friend of Congressman Garfield and president of Hiram College. They took the steamer *Perry* from Ohio to the Queen City, arriving on Thursday, August 1, 1878. Garfield's diary entry from that date describes the day best:

> Awoke in sight of Buffalo, and at 9 a.m. were in the Harbor. After breakfast Burke and I and the boys went uptown, and at noon took the train to Niagara where we spent the day until six-thirty, looking at the points of interest on both sides [of] the river and falls. Boys were greatly delighted with the trip. At 6:35 we took train and reached Buffalo in an hour. The captain's cutter was waiting for us at the foot of Main Street and took us to the Perry where we spent the night.[21]

The Garfield diary also describes the next, and final day of this short vacation:

> Jim was up before the rest of us, and managed to fall into the river from the dock, and get himself out and dried in time for breakfast. Several citizens called during the forenoon. At 12:50 went with the boys to the Depot to meet Mr. Warren of Boston who comes to get his son. We asked him to go on board the cutter with us, but he could not. We parted with him and Bentley and returned

to the Perry for dinner. At two we went down to the harbor to witness the experimental use of the life-saving apparatus. It was poorly handled; but the result was otherwise very satisfactory. At eight we were about leaving Buffalo, when the ding[h]y with three men was upset, and one of the men came near drowning. At nine we were outside and steaming up the lake [for Ohio].[22]

In September of 1879 Mr. and Mrs. Garfield dropped off their sons for school in Concord, New Hampshire. Two diary entries put them around or in Buffalo at that time, "Dinner at East Buffalo..."[23] and, "We dined at East Buffalo."[24] It is not clear from these brief mentions whether they dined aboard the train, or whether they actually alighted and ate at a local Buffalo restaurant. They could possibly have stopped at the old Union Depot, which was at the site of the present Central Terminal in East Buffalo, and which had restaurant facilities.[25]

Close to Election Day that year Garfield was on the road again, campaigning for Republican candidates. On Thursday, October 30, 1879 he arrived at the Exchange Street Station where he was met by a committee of Republicans. He enjoyed his luncheon at the Tifft House, and then went to St. James Hall at two o'clock for a rally. The hall was filled to standing room. Buffalo lawyer and State Senator Sherman S. Rogers introduced Garfield and he was received with tumultuous applause. He proceeded to speak for one and three quarters hours. The speech was typical partisan Republican fare for the time. Garfield equated the Democrats with rebels, suggesting that should they take control of the federal government, the country would see ex-rebels and their ideas take control of the United States. Garfield was heartily cheered at the conclusion of his talk.

Afterward, the Congressman dined at Senator Rogers' home, attended a performance by a church choir, and later returned to Tifft House for the night. He took the train to Lockport the next morning for his next speaking engagement.

Garfield, Harrison and McKinley

On August 3, 1880 a unique event occurred in Buffalo, one which had never happened before, and has not happened since. That was the joint appearance in the city of three future American presidents – James A. Garfield, Benjamin Harrison and William McKinley.

Garfield had been nominated in June to be the Republican Party's presidential candidate for 1880. He would go on to win the election and become our twentieth president. Harrison, of Indiana, was a member of the Mississippi River Commission. Although not yet having held a significant political office of national prominence, he was an active Republican Party operative who would go on to become our twenty-third president in 1889, sandwiched in between the two terms of Buffalonian Grover Cleveland. McKinley, then a Congressman from Ohio, would of course become our twenty-fifth president and meet his tragic fate during another stay in the Queen City in 1901.

These three gentlemen, accompanied by six others, were on their way from Garfield's home near Cleveland to New York City to attend to Republican Party matters, and it was decided that they would stay overnight in Buffalo and do a little whistlestop campaigning while en route. That alone was unusual for the time, when presidential candidates did not routinely travel to campaign on their own behalfs.

Several dozen prominent Republicans from Western New York and elsewhere took a special train from Buffalo to Dunkirk to meet General Garfield's train and escort him to the Queen City. They included Sherman S. Rogers, who as a partner of the law firm Rogers, Bowen and Rogers had under his employ for a time a young Grover Cleveland. Initially a Democrat in his political leanings and one of those who had influenced Cleveland to also become a Democrat, Rogers converted to the Republican Party during the Civil War, while Cleveland remained loyal to the Democrats.

Local Republicans had planned and organized a grand welcome for their presidential standard bearer, including a parade to his hotel after a hearty welcome at the railroad station. Garfield's train rolled into Buffalo's Exchange Street Station more than an hour late, at around 9:30 p.m. Depending on which account of the welcome ceremonies one believes, either the pro-Republican or the pro-Democrat ones, what ensued was either an event of "exultation" and "nearly unparalleled enthusiasm," or one that "showed a want of organization and enthusiasm and fell far short of being a success."[26]

Thousands of Garfield's supporters had gathered on the platform and in the concourse of the station. Some of them, who had been organized by Republican ward clubs, carried torches and Chinese lanterns. A loud cheer went up as their candidate alighted from his car and was quickly escorted with his entourage to waiting carriages. A procession was formed down Exchange Street which moved west onto Main northward. It was led by a platoon of policemen, a band, a veterans' group, carriages containing Garfield and finally the various Republican clubs marching behind. The marchers were carrying torches, lanterns and campaign banners and were greeted by cheering crowds along the route. From Main west onto Huron then north onto Niagara Street, and then Porter and Prospect to their hotel destination, many houses and businesses along the way were illuminated, and there was an occasional pyrotechnic display.

Once the hotel was reached, a huge cheer went up from the huge throng that had gathered around it. This was Pierce's Palace Hotel, which stood on Prospect Avenue between Porter and Connecticut Avenues facing Prospect Park. A magnificent six story structure, it existed for only three years before a fire destroyed it in 1881. The site is now occupied by the D'Youville College campus. The hotel was splendidly illuminated, and General Garfield and the guests exited their carriages and stepped onto a temporary platform that had been erected near the hotel's entrance. Sherman S. Rogers advanced to the front of the platform and with a short speech introduced Mr. Garfield, who of course was enthusiastically cheered.

In a very short address, he simply thanked the community for its great greeting, but he said he was in Buffalo "not to discuss politics, not to make speeches." He let others do that for him. Benjamin Harrison was introduced. He gave a somewhat lengthy campaign speech in which he praised Buffalonians for the prosperity of the country and excoriated Democrats as supporters of the rebellion, traitors to the United States, and general ne'er-do-wells. The next speaker was William McKinley. In his remarks, he warned that the Democrats, if elected, would curtail liberty, deny certain people the right to vote, and place loyalty to their party above the interests of the nation.

By the time the speeches were finished it was nearly midnight. Garfield held a brief reception on the hotel's veranda, during which many persons had the opportunity to shake the candidate's hand. He and his party then retired to their rooms, but were up promptly at 5 a.m. the next morning. Their special train left for points east at 6:30.

On the way back from his New York jaunt, Garfield stopped at the Chautauqua Institution where he spent two nights. On Sunday, August 8, he attended a church service, a YMCA meeting, heard singers and listened to an explanation of the Chautauqua scheme. On Monday morning five thousand people assembled in front of Garfield's hotel to greet him. He spoke to them for fifteen minutes before leaving for Ohio.[27]

Benjamin Harrison in 1870 had visited Niagara Falls from Indiana with his family.[28] This would have required them to alight from their train at Buffalo's Exchange Street Station and either walk or take a carriage or trolley across Washington and Main Streets to the Erie Station, where they would have boarded a train for the Falls. If arriving by lake steamer, they still would have most likely disembarked in Buffalo.

Chester A. Arthur Not Quite In Buffalo

President Garfield succumbed to an assassin's bullet on September 19, 1881 and Vice President Chester A. Arthur then became the twenty-first president of the United States. He was born in Fairfield, Vermont on October 5, 1829. His father William was a Baptist abolitionist preacher who relocated every few years. In April 1835 the Arthur family moved to Perry, Wyoming County, New York, when young Chester was just five years old.[29] The village of Perry is located on Silver Lake just west of Letchworth State Park and is about fifty miles east of Buffalo.

William Arthur became pastor of the First Baptist Church in Perry. This church building no longer stands but the parsonage where the Arthur family lived still exists, in back of the present church building on Main Street, but not in its original location. It is still in use as a fellowship hall and Sunday school.[30] In September of 1837 the Arthurs moved from Perry to York, New York in Livingston County where they lived for five years. The village of York is several miles north of Letchworth State Park and is about sixty miles east of Buffalo. Reverend Arthur became pastor of York Baptist Church. That church building no longer stands. Young Chester at this time attended old brick schoolhouse number eight, long gone, but a historical marker designates its former location on Main Street in the village. Chester's one year old brother George died while the family lived in York and his grave is in Pleasant Valley Cemetery near there. In 1842 the family moved to Union Village (now Greenwich, New York) in Washington County, not far from Saratoga Springs.[31]

Charles Julius Guiteau

The murder of President Garfield that resulted in Chester A. Arthur succeeding to the presidency was committed by one Charles Julius Guiteau, a man some might describe as being quirky, and in a more harsh manner as being insane. When he was young he joined the Oneida Community in Central New York State, a group known for its practice of "free love" and "Bible communism."[32]

The eccentric Guiteau never really fit in to the community so he was expelled in 1866. He went to Chicago where he managed to pass the bar examination. Unable to make it as a lawyer, he turned his attentions to religion and decided to become a preacher. He actually wrote a book espousing the Second Coming of Christ. In 1877 he hit the road with his message, traveling throughout the Midwest and northeast, from Wisconsin to the eastern seaboard. One of the cities in which he stopped was Buffalo.

Constantly low on funds, Guiteau would usually board trains without a ticket and be tossed off by the conductor at the next stop. He would sleep and take his meals at hotels or boarding houses and usually skip out on his bills, often one step ahead of the law. Guiteau's usual practice was to arrive in town and try to impress a pastor or manager of a hall to allow him to speak in his establishment, either for a set fee or part of the proceeds. Once such permission was secured he would pass out handbills advertising his appearance. Perhaps a newspaper would run a small notice about his upcoming lecture, as did the *Buffalo Courier* the day before Guiteau's speech in the Queen City.[33]

During his trial in 1881 for the assassination of President Garfield, Guiteau was questioned about his travels and remembered this about his journey to Buffalo:

> I took a train, and without any money, and the fare was $5 from Cleveland to Buffalo. The conductor was a very clever fellow. I guess he was a Christian man, and I says, 'I have not got any money. I expected to lecture here and get some money, and I am going to Buffalo to lecture.' He says, 'Never mind, never mind.' So he let me pass from Cleveland to Buffalo.[34]

The date of Guiteau's arrival in Buffalo is not known, nor is the place or duration of his stay. It is known that he delivered a lecture at the First Presbyterian Church on September 18, 1877. That building was located at Main and Church Streets directly across Church from St. Paul's Episcopal Cathedral. It was torn down in the late nineteenth century and the site became part of the bustling Shelton Square. It is now the site of the Main Place Tower office building.

At his 1881 trial Guiteau recalled his experience speaking there:

> I lectured there in the basement of one of the high-toned Presbyterian Churches. I was well advertised, and had a three or four hundred house, one of the most respectable houses I ever had. The lecture was free, and I took up a contribution, and I think I had four or five dollars.... I got a pretty good newspaper report of it in the *Buffalo Courier*.[35]

Perhaps more than four years after the fact, and considering his mental status, Guiteau's recollection was faulty, for the *Courier* reported on his lecture thusly, under the heading "Christ's Second Coming:"

> Mr. Charles J. Guiteau, who styles himself 'a Chicago lawyer and theologian,' is a peculiar person with peculiar ideas, as he demonstrated last evening in the lecture room of the First Presbyterian Church. The announcement that he would deliver his 'great lecture' on 'Christ's

Second Coming' attracted only a small audience to that place....This kind of work could not be presented without means in the way of lucre...and the contribution boxes were handed round. Mr. Guiteau then proceeded with a somewhat lengthy lecture...[36]

The review actually covered several column inches. The *Express* and *Commercial Advertiser* also covered the meeting, but in shorter, more matter-of-fact pieces, with the Express calling it "an interesting lecture."[37]

Guiteau moved on to Rochester next. Eventually, he turned his attention to political matters. He became deluded with the idea that he was responsible for the election of President Garfield in 1880 and became upset with him that he failed to reward him with a presidential appointment. Apparently, the theologian in Guiteau never left him, for he later claimed that God told him to fatally shoot the president on July 2, 1881.

After the Garfield shooting, the editor of the *Express* recalled Guiteau visiting his offices asking for a newspaper notice about his upcoming lecture. The editor said that the assassin brought with him circulars which conveyed the impression that the author was mentally unbalanced. He recalled listening to Guiteau's lecture and thinking that he was "either an ignoramus or a lunatic," but not capable of committing the attack on the president.[38]

Whether he realized it or not, Guiteau had had an uncle who had lived in Buffalo for several years. Julius Guiteau was born in Oneida County and migrated to Buffalo. He worked as a druggist and was postmaster of the village of Buffalo from 1818 to 1831. In 1836 he moved to Mauch Chunk, Pennsylvania, where he collaborated on starting the first anthracite blast furnace in the world. He died in Illinois in 1845.[39]

One of Charles Guiteau's defense attorneys at the Garfield murder trial was Charles H. Reed. Reed had been born in Strykersville in Wyoming County in 1834 and studied law in Lancaster, New York in the office of Johnson Parsons. He moved to Chicago and became a state's attorney there. In 1868 he administered the law examination that Guiteau passed to be admitted to the bar. In 1877 he successfully co-prosecuted the two men charged with attempting to steal Abraham Lincoln's body from its tomb in Springfield, Illinois. Reed consequently got involved in investment fraud and died an alcoholic at the age of fifty-eight in 1892.[40]

Belva Ann Lockwood

Belva Ann Lockwood was a native of Niagara County who was an educator, lawyer, women's rights and peace activist, as well as a presidential candidate in 1884 and 1888.

Born Belva Ann Bennett on October 24, 1830 on a farm in Royalton,[41] she was the second of five children. She was a bright girl who learned her lessons well, and by the age of fourteen she was already teaching school. She was first married to a young farmer and sawmill worker named Uriah McNall in 1848. They lived on a farm just north of Gasport and had a daughter. Uriah died in 1853, leaving Belva a widow at the age twenty-two.

It was perhaps her experience as a single parent that first opened Belva's eyes to the inequality of opportunity and rights that women had to endure. Determined to make her own way and contribute to society despite the roadblocks thrown in her way, she attended and in 1857 graduated from Genesee College, which later became part of Syracuse University. She then became a teacher, and eventually became headmistress of a Lockport school.

But Belva Ann McNall wanted to become a lawyer. She sensed a greater opportunity to do so in Washington, D.C., so she moved there in 1866 and soon became active in the cause of equal rights for women. She married Ezekial Lockwood in 1868, entered National University Law School (now George Washington University) and graduated from there with a law degree in 1873. She was widowed a second time in 1877.

Belva Ann Lockwood fought for and won the right to argue before the United States Supreme Court, becoming the first female to do so, in 1880. In 1884 she was persuaded to run for president as the candidate of the Equal Rights Party. The nominee of the Democratic Party that year was Buffalo's Grover Cleveland. Women did not yet have the right to vote (with a few exceptions), and she famously said, "I cannot vote, but I can be voted for."

Lockwood outlined a fifteen-point platform and tried to arrange for a debate with Cleveland and Republican candidate James G. Blaine.[42] Some consider her to be the first female presidential candidate, although Victoria Claflin Woodhull ran for president in 1872 on the Equal Rights ticket. However, Woodhull would not have qualified for the presidency based on her too-young age, so many historians do not take her candidacy seriously. Lockwood received fewer than five thousand popular votes and, of course, no electoral votes for president in 1884. She ran again in 1888 and once more received only a tiny tally of votes.

In her later years Lockwood continued advocating for equal rights for women and became devoted to the international peace movement. She visited Buffalo at least once in adulthood, in 1901 to visit the Pan American Exposition. She died in Washington D.C. on May 19, 1917.

Governor McKinley Campaigns in Buffalo

On September 15, 1892 Buffalo was hosting the national convention of the Republican National League, an organization founded to promote to young men the principles of the Republican Party and to encourage them to become future party leaders.

On that day, in the midst of a presidential campaign, former Congressman and then Ohio Governor William McKinley was in the city as the main speaker to address the conventioneers at the Music Hall on Main Street near Edward. One of several speakers that evening, McKinley was loudly cheered for several minutes upon introduction to the packed house. His speech centered on support for a high protective tariff in opposition to the free trade policies of the Democrats, and on opposition to a rise of state banks.

In 1894 Governor McKinley stopped in Buffalo for another short visit. He was making a campaign swing across New York State in support of Republican Congressional candidates. He alighted from his train at the Exchange Street Station at 7:05 p.m. on Thursday, October 25, and was greeted by fifty local Republicans and escorted to the Iroquois Hotel.

After a short stop there, McKinley was off to Wesp's Hall at Clinton and Watson Streets. He was accompanied by Fred Grant, son of the late General Grant, who made the trip to Buffalo with him, and local Republican officer John R. Hazel, among others. Ironically, Hazel would be appointed a federal judge by McKinley when he became president, and Judge Hazel would swear in Theodore Roosevelt as president after McKinley's death in Buffalo in 1901.

Governor McKinley received a great ovation when he entered the auditorium, which was packed to the rafters. He confined his twenty-minute talk to the issue of the national tariff. McKinley was known as the Champion of Protection and the Great Protectionist for his advocacy of extremely high customs duties on goods imported into the United States. The Tariff of 1890 bore his name because he had shepherded it through Congress as head of the House Ways and Means Committee that year. It was replaced by a lower tariff by the Democrats in 1894, and McKinley was now campaigning for a return to a higher tariff, urging the election of Republican Congressional candidates who would support such a measure. He stressed the purported advantages to working men of a high tariff.

"Will you help do it, workingmen of the city of Buffalo?" McKinley inquired.[43]

As the McKinley party left the hall, fireworks burst in the air and the audience surged outside to see the men off.

Governor McKinley's next stop was the Music Hall on Main Street. He received a huge ovation when he walked inside and prolonged cheering and hat waving after he was introduced. He proceeded to assail the Democratic administration of President Cleveland for ruining the economy and again hit the theme of the tariff. He equated a low tariff rate with low wages for the working man. He closed with an appeal to elect Republicans to Congress.

Following his hour-long speech, McKinley was driven to Harmonia Hall at 264 Genesee Street at Ash Street, now a parking lot for the Maritime Charter School. It was close to 10:30 when the governor entered, and as at the other two venues, he received a wildly enthusiastic welcome from a packed hall. Here, as at Wesp's Hall, the governor tailored his speech more toward the laborer, since he was in a working-class neighborhood. He once again emphasized the advantages of a high tariff to the working man.

"You've got your opportunity this fall to vote for your wages, your homes, your family and your own highest well being. Men of Buffalo, I hope you'll do it," he urged.[44]

After the conclusion of this address McKinley headed back to the Iroquois Hotel, where he spent the night. He left for points east at 7:30 the next morning.

McKinley's opponents claimed that he had spoken at Wesp's and Harmonia Hall to keep the working-class people of those areas away from the more upper class citizens who attended his talk at the Music Hall. Such a charge was easily countered by his supporters, who could say that he went to the two East Side venues because he respected the laborer enough to meet him in his own community.

GALLERY OF IMAGES

VIEW OF LAKE ERIE AND THE BAY FROM BUFFALO IN 1816.

View of Buffalo Harbor as General Harrison would have seen it in 1813.
(Courtesy of the Buffalo History Museum)

View of Court House Park, now Lafayette Square. The Liberty and Free Soil parties held national conventions there. The building in the center background is the old County Court House. Sheriff Grover Cleveland sprung the trap of the gallows for two felons in the rear courtyard of the building. Site is now the Central Library.
(Courtesy of the Buffalo History Museum)

The Niagara Falls Suspension Bridge, the first span across the Niagara River. President Taylor crossed the bridge in 1849 to become the first president to leave the U.S. while in office. (*Library of Congress*)

Depiction of the crowd on Main Street welcoming President-elect Lincoln to Buffalo in 1860. (*Leslie's Illustrated Newspaper*)

Academy of Music Building, formerly the
Metropolitan Theater, where John Wilkes Booth
performed in the early 1860s.
(*Courtesy of the Buffalo History Museum*)

St. James Hall interior. Abraham Lincoln attended a lecture here with Millard
Fillmore. Lincoln's body lay in state in the Hall in 1865. James A. Garfield
spoke here.(*Courtesy of The Buffalo History Museum*)

The Castle Inn on Niagara Square. It was formerly Millard Fillmore's home, and he died there in 1874. It is now the site of the Statler Building. (*Library of Congress*)

Millard Powers Fillmore (1828-1889), son of Millard Fillmore, and friend of Grover Cleveland. (*Courtesy of The Buffalo History Museum*)

Governor Grover Cleveland parading down Main Street during the 1884 presidential campaign. (*Library of Congress*)

The Tifft House on Main Street. James A. Garfield and Theodore Roosevelt stayed here. Former President Grant reviewed a parade from the front of the hotel in 1880. (*Library of Congress*)

Pierce's Palace Hotel on the West Side. James A. Garfield, Benjamin Harrison and William McKinley made a joint appearance here and stayed overnight in 1880. (*Courtesy of The Buffalo History Museum*)

The Weed Block building at Main and Swan. Grover Cleveland maintained a second floor law office there for several years and lived in an apartment in the attached rear building. (*Courtesy of The Buffalo History Museum*)

President McKinley reviewing parading veterans at Symphony Circle during the 1897 GAR encampment. (*Library of Congress*)

The Milburn house on Delaware. President McKinley died in a upstairs room. Vice President Roosevelt was once an overnight guest, and former President Cleveland spent a day there. (*Library of Congress*)

The Buffalo Club. Fillmore and Cleveland were members and several presidents were guests. The cabinet met there in 1901 during the McKinley assassination period. (*Library of Congress*)

President Taft on the front porch of the Wilcox House during his 1910 visit to Buffalo. Theodore Roosevelt took the oath of office here in 1901. (*Library of Congress*)

The Elmwood Music Hall-Convention Hall at Virginia and Elmwood. Theodore Roosevelt, William Howard Taft, Herbert Hoover and FDR all gave talks there. (*Courtesy of The Buffalo History Museum*)

The Exchange Street Station, Buffalo's main railroad depot, operated from the 1850s to 1929. At least sixteen future, former and incumbent presidents passed through the station during that time. (*Courtesy of The Buffalo History Museum*)

Lafayette Square with Lafayette Hotel to the immediate right of the monument. Wilson, Hoover and FDR were guests here. This was FDR's preferred Buffalo hotel. (*Library of Congress*)

The Iroquois Hotel at Main and Eagle. Cleveland, McKinley, T. Roosevelt, Taft, Wilson and Harding were all guests here. (*Library of Congress*)

CHAPTER 8

PRESIDENT MCKINLEY AND THE PAN-AMERICAN EXPOSITION

President McKinley at the GAR in 1897

Any Buffalonian with even a casual interest in history knows that President William McKinley traveled to Buffalo in 1901 to attend the Pan-American Exposition, a trip that ended in tragedy for him and the nation. Most believe that was his only visit to Buffalo as president, but that is not correct. Four years earlier he made a well-publicized festive visit to the Queen City to attend the thirty-first Encampment of the Grand Army of the Republic (GAR).

The GAR was the organization of Union veterans of the Civil War, which boasted almost half a million members at its peak in 1890, and still counted 319,456 members in 1897.[1] It rotated its Encampments, or national conventions, among various American cities, and now it was Buffalo's turn to host. Because of the presidential visit, there was a great deal of excitement and anticipation in the air as the Encampment began its week-long run on Tuesday, August 24, 1897. Veterans began arriving in Buffalo as early as Saturday and soon became a flood of thousands. About 50,000 of them descended on the city for the big gathering, along with perhaps another 100,000 other participants, supporters and family members. Some 4,000 or so were put up in actual shelters set up in a tent city overlooking the Niagara River near Fort Porter in Front Park, now the site of the Peace Bridge Plaza.

This mini-city was called Camp Jewett, after Buffalo Mayor Edgar B. Jewett, a Civil War veteran. This tenting feature, a recreation of the army field camps so common during the war, was the reason these reunions were called Encampments. Other veterans crowded into hotels, were housed in schools, or roomed in boardinghouses and in Buffalonians' homes, who graciously offered accommodations to them.

President McKinley and his entourage arrived at the Exchange Street Station in the Queen City precisely on schedule at three o'clock on the afternoon of August 24. His party included First Lady Ida (Saxton) McKinley, Secretary of War Russell Alger, New York Governor Frank Black and a group of staffers. McKinley himself was a Union Civil War veteran and member of the GAR and he intended to attend the Encampment as a fellow veteran in the spirit of comradeship. But given the fact that he was the president and commander-in-chief of the United States, his presence dominated the gathering and he was the center of attention.

A crowd of thousands gathered in and near the train station to greet the president and many thousands more lined Exchange, Main and other streets along the route to his hotel. The police kept perfect order as the esteemed guests were escorted out of the depot and into waiting carriages. Into the first carriage climbed President and Mrs. McKinley, Augustus Scheu, who was chairman of the Buffalo Citizens' Committee to welcome the GAR and the president to the city, and Thaddeus S. Clarkson, who was commander-in-chief of the GAR. Several other carriages were occupied by additional dignitaries and aides.

A squad of mounted policemen led the way from the depot down Exchange to Main as the throng of people lining the streets cheered. Every building sported American flags and other patriotic decorations. The carriages moved briskly up Main through two specially constructed arches, then west on Chippewa to Georgia as the applause rolled through the crowds of curbside spectators. North on Prospect to Porter

Avenue, where the jam of people was great, the carriages pulled to a stop at the Niagara Hotel to the strains of "Hail To The Chief."[2,3] A huge crowd had gathered round the hotel, many of them GAR veterans who had walked over from nearby Camp Jewett.

In front of the hotel were four companies of infantrymen from Fort Porter accompanied by the band that had kept the waiting crowd entertained. Local posts of the GAR stood in formation off to one side. The president's carriage was driven between the troops and the veterans, and he and his companions quickly entered the hotel. The soldiers and veterans marched away, restraining ropes were removed and the crowd of onlookers soon pressed forward toward the hotel's balcony. The band played and the people cheered and called for the president. After several minutes, they were rewarded as McKinley stepped out onto the upper balcony and received a hearty greeting. He then disappeared and reappeared on the lower balcony with Secretary Alger and a few others. The president made some brief remarks, saying how happy he was to be in Buffalo and how grateful he was for the generous welcome. "I am glad to be in Buffalo with my comrades of '61 and '65, and my comrades now," he said.[4]

He left the veranda, Secretary Alger made a short speech and then the crowd dispersed. Once the obligatory greetings were made inside the hotel, President and Mrs. McKinley settled in for a couple of hours of rest. The first lady, an epileptic in delicate health, did not take part in much of the upcoming festivities, but the president was kept busy. Early in the evening he was due at a banquet at the Ellicott Square Building. The largest office building in the world at ten stories tall, it had only opened the previous year. The dinner was to be held in the club rooms of the exclusive Ellicott Club on the top floor of the building and was sponsored by the Columbia Post of the GAR from Chicago.[5] The 400 invited guests began arriving around 6 p.m.

As news of the pending arrival of the president spread, a crowd gathered outside the Ellicott Square entrance as well as in the lobby and corridors within. Shortly after 6:30 President McKinley's carriage pulled up, led by the Columbia Post marching band. The crowd surged around the carriage as the president, still seated, bowed to his left and right. People offered their hands to him and he was kept busy shaking them until the carriage pulled into place and he alighted to a rousing cheer. One of the men accompanying him was Wilson S. Bissell, former President Cleveland's old friend.

McKinley was escorted through the lobby to a waiting elevator whose interior was fitted with special decorations and a large plush seat. The president exited on the tenth floor and strode into the Ellicott Club parlor rooms as a cheer went up. A short reception was given by McKinley and GAR Commander Clarkson. At 7:30 they were escorted to their seats at the main table in the banquet hall to a loud standing ovation. From the high ceiling of the gold and white dining hall were suspended red, white and blue bunting and from them to all points of the room were connected streamers of the same colors. On the wall above the table of honor hung a painting of President McKinley framed in flags and banners. Above it was a huge reproduction of the GAR insignia. Flags, shields and streamers bedecked the other walls of the room. In front of the main table were spread the dining tables for the 400 attendees, almost all prominent GAR members.

After the meal was served, it was announced that McKinley and Clarkson would leave for a short time to attend previously scheduled engagements, but would return to speak. It was 8:45 when they left the room to polite applause. The reason for their exit was to attend a couple of GAR "campfires." These were not actual campfires but rather meetings of GAR members at different venues in the host city, usually churches, where the veterans reminisced, prayed and honored the memories of departed comrades.

The first campfire at which President McKinley and Commander Clarkson arrived was at the Delaware Avenue Methodist Episcopal Church, which was filled to overflowing. Preliminary speeches were made, there was some singing accompanied by organ and band, and shortly after 9 p.m.[6] McKinley and Clarkson appeared. They were greeted by the ladies and gentlemen present with a storm of cheers.

Commander Clarkson was introduced first, made a short address in which he praised Buffalo's hospitality, and then introduced the president. McKinley then appeared at the rostrum and was applauded for five minutes as he bowed in acknowledgment. He made some brief remarks concerning the purpose of his visit.

"I am only come to this splendid presence tonight that I may pay my respects to my old comrades and lay at their feet my tribute of love and appreciation and affection," he declared.[7] He bid the audience good night and he and Commander Clarkson were off to the next campfire. This one was close by, the Asbury Methodist Episcopal Church at the northwest corner of Pearl and Chippewa.[8]

It was a little after 9 p.m. when the two men entered the church to a tumultuous cheer. Commander Clarkson spoke first, very briefly, and then President McKinley gave a short address in which he lamented the loss of old soldier comrades who had gone on to their rewards.

"I thank you, ladies and gentlemen, for this moment that you have given me to pay my respects to that noble army of volunteers, the sacrificed giants who cleft darkness asunder and thus assured our national existence," he said.[9]

Loud and prolonged applause followed, after which the campfire was concluded and McKinley and Clarkson hurried back to the Ellicott Club. Reentering the banquet hall at around ten o'clock, the two men were greeted with a loud welcome. The head of the Chicago GAR post introduced the president in verse, after which McKinley arose to a tumult of applause, bowing right and left to acknowledge it. In a speech that lasted but a few minutes, interrupted many times by cheers, he extolled the country's reigning peace and the sacrifices made by the young men in the late war. Other speakers followed, and it wasn't until the wee hours of the morning that the meeting broke up and the participants dispersed.

The next day, Wednesday, September 25, was another great one weather-wise, and the day of the Grand Parade. Though parades of various lengths and durations were held each day of the Encampment, this was the big one, the focal point of the entire Buffalo meeting. Early in the morning the 50,000 veterans began arriving near its starting point at Main and Terrace. Just after 10 a.m., led by mounted police and a military band, then carriages containing President McKinley and other dignitaries, the old soldiers began their march up Main Street. Bands and drum corps were interspersed within their ranks, and they provided a steady cadence and patriotic air. Along the entire route of the parade were throngs of spectators at curbside, on porches, on rooftops and in windows; by some estimates there were 200,000 of them.

Moving north on Main, the blue-clad veterans encountered a huge arch spanning the street, formed by the letters G-A-R. They passed underneath the letter A. Some sixty feet high and topped by an eagle and an American flag, it was decorated with electric lights that glowed in the night time. A little farther up the street was a triple white arch adorned by two buffaloes at the top and the letters GAR painted above the three arches.

All along the route the buildings and homes sported a sea of American flags and other patriotic emblems. The marchers turned westward at Chippewa Street to Delaware Avenue. At that intersection was perhaps the most interesting feature of the Encampment. It was called the Living Shield, and it was composed of 2,000 children dressed in red, white and blue, all positioned on a grandstand in the formation of an American flag shield. For a few hours each day these children sang patriotic songs in formation in two shifts, and they did so during this Grand Parade.[10] When the president's carriage approached, it halted for a moment as the children cheered and waved handkerchiefs, and the president waved his in response. There was a brief scare as the lead horses of his carriage reared up, but they were quickly brought under control.

Continuing up Delaware the procession headed west on North Street and reached the Circle (now known as Symphony Circle) at 11:20 p.m. As President McKinley, Commander Clarkson and Governor Black left their carriages, a storm of applause and cheers rang out from the thousands of spectators gathered in the vicinity. A reviewing stand had been set up at the north part of the Circle at the end of Richmond Avenue and the president and scores of other dignitaries occupied places underneath its white canopy. As wave after wave of marchers made their way past the stand, McKinley bowed and waved his black silk hat. Many passing veterans tossed goldenrod into the president's box, others tried in vain to shake his hand, which was too high out of reach.

After a couple of hours, the president disappeared into a tent in back of the reviewing stand for a few minutes to have sandwiches and a cup of coffee, and then reappeared. Back at the starting point of the parade on Main Street, it was almost 4 p.m. before the last of the marchers were on their way, and they managed to reach the president's stand just after five o'clock. The last contingent was the Chapin Post of Buffalo, and after it passed Mr. McKinley's carriage was wheeled around and driven to a nearby home to pick up the first lady. President and Mrs. McKinley were then taken back to the Niagara Hotel. The president expressed his pleasure with the ceremonies, and then enjoyed a few hours of rest.

That evening President McKinley once again left the hotel to attend some engagements. His first stop was a public reception at the Buffalo Music Hall on Main Street. Accompanied by Governor Black, Bishop Ireland of the Episcopal Church and a few others, he arrived at 9 p.m. Men and women had already lined up for admittance two hours earlier. When the doors opened, 1,200 were allowed to take seats in the balcony.

Once the president was ready to receive, people were hurried along at a fast pace, some getting in a word or two with a quick handshake. McKinley greeted each person with a handshake and a "Glad to see you." "Thank you." About 2,000 in all made it through the line in forty-five minutes before the president had to leave, disappointing thousands more still awaiting their turn.

The president's next stop was the headquarters of the Military Order of the Loyal Legion, which was housed in a mansion on Eagle Street across from City Hall. The Loyal Legion, of which McKinley was a member, was a national Civil War officers' organization formed even before the GAR, but was not affiliated with it. The president and his entourage arrived about ten o'clock. He received well-wishers for about an hour and then proceeded to the Buffalo Club on Delaware Avenue. There he held a reception for club members before returning to his hotel.

The next day, Thursday, September 26, was President McKinley's last day of his Buffalo excursion. He and Mrs. McKinley both took breakfast at the hotel, then he met a GAR delegation from St. Louis. At 10:30 the president, Secretary Alger and William Hengerer entered a carriage, and with another filled with four dignitaries, headed out on a trip to Niagara Falls. McKinley expressed his wish to be driven through the tent city, but a policeman at the entrance would not let the carriage in. He said that he was just following his orders not to let any vehicles into the camp, no exceptions. Though criticized by some, he was roundly praised by many veterans, Buffalo Police Superintendent Bull, and even the president. The carriages drove on to the foot of Porter Avenue where the party entered a special rail car that carried them to the LaSalle area of Niagara Falls.

Arriving at LaSalle in a few minutes, shortly before 11 a.m., the president was warmly greeted by a huge crowd of residents as he disembarked from the train, shook hands with several people and entered a carriage. He was then driven across a bridge to Cayuga Island. His purpose was to drive the first stake in the layout of the Pan-American Exposition, scheduled to take place on the island in 1899. Cayuga Island hugs the shoreline of the Niagara River directly north of and opposite Grand Island and is today a residential neighborhood of the city of Niagara Falls. The North Grand Island Bridge is directly west of it. With the outbreak of the Spanish American War in 1898, the Exposition was postponed and rescheduled for 1901. By that time officials had changed their minds and decided to move the fairgrounds to the city of Buffalo, where the Exposition was ultimately held.

The president was handed a large mallet into which was carved "McKinley," and as he drove a pre-positioned stake into the ground a large crowd of onlookers cheered. He shook hands with hundreds of people, and then was driven around the island. By 11:30 he was back on the special train and at noon back in Buffalo where he was taken back to his hotel.

After a few minutes, he reemerged and was driven to the Buffalo Club on Delaware for an informal luncheon. Arriving there about one o'clock, the president was promptly seated in the dining hall, which was tastefully decorated with flags and banners. The meal was served and then a toast was proposed to President McKinley. After much applause, he rose from his chair and said, "I can only assure you that I will carry with me the dearest and sweetest memories of my visit to Buffalo. I cannot forbear to thank you for your hospitality and for your cordial welcome, not only to me, but to my comrades of the Grand Army of the Republic. I bid you goodbye."[11]

Another round of cheers filled the room and the president left the building. He was rapidly driven away through a crowd of onlookers to the foot of Main Street where he boarded the *Comanche* at the harbor. This was the yacht of Senator Marcus Hanna of Ohio, who had also been in Buffalo. Mrs. McKinley had earlier boarded the boat. It was 3 p.m. as the yacht pulled away en route to Cleveland, with a salute of steam whistles from nearby watercraft, and one of twenty-one guns from another yacht.

This thirty-first Encampment of the Grand Army of the Republic was generally viewed as a huge success by Buffalonians and visitors alike, with President McKinley's presence making it especially memorable. Once he had departed, the Encampment was for all practical purposes over, and for the next couple of days the visitors left the Queen City for their home towns.

Vice President Roosevelt At The Pan-American Exposition

The Pan-American Exposition opened to the public on May 1, 1901, but it was not officially dedicated until May 20. That was designated as Dedication Day and the guest of honor to headline the ceremonies was Vice President Theodore Roosevelt.

At 8 p.m. on Sunday, May 19, the vice president, his wife, their daughter Alice and Mr. Roosevelt's sister and brother-in-law arrived at the Exchange Street Station. The party was met by Exposition President John G. Milburn. Through an applauding crowd, the Roosevelts were escorted to a waiting automobile and driven directly to the Milburn home at 1168 Delaware Avenue where they would spend their time in Buffalo as guests of the family. Though it is not actually known, Vice President Roosevelt quite possibly may have slept in the same room in which President McKinley was to die four months later.

Monday, May 20, was declared a local holiday and most schools, businesses and government offices were closed for the day. The weather started out gloomy, but a threat of rain never materialized. The whole city seemed bedecked in American flags and other decorations. A grand parade to the Exposition grounds was scheduled to start at 10 a.m. from City Hall on Franklin Street and the route began to line with spectators from an early hour.

In all the streets around City Hall were arranged marching bands, soldiers, Exposition concessionaires and over a hundred carriages for various officials. A little after ten Vice President Roosevelt and Mr. Milburn arrived and the parade began. Led by a contingent of mounted police, the bands and troops marched off, followed by the carriages of Roosevelt and the hundreds of other distinguished guests, from governors, senators and foreign diplomats to state and local officials including Buffalo Mayor Conrad Diehl and dozens of Exposition officers. The procession moved south on Franklin to Seneca, up Main, west on Chippewa, north on Delaware to Chapin then Lincoln Parkway and into the fairgrounds. The whole way was lined with some 200,000 cheering spectators.

Bringing up the rear of the parade were the costumed, diverse personages from the Exposition's Midway, who fell into line from the Terrace downtown. It was described by one Buffalo newspaper as:

> ...a world caravan, a grotesque procession, a winding, irregular, gorgeous, garish, gay, gleeful, rip-snorting, hulabalooing, side-splitting, eye-pleasing, bewildering conglomeration of curiosities from the Esquimau of the North, the Indian of the West, the Jap of the Far East, the Dervish of the Mediterranean shore.[12]

Cleopatra, gondoliers, old plantation slaves, Hawaiian villagers, Arabs, donkeys, camels, elephants, monkeys, all these and more were part of the passing pageant.

At noon the head of the parade entered the Exposition grounds. In the middle of the fairgrounds Vice President Roosevelt and the other dignitaries alighted from their vehicles and in a two by two column walked in their black high hats and frock coats. Through the middle of this gleaming "Rainbow City" of colors, they gazed at the monuments and buildings. They entered the Temple of Music, the building dedicated to musical concerts and oratory, now joined by Mrs. Roosevelt and Alice. The guests were seated, but two dozen of them, including the vice president and Mr. Milburn, took seats on the stage in front of a chorus and band. The public was let in and quickly filled the auditorium.

The program started at 1 p.m. with the band playing "Alleluja." The bishop of the Methodist Church in Buffalo said a prayer, a poem was recited, a message from President McKinley was read, the orchestra and chorus did a number, then Mr. Roosevelt was finally introduced. He smiled and bowed to the cheering audience, then gave a thirty-minute forceful, energetic dedication speech. It was basically a paean to the accomplishments of America laced with warnings and suggestions as to what must be done to move forward the progress of the nation and the world.

Once the ceremonies at the Temple concluded, Milburn and another Exposition officer escorted the vice president on a walking tour up and down the fairground's Grand Esplanade. They boarded a carriage and were driven to the Milburn house where Roosevelt and his wife were guests at a tea. At 9 p.m. Vice President Roosevelt toured the Exposition at night and enthusiastically praised the illumination of the grounds in the highest terms. He returned to the Milburn home at eleven o'clock for a very late dinner.

On Tuesday, May 21, the vice president was scheduled to attend a ten o'clock breakfast at the Buffalo Club in honor of Senator Marcus Hanna of Ohio. However, he arrived an hour and a half late. After chatting with several of the guests, Roosevelt and Hanna left for a reception at the Merchants' Exchange Building at the northeast corner of Seneca and Pearl Streets.[13]

Sponsored by the Board of Trade, the reception was attended by a veritable "who's who" of 500 Buffalo businessmen. Both Roosevelt and Hanna gave short speeches in a large hall decorated with flags and bunting, after which they shook hands with audience members for a half hour.

At 1 p.m. it was off to the Ellicott Club on the top floor of the Ellicott Square Building where the two men were luncheon guests of the trustees of the Merchants' Exchange. No speeches were made, and by two o'clock Vice President Roosevelt hurried away to join Mrs. Roosevelt at a reception at the home of Mr. and Mrs. George L. Williams at 672 Delaware. This is the structure now known as the Butler Mansion, which still stands and is today used as a University of Buffalo training center. From there Mr. Roosevelt was taken to the Women's Building at the Exposition for a reception. In the evening, Vice President and Mrs. Roosevelt attended a reception and elegant dinner at the Twentieth Century Club at 595 Delaware, a structure that still stands today and still operates as the club.

On Wednesday, the Roosevelts boarded a special train at 10 a.m. for an excursion to Niagara Falls. Their dozen or so companions on the trip included Mr. and Mrs. John Milburn. They took the trolley up to Lewiston in a drenching rain and dined at Prospect House restaurant in the Falls before returning to Buffalo. The Roosevelts enjoyed an early evening dinner at the opulent mansion of Mr. and Mrs. John C. Glenny at 1150 Amherst Street. A stately, gleaming, white columned structure, it was sadly abandoned and torn down in the 1950s and the site is now an athletic field for Nichols School.

After dinner and late in the evening, at about ten o'clock, Mr. Roosevelt was invited outside to see an old log cabin which stood on the property. A joke was about to be played on the vice president. As he entered the cabin, two brawny Indians in full regalia and war paint seized him. Other Indians outside waved tomahawks, fired rifles and whooped and jumped up and down. They were from the Indian Congress at the Exposition and they invited the vice president to stop at their exhibit, along with a more serious plea to help save Indian lands. Roosevelt good-naturedly accepted the invitation and said he would do what he could to help protect their land.

The next morning at 10:30 Vice President and Mrs. Roosevelt once again visited the Exposition. Their first stop was at the Indian Congress where Mr. Roosevelt "christened" a newborn Indian baby and watched the Indians perform. By 11:30 they were at the Exposition zoo to get a look at the animals and watch a lion tamer perform. They also took a boat ride on Mirror Lake from the New York State Building.

By 7 p.m. the Roosevelts were at the Ansley Wilcox mansion at 641 Delaware, that place to become so famous four months hence. Among the guests were Mr. and Mrs. Milburn. They then retired for the evening to the Milburn home. The next morning at 9:30, and with no prior announcement, they departed from the train station for their home in Oyster Bay, Long Island.

President McKinley Attends The Pan-American Exposition

The Pan-American Exposition grounds were located on 342 acres on the west side of Buffalo between Elmwood and Delaware Avenues, north from what is now Delaware Park Lake, up to the Belt Line railroad tracks just north of what is now Great Arrow Parkway.

This was the world's fair of its day, a summer-long carnival, theme park and meeting place featuring cultural, scientific, industrial and educational exhibits. Though they were temporary structures, the various exposition buildings were a beautiful sight, painted in a variety of different hues. The focal point was the 400-foot-tall Electric Tower, which sported a signal beacon atop it that could be seen for many miles at night. Fountains, canals and statues graced the wide walkways and at night 200,000 electric bulbs attached to the buildings and fixtures illuminated the grounds.

President and Mrs. McKinley were on a national tour when it opened on May 1, and Mr. McKinley sent a congratulatory message from the road to the offices of the Exposition. The McKinleys were scheduled to stop in Buffalo to visit the fair on June 12, toward the end of their journey, but that did not happen because the first lady fell ill in California. The president canceled the remainder of the tour and his train headed straight to the McKinley home in Canton, Ohio where Mrs. McKinley recuperated. President McKinley's visit to the Exposition was rescheduled for early September 1901 and on Wednesday, September 4 the train bearing him and Mrs. McKinley arrived at 6 p.m. in downtown Buffalo.

It was a short three car train and it slowed to a stop at the Exchange Street Station as a din of horns, whistles, guns and bells sounded a welcome to the chief executive. As it passed the Terrace Station the train slowed. A cannon salute was fired off but was mistimed and blew out several windows of the train's front car, startling everyone but causing no injuries. The McKinleys were not in that particular car and were not in danger at any time.

The train continued on through the western loop of the Belt Line and into the Exposition rail station at the northern end of the grounds at around 6:15 in the evening. Mr. and Mrs. McKinley, members of their party and escorts, including Buffalo Mayor Diehl and Exposition President Milburn, alighted from the train to the sound of bells and whistles and the cheers of thousands of fair-goers who had gathered round.

Police, railroad detectives, a few soldiers and the Secret Service, which only a few years earlier had started accompanying the president on his trips, kept a path clear to waiting carriages for the honored guests as the president lovingly guided his wife along. The carriages moved southward through the colorful panorama of the Exposition grounds as onlookers cheered their approval, waving hats and handkerchiefs. The carriages exited onto Delaware Avenue and to Mr. Milburn's residence. There, the McKinleys were to be the guests of the Exposition president for their scheduled three-night stay in Buffalo, just as Vice President and Mrs. Roosevelt had been the Milburns' guests in May.

The next day was President's Day at the Exposition, in honor of Mr. McKinley. At 10 a.m. the president, Mrs. McKinley and Mr. Milburn emerged from the Milburn home and entered an open carriage. A squad of mounted police and soldiers escorted the vehicles up Delaware Avenue to the Lincoln Parkway entrance of the grounds as they were cheered by thousands of street-side spectators along the way. It was a gleaming, sunny day.

The president was welcomed by a twenty-one-gun artillery salute and the Marine Band led the carriage through tens of thousands of applauding, hollering spectators who lined the route of the procession. At the center of the Esplanade, off to one side, loomed a stand built for the president and invited guests, a big purple-canopied structure adorned with American flags and seating for 500 VIPs. When his carriage stopped, President McKinley stood up and bowed, and a roar burst forth from the crowd as kerchiefs, hats and parasols were waved. As the president helped Mrs. McKinley to her feet, the applause deepened.

Through a cordon of army officers strode the McKinleys and Mr. Milburn onto the stage. They faced the audience for a moment, the gentlemen in their black frock coats and gray trousers, the first lady dressed in gray gown and bonnet, the Marine Band playing. Then the president helped his wife to her seat. Mr. Milburn introduced the president to tumultuous cheers. It was estimated that the crowd of spectators numbered 50,000, and it stretched all along the Esplanade, walkways and open spaces.

At 10:37 a.m. President McKinley began to deliver his prepared speech from the front of the stand. He spoke strongly and eloquently, though only the first several rows of people could hear him clearly in these days before the microphone. He talked for thirty minutes about the shrinking globe, the importance of sensible trade agreements and the progress of the world. At the conclusion, Mrs. McKinley was driven to the Women's Building for lunch, then back to the Milburn home. The president shook hands with the various dignitaries on the stand, then he and Milburn rode to the Exposition stadium through more hollering, applauding crowds.

The president walked into the stadium to a burst of cheers from the 10,000 spectators seated inside. He approached a reviewing stand and looked down upon a field full of soldiery in all their colorful, glittering splendor. He then left the stand to review the troops, walking left and right around the field as the crowd applauded. He returned to the stand, then all the troops marched by their commander-in-chief to the air of "Hail To The Chief" and other patriotic tunes. By noon the president had departed the stadium and made quick visits to various Exposition buildings. He was at the New York State Building for lunch, now the headquarters of the Buffalo and Erie County Historical Society and known as the Buffalo History Museum. This was the only building built as a permanent structure for the fair, the others being primarily of plasterboard and wood meant to last only through the summer.

The president was greeted inside by the heads of the New York Commission and the building soon began to fill with the 200 or so government officials and other guests who had been invited to the luncheon. Included was Wilson Bissell, Grover Cleveland's former colleague. It was held in the main hall on the first floor, with some guests seated in the assembly hall, and began at two o'clock. An orchestra on the above balcony played various musical selections throughout the meal. At close to half past three the president departed for the Government Building on the grounds, where another mass of people cheered him.

The president took a quick tour of the building, then held a short reception within it. At about four o'clock McKinley left for the Milburn home for a well-deserved rest and reunion with his wife. After dinner, carriages awaited the McKinleys and their party and they left the house for the Exposition, arriving there at 7 p.m. The carriages stopped at the south end of the Esplanade, giving the first couple a view straight up to the Electric Tower. Mounted police and detectives kept the people well away from them. As all watched darkness slowly fell, and then the thousands of light bulbs on the buildings began as tiny specks of orange, growing steadier until the whole Exposition was gloriously illuminated and the Electric Tower beacon began its display, a display that awed thousands each night at this dawn of the age of electricity.

After several minutes the carriages moved on to the Art Gallery landing on Delaware Park Lake. The president and Mrs. McKinley and the others were ferried in boats to the Life-Saving Station on the lake. An army band on a floating stage in the middle of the lake played, illuminated in red light. There were dancing girls and acrobats and fireworks over the water, a "battle of the ships" and fireworks set off proclaiming "McKinley, Chief of Our Nation," and a portrait of him was displayed. After this, the presidential party was taken back to the landing and they were back at the Milburn house by ten o'clock.

Friday, September 6, 1901 was President McKinley's last scheduled full day on the Niagara Frontier. He was fond of early morning walks and on this day he rose ahead of time and exited the front door of the house at 7:10. With a nod to the sentries and Secret Service men stationed out front, he set off alone south along the west side of Delaware Avenue. Formally dressed for the day in black frock coat, gray trousers, bow tie, white shirt and silk top hat, he crossed the street at West Utica and returned along its east side. The Secret Service men did not follow him, but they never let the president out of their sight.[14]

At 8:30 the president reemerged from the Milburn house with Mrs. McKinley and John Milburn. They climbed into a carriage with Mary Barber, the first lady's niece. Another carriage contained the president's secretary George Cortelyou, the McKinleys' physician, Dr. Presley M. Rixey, Mrs. Rixey and Secretary of Agriculture James Wilson. Into a third carriage clambered detectives and the Secret Service agents.

They drove north on Delaware and onto the Exposition grounds, the whole route already lined with enthusiastically cheering people as the horses trotted past. The carriages stopped at the Exposition railway station where the presidential party was joined by a hundred other guests which included military officers, diplomats and a bevy of Buffalo's social elite. They climbed into a special train of four cars and headed for Lewiston. Once there, Mr. and Mrs. McKinley and all the others transferred to trolleys of the Gorge Route which took them along a scenic way a few yards above the rushing waters of the lower Niagara River, Devil's Hole and the Whirlpool. The president was in a jolly mood and the first lady was delighted.

The trolley reached the end of the line shortly before noon in Niagara Falls where cheering citizens, loud bands and displays of flags welcomed them. He and his guests got into a long line of carriages and they drove onto the Falls View Bridge between the United States and Canada for a better view of the falls.

It was thought that no American president had ever left the United States while in office, and President McKinley had no intention of doing that now, especially when he had not been invited by the Canadians.[15] In preparation, a chalk line had been drawn to mark the international boundary on the span and the president's driver was warned not to cross it. The coachman successfully observed the line, the president got a spectacular view of the falls, the presidency was supposedly preserved and a grave international crisis was avoided.[16] Indeed.

Mrs. McKinley was dropped off at the International Hotel and then the remainder of the entourage rode around Goat Island. After returning to the hotel, the president and a few select guests were served a luncheon. At two o'clock the president rode to the railroad station to see Mrs. McKinley aboard the return train, then went to the Niagara Falls powerhouse to observe the workings of the electric dynamos that produced the electricity that lit up the Pan-American Exposition.

By three o'clock he and the rest of the touring group were back aboard the train and ready for the return trip to Buffalo. At every point during his Niagara Falls visit crowds had heartily cheered McKinley, a testament to his popularity. At 3:30 the train arrived back at the Exposition. Mrs. McKinley, her health being delicate, was driven to the Milburn home accompanied by Dr. Rixey while the president, Cortelyou and Milburn were taken to the Mission Building. Afterward the president was driven to the Temple of Music where he was to hold a public reception. A crowd of people had been gathering for hours near the building hoping to gain entrance and get a chance to shake President McKinley's hand. Among those in the crowd was a strange and troubled young man by the name of Leon Czolgosz.

Czolgosz was the twenty-eight-year-old son of Polish immigrants. He had been an industrial worker, described as shy and law abiding, living on the family farm near Cleveland, Ohio. Then in 1898 something happened to him mentally and emotionally. He quit his job, became moody and lazy, railed against religion and fancied himself an anarchist. He began reading anarchist literature and attended some of their meetings.

On July 6, 1901 Czolgosz came to West Seneca, New York and took a room at the farm of Antoni Kazmarek and his wife on Ridge Road, now part of the city of Lackawanna, for a stay of six weeks.[17] He was secretive, not saying much about what his business was, except that he went into Buffalo two or three times a week to "attend meetings."[18] He hired a boy to bring him food, never going out for meals. Why Czolgosz came to Western New York at that time is a matter of conjecture. He himself later claimed that he was looking for work. He could not have come to plot an attack on the president, for McKinley's visit to the Exposition was not announced till August, after Czolgosz had arrived in West Seneca. Perhaps wanting to get away from his family, with whom he quarreled, he chose the area because of special low fares to Buffalo for the Exposition and the familiarity of a large Polish American population.[19]

It appears that fate brought Czolgosz to Western New York that summer. Once here, his disturbed mind decided to take advantage of the coincidence of the McKinley visit, and the seeds of his intention to kill the president took hold. Czolgosz vacated the Kazmarek farm and returned to Cleveland on August 30, probably to collect a family debt owed to him.[20] He was back in Buffalo on Saturday the thirty-first but this time checked in to John Nowak's Inn, a saloon hotel in the heart of the predominantly Polish American Broadway-Fillmore district. Nowak's was located at 1078 Broadway. That building was torn down and the site is now occupied by a restaurant parking lot.

Czolgosz checked in under the name John Doe and went by the alias Fred Nieman. He said that he was in town to sell souvenirs of the Pan-American Exposition. To proprietor Nowak he seemed to be a decent young man, but his clerk thought him odd. Czolgosz visited the Exposition grounds, took walks down Broadway, visited a local barber for shaves, but did not spend much time at the saloon at Nowak's. One night he attended St. Casimir's church in Kaisertown. One fateful trip he made was to the Walbridge Hardware Store at 392 Main Street, where the Main Place Mall now stands, to buy a .32 caliber pistol.

On September 4 Czolgosz was in the crowd when President McKinley alighted from his train at the Pan-Am railroad depot. It was on the next day that the demented young man intended to kill the president. He was only a few feet away as McKinley gave his speech on the Esplanade, but the crush of the crowd against him made it impossible for him to draw his weapon from his pocket. Czolgosz said he followed McKinley to Niagara Falls the next day, but he did not act there. Finally, that afternoon found him amongst the crowd outside the Temple of Music where he managed to get into the receiving line forming to greet the president.

At four o'clock the president's open carriage pulled up to the building. Topped by a gilt-edged dome, the 180-foot-high rotund Temple sported a salmon hue with red trim and touches of aqua. It featured concerts and speeches. As he alighted from his vehicle the president bowed and smiled to the cheering crowd of thousands that had gathered round the building in the sunny, unseasonable eighty-degree heat. Some 3,000 people had already been admitted to observe the reception and they filled the galleries and many seats on the main floor. Accompanied by Milburn and Cortelyou, President McKinley entered to the strains of "The Star-Spangled Banner" and took his place at the bend of a curving aisle formed by the backs of chairs hung with light blue cloth. It was here that he would greet a few hundred lucky persons who had lined up to shake his hand.

McKinley stood in front of a backdrop of potted palms and an

American flag, with Milburn to his left and Cortelyou on his right. Four Buffalo police detectives stood nearby and two Secret Service agents were positioned directly across the aisle from the president with soldiers, and Exposition guards also strategically placed.[21] The doors opened as a Bach sonata was playing on the house organ. The public filed quickly by for a brief grasp of the president's hand. After a few minutes Czolgosz approached. He had wrapped his pistol in a handkerchief in his right hand, making it appear to be bandaged.

It was 4:07 p.m. The president's right hand reached for Czolgosz's left hand, but Czolgosz pushed it away and quickly fired two shots through the handkerchief at McKinley's mid-section. The first was deflected by a button on the president's vest, but the second tore through his body, As he staggered backward, clutching his stomach, he was caught by one of the detectives.

There was controlled chaos in the Temple of Music as McKinley was helped to a chair and the assailant was pummeled to the floor. Screams and shouts filled the air as people rushed for the exits and those outside tried to push their way in to see what was the matter. Czolgosz was eventually taken away by the police and the president was rushed to the Exposition hospital by electric ambulance. There, in the little field hospital, McKinley underwent emergency surgery to repair the wound. By 7 p.m. the operation was over and the patient was transported to the Milburn residence for recuperation. Doctors were hopeful that the president would make a complete recovery.

By this time the world was well aware of what had happened in Buffalo. At 9 p.m. doctors issued their first bulletin, which expressed their expectations for recovery. "MCKINLEY SHOT BY AN ANARCHIST" exclaimed one Buffalo newspaper headline in bold front page letters the next morning, and others in the Queen City and around the country sported similar banners. A crowd of people was gathered near the house on Delaware Avenue, but all horse and carriage traffic was blocked. An army regiment was camped across the street in a vacant lot to guard the house along with local police. Members of the press were housed in big tents.

Meanwhile, cabinet members and Vice President Theodore Roosevelt rushed to Buffalo upon hearing the news of the shooting. Roosevelt was vacationing near Burlington, Vermont and on Saturday morning he boarded a special train for Buffalo. By early evening on Friday an angry mob of men had gathered outside Buffalo Police headquarters. Thousands of restive citizens took over the area of Seneca, Franklin, Erie and Main Streets with cries of "Lynch him!" directed toward Leon Czolgosz, who was being held inside.[22] Policemen, mounted and on foot, pushed the crowd back and ordered them to disperse, but it took till midnight before the area was calmed down. In New England, former Buffalonian and former President Grover Cleveland said, "With all American citizens, I am greatly shocked at this news. I cannot conceive of a motive. It must have been the act of a crazy man."

On Saturday September 7 at 1 p.m. Vice President Roosevelt arrived at the Exchange Street Station and was met by an escort of mounted police. With solemn countenance, he quickly entered a carriage before a crowd of onlookers, waved away newspapermen and was driven to the Iroquois Hotel at Main and Eagle. From his carriage at the Eagle Street entrance he conversed with Ansley Wilcox. The two men were then driven to the Milburn house where the vice president stayed for about a half hour inquiring about the president. He was then conveyed to the home of his friend Carlton Sprague at 810 West Ferry Street near Delaware, and then to Wilcox's home at 641 Delaware.[23] Mr. Wilcox had invited Roosevelt to stay with him while he was in Buffalo and the vice president accepted the invitation. The two men had been acquainted with each other since the 1880s when TR was a young New York State assemblyman, through their work on commissions on civil service reform and to create Niagara Falls State Park, having been appointed by Governor Grover Cleveland. Also, as governor of New York, Roosevelt had appointed Wilcox to commissions to investigate mistreatment of state prisoners and to investigate the district attorney of New York County.

By late afternoon all the cabinet members except Secretary of State John Hay and Secretary of the Navy John D. Long were in Buffalo. Hay would arrive later. It was decided that the Buffalo Club on Delaware, just south of the Milburn and Wilcox residences, would be the headquarters where they would meet. Communication links to Washington were installed. Visitors of all manner called at the Milburn home, mostly government officials, but no one was allowed into the second-floor sick room to disturb the president. One of the callers was Comptroller of the Currency Charles G. Dawes, who would serve as vice president of the United States from 1925 to 1929. The house next door to the south was used as the federal government's administration building, with a direct telephone link to the White House.

At this point a brief history of the Ansley Wilcox house is appropriate. The site was originally part of what was called the Rathbun parcel. Benjamin Rathbun, a speculator and financier, had owned it but went bankrupt in 1836. Management of the property was then assigned to a legal team that included Millard Fillmore. It was sold to Ebenezer Walden, who was later to become mayor of Buffalo. It became known as Walden Hill, and an eighteen-acre portion of the property extending from Delaware to Main Street was leased by the federal government in late 1839 for construction of a temporary army base.

Brick barracks and other structures were built beginning in October, with completion in early to mid-1840. There is evidence that a brick federal style two and a half story house probably already existed on the parcel, near Delaware Avenue, most likely built in 1835-36.[24] The whole complex was named the Poinsett Barracks after the secretary of war, but was also known as the Buffalo Barracks. The army post became a center of social activity in the city and among the guests who visited were said to be Millard Fillmore, and probably Grover Cleveland.

By 1845 the army abandoned Poinsett Barracks for the new Fort Porter on the Niagara River in Black Rock. All the military buildings except the officers' quarters were demolished. That structure was the aforementioned brick federal style house probably built in 1835-36. The army's lease was terminated in 1847, whereupon Mr. Walden sold the parcel on which the house stood to Joseph Masten, who made major additions to it, including switching the front portico from the east to the west side of the house.

Masten sold it to a bank ten years later and in 1863 it was bought by Alfred P. Laning, who was Grover Cleveland's law partner from 1869 to

1870. As such, Cleveland was most likely a guest at the house on more than one occasion. Another visitor to the house while Laning lived there was Mr. Fillmore.[25]

In 1880 the Bell family owned the property and it was bought by Dexter P. Rumsey in 1883 as a wedding gift for his daughter and her new husband, Ansley Wilcox. The Wilcoxes made major changes to the mansion, and it assumed its current appearance. After the Wilcoxes died in the early 1930s the property became a restaurant operated by Kathryn and Oliver Lawrence, who lived upstairs. Major interior alterations were made during this period. When Mr. Lawrence died in 1959, the restaurant closed and the building was sold to a developer who planned to demolish it, but in 1963 Liberty Bank bought it and saved it.

Through community efforts, it was declared a National Historic Site in 1966 and purchased by the federal government in 1969. Major changes were made to restore the interior to its 1901 appearance, when Theodore Roosevelt took the oath of office there. On September 14, 1971, the Ansley Wilcox mansion opened as the Theodore Roosevelt Inaugural National Historic Site. What is now the north-western-most part of the mansion is the original portion that was the officers' quarters of Poinsett Barracks.

On Sunday, September 8, cabinet members called at the Milburn house in late morning. They were joined by Vice President Roosevelt and Ansley Wilcox at noon, who had both attended services at the First Presbyterian Church at North and Symphony Circle and then had walked to the Milburn residence.[26] The attending physicians released encouraging news about President McKinley's condition and continued to issue regular, optimistic bulletins to reporters.

On Monday Roosevelt called at 12:30 p.m. Cabinet members and many others came and went throughout the day, and all left the house in a cheerful mood as doctors became more optimistic for a full recovery for the president. By Tuesday the ninth, McKinley was considered to be completely out of danger and well on the way to recovery. Cabinet members, family and others began leaving Buffalo. At 9:30 p.m. Vice President Roosevelt left the city. By Wednesday the president was alert and wanted to talk, read a newspaper and smoke a cigar. These requests were denied, and visitors were restricted to Mrs. McKinley and Cortelyou.

On Thursday morning, the president was given solid food for the first time since the shooting. He seemed to tolerate it well but by mid-afternoon he complained of nausea, fatigue and headache. First blamed on indigestion, the doctors soon realized that it was much more serious. The patient appeared to be sinking fast. The pulse raced and the heart weakened, failing to respond to treatments. It was a full-blown relapse.

By Friday morning McKinley's condition was extremely serious. Telegrams were sent to call back the family, government officials and Vice President Roosevelt. The mood of the country grew gloomier as newspapers headlined the alarming turn of events. As near as they could get to the Milburn residence, people kept vigil on the street and on front lawns along Delaware and West Ferry. Main Street between Exchange and Swan became impassable as citizens crowded around newspaper offices for the posting of the latest bulletins on the president's condition.

In the afternoon, the president began to lose consciousness and a 6:30 p.m. bulletin conceded that "the end is only a question of time." Respiration ceased at 2:15 a.m. on Saturday, September 14, 1901. Cortelyou went downstairs and announced to those gathered in the parlor, "Gentlemen, the president has passed away." He signed the final bulletin, which simply read, "The president is dead."

Vice President Roosevelt had been contacted with great difficulty at a remote retreat in the Adirondack Mountains. He immediately raced for the nearest railroad station where he learned that he had succeeded to the presidency. He arrived in Buffalo just before 2 p.m. Saturday and was met at the Terrace rail station by his secretary William Loeb and John Milburn. Carriages ahead and behind him as well as mounted police formed an escort as the new president was driven up Delaware to the Wilcox mansion. After a short stop there, Roosevelt went to the Milburn house. Dressed in borrowed frock coat and top hat, he went into the house where he expressed his sympathies to the family and met briefly with Cortelyou, then was driven back to the Wilcox residence.

Secretary of War Elihu Root had made arrangements for a swearing-in ceremony for Roosevelt. He had also been present at the swearing in of Chester A. Arthur in New York City twenty years earlier when Arthur became president upon the death of James A. Garfield. U.S. District Judge John R. Hazel, appointed to the bench by President McKinley, was called to administer the oath of office to Roosevelt. Forty-three persons were crowded into the small library of the Wilcox mansion, including five cabinet members and about twenty members of the press. Roosevelt stood in the bay window alcove of the room, with the furniture draped in dust covers, and recited the oath.

A short cabinet meeting was held after which President Roosevelt issued a proclamation for a national day of mourning on the following Thursday, the planned day of the funeral. Secretary Root and the new president then went for a walk up the east side of Delaware to Highland Avenue, where the two parted company. They were guarded by Secret Service men, who kept a respectful distance. A great crowd of people had gathered around the Wilcox mansion during the oath taking and had followed the president on his walk to and from the house. By the time he returned it was 5 p.m.

President McKinley's body remained in the bedroom where he had died. Military corpsmen had been posted to guard the remains. Senator Marcus Hanna, a close friend of the McKinleys, went downtown to undertakers Drullard and Koch to ask them to handle funeral arrangements and to order a casket. Their establishment was located at 11 Niagara Square at the southeast corner of Delaware.

Beginning at 11:45 a.m. two pathologists conducted an autopsy on the late president in the room where he had died, in the presence of army surgeons and the doctors who had tended to McKinley. It lasted three hours. Specialists from Drullard and Koch embalmed and prepared the body. A death mask was made. On Monday the sixteenth the body was carried downstairs and laid in a mahogany coffin lined with cream colored silk. The late president was dressed in the formal attire of a black frock coat. A soldier and a sailor were stationed behind the casket.

Outside the house citizen mourners began gathering at an early hour to pay their respects, though they were kept at least a block away in all directions. About 9 a.m. carriages began arriving with family members and other mourners. Finally, at eleven o'clock President Roosevelt's carriage pulled up. In it also were Mr. and Mrs. Wilcox.

In the first floor parlor where the body lay, the president approached the bier and took his place near the head of the casket. Mourners filled all the rooms on the first floor. Mrs. McKinley and family members were at the head of the stairs on the second floor. A simple Methodist funeral service was held and was over by 11:30. The casket was closed, carried out of the house on the shoulders of four soldiers and four sailors and placed in a horse drawn hearse. President Roosevelt led the mourners out of the house and they entered carriages as an army band played "Nearer, My God, To Thee."

Led by the police, the army band, infantry and Marines, the funeral cortege moved slowly down Delaware in time to solemn music as church bells tolled. The soldiers and sailors walked alongside the hearse. Some 50,000 people lined the flag-bedecked avenue, whose house were decorated in signs of mourning. As the cortege reached Niagara Square it began to rain. By the time it turned onto Eagle Street it was pouring.

The hearse pulled up in front of the Franklin Street entrance of City Hall at 1 p.m.[27] President Roosevelt, cabinet members and other distinguished men were quickly hustled into the building. They took places around the plain black catafalque in the main lobby. Several floral offerings and potted plants had been placed there. American flags hung from the ceiling and black bunting was draped all around. Into this hall the soldiers and sailors bore the casket of their late commander-in-chief and laid it on the catafalque to the melody of "Nearer, My God, To Thee."

Undertaker Drullard removed the upper coffin lid. Its lower part was covered by an American flag on which were laid arrangements of red and white roses. President Roosevelt, the cabinet, the family and other principal mourners paid their respects then left the building. A military honor guard took positions around the coffin, then the public was admitted.

A huge crowd had been gathering near the building for hours and a heavy rain was now falling. The people came in the Franklin Street entrance in two columns, passed by the bier, and left out the Delaware Avenue doors. Many of them left a flower at the catafalque as they passed.

At times the line extended for half a mile. The hall remained open for ten hours during which an estimated 80,000 to 100, 000 people passed through to view the body of the late president.

Immediately after leaving the City Hall, President Roosevelt was driven back to the home of Ansley Wilcox. Plainclothes police on bicycles followed behind for security. Though the new president personally eschewed increased protection, since succeeding to the presidency he had been discreetly observed by police and Secret Service men, and a burly bodyguard was usually stationed near the door of whatever room in which he happened to be. Mr. Roosevelt took lunch at the Wilcox home and a constant stream of callers came to see him, some of whom were admitted to meet with him. Woodrow Wilson, then a professor at Princeton University, apparently came and was greeted by the new president. He was returning from a vacation at Rosseau Falls, Ontario.[28] The president remained in the house till the next morning.

Back at City Hall the late president's bier had been guarded throughout the night and just past 7 a.m. on Monday morning the Franklin Street doors were reopened. On this day the body would be taken from Buffalo to the nation's capital. Ranks of military men were in formation outside the entrance. Carriages carrying cabinet members drew up the driveway. At precisely 7:45 the coffin, borne by the soldiers and sailors, emerged form the doorway, the flag-draped casket on their shoulders. They placed it in the hearse to the strains of mournful music.

The entire area around City Hall and along the route to the railroad depot was crowded with thousands of Buffalonians. The sad procession moved out to the sound of dirges, accompanied by the tolling of church bells. Down Franklin to Church and through Shelton Square, past St. Paul's Cathedral, the cortege turned south on Main to Terrace, past the black-draped downtown buildings, arriving at the Terrace train station after thirty minutes. President Roosevelt was waiting there, having gone straight to the depot from the Wilcox mansion. Others who had been invited to partake in the funeral ceremonies in Washington were already aboard the train. They included Mrs. McKinley who, despite her precarious health, was coping with the whole ordeal remarkably well. President Roosevelt and a few other gentlemen escorted President

McKinley's flag-draped coffin from the hearse to the train where it was placed in the observation car. At 8:30 a.m. both presidents were aboard and the train pulled out.

So ended Buffalo's eleven days at the center of the nation. The Pan-American Exposition had remained open after the shooting of the president, but on Friday, September 13, when McKinley was near death, it closed early and remained so till the following Monday. A pall was cast over the last few weeks of the season and it wound up losing money for its investors.

Former President Cleveland made no statement following President McKinley's death. But on September 19, five days afterward, he delivered a eulogy to the students of Princeton in which he praised the late president and denounced anarchy.[29]

CHAPTER 9

INTO THE TWENTIETH CENTURY

Future President Theodore Roosevelt in Buffalo

The three trips that Theodore Roosevelt made to Buffalo in 1901 in connection with the Pan-American Exposition and assassination of William McKinley were not his only visits to the Queen City. He made several other journeys to Buffalo, both formal and informal, before and after his presidency.

In 1883 he visited the Badlands of North Dakota and bought a ranch there. After his first wife died in 1884, he spent much of the next two years playing cowboy at the ranch, trying to drown his sorrow. In the following years, even after moving back to New York, he made several visits to the ranch. And it was during these train trips to and from the Badlands that he may have stayed overnight in Buffalo.[1] It is known that he checked into the Tifft House hotel on November 18, 1883, but his business in the city is not known.[2]

TR's first formal visit to Buffalo was to deliver a speech to the Liberal Club of Buffalo on January 26, 1893. At the time, he was a member of the U.S. Civil Service Commission. This club was an organization of the most prominent citizens of the city, and its purpose was to discuss subjects having to do with morals, education and public affairs in order to shape public policy.

The club usually met at the old Genesee Hotel at West Genesee and Main Streets, but on this occasion the meeting was held at the Chapter House, believed to be the chapter house of the Women Teachers Association. It was located at 95 Johnson Park, it still stands today and is known as the New Phoenix Theater.

Roosevelt had arrived in Buffalo at 9 a.m. and was the guest of lawyer Sherman S. Rogers, whose residence was at 698 Delaware Avenue.[3] His speech followed a 7 p.m. dinner and meeting at the Chapter House. In the talk, entitled "Duties of American Citizenship," he spoke about the importance of political participation and cooperation while also touching on civil service reform and Americanism:

> The first duty of an American citizen, then, is that he shall work in politics; his second duty is that he shall do that work in a practical manner; and his third is that it shall be done in accord with the highest principles of honor and justice.[4]

His speech was continually interrupted by enthusiastic applause. He left Buffalo for Washington, D.C. at the ungodly hour of 4:00 the next morning.

Roosevelt returned to Buffalo in 1895. He was then Police Commissioner of New York City. On the evening of September 10 he spoke to the Liberal Club at the Twentieth Century Club Building at 595 Delaware Avenue.[5] He sat at the main table as the guest of honor, flanked by club President John G. Milburn and Wilson S. Bissell, who had recently finished a stint as President Grover Cleveland's postmaster general. Also present was Sherman S. Rogers.

Mr. Roosevelt spoke before the club that night on the subject of Americanism and how important it was for Americans to put aside their differences of race, creed and national origin to work together for the good of the United States. He probably stayed at the Iroquois Hotel that night. The next morning Roosevelt visited Central High School, which was located on Niagara Square and Court Street, a site now occupied by the Mahoney State Office Building. He spoke to the students and especially thrilled the boys with tales of big game hunting, and he congratulated them upon their academic achievements.

That evening Roosevelt gave a speech at the Music Hall on Main Street. The place was packed to capacity with citizens anxious to hear TR speak on the Sunday laws that severely curtailed business activities on the Christian Sabbath.

With several clergymen in attendance, Roosevelt defended the Sunday laws, especially those restricting the sale of alcohol. He equated the freedom to sell liquor on Sunday with the liberty to commit crime, and argued that a liberalization of the law would lead to a collapse of morality and decency in America.

TR's 1898 visit to Buffalo was as raucous and boisterous as they come. Then running for governor of New York, his campaign stop was indeed a high-spirited affair. And only a few months after his exploits at San Juan Hill during the Spanish American War, he was probably the most celebrated man in America.

Now popularly referred to as Colonel Roosevelt, he arrived at the Exchange Street Station at 4:30 in the afternoon of October 25. Long before his train rolled in thousands of people occupied places around the depot. Dressed in gray overcoat and suit and Rough Rider hat, Roosevelt was escorted out a side entrance as mighty cheers arose from the people, who not only surrounded the station, but shouted from a departing train, the tops of box cars, rooftops, windows and a nearby bridge.

A formation of Rough Riders on horseback waited outside as the colonel waved his hat and bowed, and entered one of many carriages. He was accompanied by leading citizens of Buffalo, including Chauncey Depew, Sherman S. Rogers, George Urban and Edward H. Butler. Led by the Rough Riders, Roosevelt's carriage pulled out first, followed by five more. Down Exchange and then up Main Street the short procession moved to its destination, the Iroquois Hotel.

The entire route was packed with people, waving, shouting and applauding, from the sidewalks, windows and rooftops. Several times the colonel's open carriage was slowed down as it was swarmed by the crowd. The Iroquois was surrounded by a noisy mass of people and when Roosevelt's carriage pulled up, he could barely make his way into the hotel lobby. The inside was jammed with a cheering, hollering mob who gave a "Hip! Hip! Hooray!" to the colonel several times as he struggled to get to the elevator.

Roosevelt came out on the mezzanine level, which was also packed with people. Some semblance of order was instituted, and the colonel began greeting everyone in a reception line. He wanted to shake everyone's hand, but as 6 p.m. approached his aides ended the ordeal so that TR could get some dinner and relax before his busy evening schedule.

At 7:30 p.m. Roosevelt left the hotel and climbed into a carriage to embark on a series of campaign appearances. Led by the mounted Rough Riders, his carriage and those of other members of his entourage followed behind, up Main to Chippewa, Ellicott, Broadway, Pine, William to Jefferson to Clinton to Watson Street in the waning minutes of daylight.

All along the route from the hotel onward Roosevelt was cheered by onlookers. His first stop was at Wesp's Hall at the corner of Clinton and Watson. Filled to capacity and spilling outside to surround the building, TR was loudly applauded by the crowd. When he entered, the shouting and stamping literally shook the building. He delivered a speech of several minutes in which he emphasized "that creed, color or nationality shall make no difference, that every man shall have the fullest liberty that law allows."[6]

Colonel Roosevelt's next stop was St. Stanislaus Hall at the northwest corner of Fillmore and Peckham Street, a site now occupied by a parking lot. The hall was on the top floor of St. Stanislaus parish school across from the church. Roosevelt strode into the room filled with 1,500 people, escorted by parish priest Reverend Jan Pitass and Judge John R. Hazel, who in 1901 would administer the presidential oath of office to TR. The now familiar thunderous applause greeted the colonel, who was introduced by Father Pitass. Invoking the name of Polish American Revolutionary War hero Casimir Pulaski, Roosevelt appealed to the Polish American audience's sense of working class fairness and promised to tend to their needs if elected.

When TR left the building, many from the audience followed his carriage up Fillmore a few blocks to the Fillmore Theater at the southeast corner of Fillmore and Broadway, a building that no longer stands, where he gave essentially the same speech that he had delivered at St. Stanislaus, to another packed house. Leaving that venue, he was driven back downtown. His destination was the Music Hall on Main Street. This large building not only contained the 5,000-seat Music Hall auditorium, but a smaller venue known as Concert Hall. Colonel Roosevelt's first stop was the Concert Hall, filled to overflowing with every space occupied by enthusiastic supporters. He had time to deliver a campaign speech only five minutes long before leaving a wildly cheering crowd for the Music Hall auditorium.

As he entered the hall at about 10 p.m. Roosevelt was once again greeted with wild shouts, waves and applause. Great flags hung from the arch over the stage and bunting fronted the boxes and balcony. A military band struck up appropriate selections. Veterans of the Spanish American and Civil Wars took up the first several rows of seats. As Colonel Roosevelt stood on stage ready to speak a sharp bugle call from a Rough Rider sounded a charge, and he responded, "My comrades, I heard the trumpets tear the tropic dawn on the day that we marched to battle at Santiago and I know what it means. I thank you for having come here, my comrades, to play them." TR's speech praised veterans and appealed to honesty, reform and concern for the working man. It was a "speech of terrific force."[7]

From the Music Hall Roosevelt was driven to the Buffalo Club on Delaware where he was a guest of George Urban at a late "luncheon" in his honor. About a hundred guests were present. So ended his long day, as he returned to the Iroquois Hotel, not showing any fatigue and apparently having thoroughly enjoyed himself.

The next morning, he left Buffalo at 9:30 after shaking hands with a gaggle of people before boarding his rail car. The short four-car train rolled northward and made several stops on its way to Rochester. The first stop was at Sweeney and Webster Streets in North Tonawanda took place as a cannon boomed and 1,800 people gathered around the rear of the train despite a driving rain. Roosevelt gave a short speech from the rear platform and was mightily cheered.

The next stop was Niagara Falls, reached just after ten o'clock. A crowd of 1,500 heard Roosevelt speak from the train and by 10:30 it moved on. It was still raining. An unscheduled stop was made near the suspension bridge and Roosevelt appeared once again to say a few words to a couple of hundred who had gathered around. Lockport was next at eleven o'clock where TR and his party detrained for a speech at the Opera House before an audience of more than a thousand. From there, the train made stops in Middleport, Medina and Albion before moving on to Rochester.

Theodore Roosevelt was victorious in his run for governor, and his next visit to Buffalo was made as chief executive of New York State. The governor's train arrived at the Exchange Street Station at 4:45 p.m. on Monday, May 15, 1899. He and his party were met at the station by area Republicans and Independent Club members. The Independent Club was another organization of prominent Buffalonians and Roosevelt was in town to speak before it.

The governor was driven to the Iroquois Hotel where he held an informal reception in the main parlor for fifteen minutes. Just after six o'clock he emerged form the hotel and was driven down Main Street to the Ellicott Square Building. The Independent Club meeting was held in the dining hall of the Ellicott Club on the top floor. Over 300 members were present in the room, including Ansley Wilcox and Judge John R. Hazel.

It was after nine o'clock when Governor Roosevelt was introduced and rose to speak. His theme was honesty and morality among public men and businessmen and their responsibilities to their communities. The talk lasted about thirty minutes, after which other speakers were heard, and then the governor chatted and shook hands with those present for about an hour. At 11 p.m. Roosevelt was taken to the station and took the 11:30 train back to Albany. Before going aboard he remarked to a reporter, "I have been delighted with my visit here. I like to come to Buffalo. I like the spirit and energy of its people. A city with such citizens cannot fail to be great."[8]

Governor Roosevelt returned to Buffalo three months later. This time he was accompanied by Mrs. Roosevelt because it was intended to be more of a vacation than an official business trip. Early in the morning of August 16 the governor's train arrived in East Buffalo, where the private car in which he was a guest was detached and reattached to a train headed to Niagara Falls.

Once there the train made a brief stop, during which Roosevelt appeared on the rear platform of his car and made a few friendly remarks to a small crowd that had gathered. The train sped on through Lewiston, stopped briefly in Wilson and arrived at Newfane at 9:30 where the governor and his party alighted. About forty wagons occupied by local farmers greeted the visitors as they entered carriages for a two-mile drive to Olcott Beach where they were to attend a huge outdoor gathering, the Pioneers' Picnic.

After a dusty ride up Transit Road the party arrived at Olcott to the booming sounds of a band as they entered Grove House hotel, a brick edifice overlooking Lake Ontario, no longer in existence. A crowd estimated at 10,000 occupied the adjacent picnic grove, cheering and applauding Governor and Mrs. Roosevelt.

In short order the couple reappeared and the crowd surged toward them on the warm, bright day. They greeted and shook hands with everyone they could as they moved about the grounds before returning to Grove House at noon for lunch. At two o'clock Governor Roosevelt followed the blaring band to a stand crowded by fifty elderly gentlemen, who were indeed pioneer settlers of Niagara County. He gave a speech of thirty-five minutes in which he honored the virtues of those pioneers, mutual self-help and defense of America.

At the conclusion of his talk Roosevelt waded through the crowd to a waiting carriage which took him and his party back to the station at Newfane where they re-boarded their train for Niagara Falls, arriving there at five o'clock and checking in to the International Hotel. The next morning, in formal attire but wearing his Rough Rider hat, same as the day before, he took an inspection tour of the Niagara Reservation, or state park, including a trip to the bottom of the gorge on the inclined railway. Later, Governor and Mrs. Roosevelt crossed the Falls View Bridge (currently the site of the Rainbow Bridge) into Canada, rode a rail car along the gorge to Queenston, crossed over the bridge into Lewiston and arrived back at the hotel at 12:30.

After lunch the governor and his wife boarded the Buffalo-Niagara Falls trolley for a quick trip to the Queen City. Passing by waving onlookers, the car rode down Delaware Avenue and at 3 p.m. it stopped on Elmwood at the Country Club where everyone alighted for a brief meeting, after which they were driven around the designated site of the forthcoming Pan-American Exposition.

TR pledged to do all he could to increase state support for the fair. He was next driven to Fort Porter, where he stopped briefly, Front Park and downtown, where at Main and Niagara he re-boarded the trolley, rejoining the rest of his party for the trip back to his Niagara Falls hotel, reaching it at 6 p.m. That evening Governor Roosevelt appeared at a reception and the next morning boarded a train which passed through east Buffalo for Silver Lake, just south of the village of Perry, New York. Two days later he was at the Chautauqua Institution where he spoke to an audience of 15,000.

Governor Roosevelt was in Buffalo yet again, in 1900, to talk at the Saturn Club, Twentieth Century Club and the Broadway Arsenal. On February 22, he arrived at the Exchange Street Station at 4:45 p.m. and was greeted by a cold rain and blowing wind. Nevertheless, the depot was overflowing with an eager crowd. Roosevelt, wearing a black overcoat and slouch hat, was quickly escorted to waiting covered carriages, along with his party. Pulling out from Exchange to Main, then Niagara to Delaware, passersby waved in the rain. His destination, the Twentieth Century Club, the women's social organization at 595 Delaware, was reached in a few minutes.

This speech was sponsored by the Daughters of the American Revolution. It being Washington's Birthday, Roosevelt's talk focused on the Father of Our Country and the duties of all citizens of the United States. It was an address of only ten minutes, after which the governor departed for the Saturn Club. This group was a men's social club located at 417 Delaware at Edward Street.[9] Arriving there at 5:30, he sat down to dinner with the members, including Ansley Wilcox. No speech was given, but before and after the dinner, Governor Roosevelt talked informally about the Pan-American Exposition, schools, industry and taxes.

He was next driven to the Broadway Arsenal on Broadway Avenue near Michigan.[10] He and his escorts arrived there at 8 p.m. The inside of the huge National Guard center was brightly lit, with uniformed guardsmen in formation throughout the floor, which was surrounded by stands filled with 3,000 spectators. "Hail To The Chief" welcomed the governor. TR walked among the troops before entering a viewing stand where the troops marched before him to a band's accompaniment. Colonel Welch, the commander of the 65th Regiment of the New York National Guard, addressed the governor and Mr. Roosevelt reciprocated with a twenty minute speech praising the regiment's participation in the late war and the importance of the National Guard.

He then observed the unveiling of a huge bronze plaque on one wall that commemorated the twenty-two men of the regiment who died during the Spanish American War. A formation of guardsmen as well as the band then moved out of the Broadway exit, as did Governor Roosevelt and his party.

It was 9 p.m. as the guardsmen marched down Broadway with the governor and others following behind in carriages through the slushy street. Nevertheless, a considerable number of spectators viewed the short parade as it passed by, on its way back to the Saturn Club on Delaware. There, before a packed house including Sherman S. Rogers, Charles W. Goodyear, George Urban, Ansley Wilcox and Dr. Herman Mynter, one of the physicians who would tend to the wounded President McKinley, Roosevelt gave a fifty-minute speech. He praised Washington and the Founding Fathers for combining the practicable with the ideal, in other words, for the ability to compromise.

TR retired to his room at the Iroquois Hotel. The next morning, he held a public reception, shaking hands and greeting all manner of Buffalonian for over an hour. At 12:30 in the afternoon he was off to the station and at one o'clock his train pulled out, headed back to Albany.

Theodore Roosevelt returned to Buffalo in late 1900, this time in full campaign mode, as when he visited in the fall of 1898. Only now he was not running for governor of New York, but for vice president of the United States. He had been placed on the ticket with President McKinley at the Republican National Convention that summer.

Coming out of Niagara Falls on Wednesday afternoon, October 31, Roosevelt's train stopped at Goundry and Main Streets in North Tonawanda where he delivered a short speech from the back of his car.

Next, the train reached Black Rock where another brief campaign talk was given before 2,000 people. At 4:30 it arrived at the Exchange Street Station. Governor Roosevelt soon emerged, at which point he was given a raucous greeting from a huge crowd. He was whisked up Main Street to the Iroquois Hotel. The lobby was jammed with people. After several minutes, he appeared on an upper balcony and addressed the crowd very briefly, then stole his way out of the hotel for a short visit to his friend, lumber baron John N. Scatcherd, at his house at 703 Delaware Avenue.[11]

At eight o'clock that evening Roosevelt emerged from the Iroquois again to a display of pyrotechnic rockets and flares. Eagle Street was clogged with onlookers as TR entered his carriage, and with mounted police forming a square around it, he was off to Michigan Avenue, then down William to Fillmore. Nearly the entire way was lit by fireworks – rockets, flares, firecrackers – from homes and businesses. Spectators lined the streets in the early evening to enjoy a festive event. The little parade moved north up Fillmore till it reached the Broadway Market. In those days, this was mostly an open-air market, in the same location as today, 999 Broadway in the heart of Buffalo's Polish American community. And it was those people who turned out some 15,000 strong to hear Governor Roosevelt.

The ensuing scene was illuminated with electric lights and a speakers' platform had been set up on the east end. The governor's carriage pulled up before it to a wildly chanting, cheering crowd. Mounting a table on the platform, Roosevelt plunged into his campaign speech, which lasted only a few minutes. He rode back downtown to St. Stephen's Hall. No longer in existence, this was the social hall of the Roman Catholic Diocese of Buffalo, located on Franklin Street south of St. Joseph's Cathedral at the southwest corner of Swan Street. The site is now a small park.

Roosevelt's speech there was sponsored by two Italian American clubs. Over a thousand people waited inside and thousands more outside as the governor's carriage pulled up at around 9 p.m. He delivered a vigorous speech imploring the audience to support the McKinley-Roosevelt ticket. Upon exiting he addressed the crowd outside with an impromptu speech.

From there he was driven to Convention Hall at 400 Virginia Street at the northeast corner of Elmwood, which later became Elmwood Music Hall and is now a site occupied by a retail store. Seventy-five hundred people stood up and cheered Governor Roosevelt as he entered the building. The inside of the hall was decorated with flags, bunting and large pictures of the candidates hanging on the walls, balcony and stage. Roosevelt was cheered mightily as he climbed onto a table on the stage. He proceeded to speak for half an hour on campaign themes such as American administration of the Philippines, the gold standard, defense, and honesty in government. At 10:15 he was finished and hurried from the hall to tumultuous applause.

He went back to the Iroquois Hotel and was the guest at an informal supper in honor of reporters who accompanied him on his campaign swing. The next morning, he was up at seven and boarded his train for Jamestown to continue the campaign.

Former President Roosevelt in Buffalo

As previously described, Theodore Roosevelt made three trips to Buffalo in 1901, two as vice president and one as president. But his next journey to the Queen City did not come until he was a former president. Roosevelt had been hired by Outlook magazine as an editor and writer, and his employers sent him on a publicity speaking tour at their expense. On Thursday, August 25, 1910, his special train stopped in Buffalo before dawn.

A reception committee from the Ellicott Club was at the depot to greet him and his entourage of twenty, and the former president was quickly taken by automobile to the Ellicott Square Building for a 5 a.m. breakfast in the Ellicott Club banquet hall. Four hundred members welcomed Roosevelt as they all sat down to their meal. Afterward, the former president spoke extemporaneously on the importance of keeping the Great Lakes pollution free, but he also attacked political opponents, as usual casting them in a dishonest light. He stayed at the club for only about an hour before he was driven back to his train to continue on his tour.

Later in 1910 Roosevelt was again in Buffalo, this time to campaign for New York's Republican gubernatorial candidate, Henry L. Stimson, whose nomination the former president had personally steamrolled through the state Republican convention that summer. Roosevelt arrived at the Exchange Street Station in the early evening of November 1, one week before the election. He was coming in after campaign stops in Albion, Lockport and Niagara Falls. After dinner aboard his train he was driven directly to the Broadway Arsenal.

Beginning at 8:15 p.m. the former president proceeded to give a fiery campaign speech before a packed house of 10,000 listeners. He was generously interrupted with applause. Upon concluding he was whisked away to Convention Hall at Virginia and Elmwood. The building was surrounded by a crowd of thousands that began to cheer as he rode up. He was escorted inside by Ansley Wilcox and Edward H. Butler. To deafening applause and the playing of a band, he took his place on the stage before a full house of enthusiastic supporters. At 10 p.m., after delivering his campaign speech, he was driven to the Exchange Street Station where he boarded a train for New York City.

Roosevelt's candidate, Stimson, lost the election. By this time, more people were looking at the former president as a controlling, authoritative figure, not unlike the Tammany Hall politicians he always railed against. Though he was a brilliant and innovative campaigner, the opposition was quick to use his own tactics against him to neutralize his popularity.

Colonel Roosevelt's last official visit to Buffalo was in 1913. He was at the time embarked on a speaking campaign to support a New York law to allow primary voting for nominees to political office. Fresh off his losing 1912 presidential campaign as the Progressive Party candidate, whose platform championed primary elections, Roosevelt arrived in Buffalo at 5:30 in the afternoon on June 10, 1913. He was met at the Exchange Street Station by Chauncey J. Hamlin, chairman of the Erie County Progressive Committee. They drove to the Hamlin home at 1014 Delaware Avenue, at the northwest corner of West Utica. Torn down in 1926, the site is now part of the Delaware Nursing and Rehabilitation Center campus.[12]

After a brief rest at the Hamlin mansion the colonel was driven to the Teck Building at Main and Edward, formerly known as the Music

Hall, where he was the guest of honor at a Progressive Club banquet attended by some 200 partisans. Flags, shields and a large portrait of Mr. Roosevelt adorned the walls. At the conclusion of the meal, he rose to speak and was greeted by waving handkerchiefs, clinking of glasses, hoots and hollers. After a brief rallying speech, he was escorted out of the building to Mr. Hamlin's waiting automobile.

Roosevelt was driven to the old Convention Hall at Virginia and Elmwood, newly rechristened as the Elmwood Music Hall, and when he walked in at 7:30 and it was all pandemonium. The hall was filled to bursting with about 7,000 shouting and cheering for the former president. After he spoke Roosevelt was to meet in an ante-room with a hundred female suffragists, but the crush of the crowd prevented him from doing so. Police did all they could to get him back out to Mr. Hamlin's car. They drove out to Hamlin's farm estate in Snyder where Mr. Roosevelt spent the night with a couple of other guests. The next morning TR was driven by automobile to Rochester.

Theodore Roosevelt passed through Buffalo one last time on August 2, 1915. His train stopped briefly at the Exchange Street Station in the early morning hours, and he had left orders that he not be disturbed. He and his wife and son Archie were returning from California to their Oyster Bay home and were most likely asleep during this short stop.

William Howard Taft In Buffalo

Theodore Roosevelt was succeeded in office as president of the United States by his hand-picked replacement, William Howard Taft. Taft was serving as secretary of war but resigned when he was formally nominated for president by the Republicans in June 1908. By this time the nominees of both parties had adopted the modern method of crisscrossing the country and campaigning for themselves. The trailblazers for this style were Theodore Roosevelt on the Republican side and William Jennings Bryan for the Democrats. Both men were charismatic performers on the campaign stage.

By late October of 1908 Taft was on his final campaign swing, traveling by rail across New York State. After stops in Utica and Batavia, his train pulled into Buffalo's Exchange Street Station at 6:35 p.m. on the thirtieth. The curtains of his car, the last one, were all drawn closed. Mr. Taft was scheduled to deliver two speeches in the Queen City, and to be driven from the station to the Iroquois Hotel for dinner. But his plans had changed, to the temporary disappointment of hundreds of who had turned out at the station to greet the candidate, including local Republican clubs. Taft had decided to take dinner on board the train and he was so engaged when a small committee boarded to bid him welcome. It included Ansley Wilcox and Buffalo Postmaster Fred Greiner, who was also the Erie County Republican Party leader. At eight o'clock Taft emerged from the train and was escorted to a carriage as the crowd applauded. By 8:30 he had arrived at the Broadway Arsenal to give his first speech.

Taft was also scheduled to speak at Convention Hall, also known as Music Hall, but, strangely, the local Republican organization refused to announce in advance at which venue the candidate would appear first, for fear of favoring one audience over the other. So the Convention Hall crowd was forced to wait an extraordinarily long time to hear their man. Roughly 12,000 people were crowded into the Arsenal. Two bands entertained them with popular and patriotic tunes as they awaited Mr. Taft's arrival. He entered from the rear and strode up a long aisle to the stage as the audience raised a robust din of shouts, claps, hoots and hollers. Thousands of small American flags, passed out to the audience earlier, were waved in the air. Lively band music added to the atmosphere.

The cheering for Taft was clocked at fourteen minutes, the candidate occasionally rising from his seat on the stage to wave to the crowd. When the noise had subsided sufficiently Mr. Taft was introduced, setting off another loud round of applause which the candidate halted as he rose to his feet and held up his hand. Taft spoke for almost an hour in a husky, careworn voice, his throat strained from days of speech making on the campaign trail. And this was in the days before microphones were in use for public speaking. Nevertheless, he could be heard by half the Arsenal audience.

He concentrated mainly on the theme of labor, mentioning unions and a recent economic downturn. He was interrupted many times by applause. After he had finished he listened to the first few minutes of a subsequent speech, but had to leave the Arsenal, at which time the speaker was interrupted as the crowd gave Taft an ovation as he exited.

Mr. Taft was driven to Convention Hall at Virginia at Elmwood. The audience had waited for three hours or more, when at 10 p.m. their man finally entered the hall through the northwest Elmwood doors and made his way to the stage to raucous applause. The auditorium was decorated with bunting and the entire audience waved small flags. A band struck up music. Taft readily acknowledged the cheers. After fifteen minutes of this he held up his hand for silence and began to speak to the packed house of 6,000. In his speech, Taft spoke of tariffs, banks and trusts, particularly the Standard Oil Company, which he denied had made campaign contributions to him. He praised the role of a strong navy. He criticized his Democratic opponent William Jennings Bryan and lauded the Republican McKinley-Roosevelt administration.

It was a much shorter talk than he had delivered at the Arsenal, less than half an hour long. He exited into the alley to the east of the auditorium where automobiles were waiting. About a thousand people were standing in the cold outside the hall to get a glimpse of Mr. Taft, as they had also been there when he had earlier entered. He and his party reached the Lackawanna Station just before 11 p.m. where his private rail car was waiting.[13] The train pulled out of the depot a few minutes later for Elmira.

Making a circuit through Central New York, Taft's train once again made its way to Buffalo, arriving at the Exchange Street Station two days later. Mr. Taft and his party arrived early on Sunday, November 1 and they were driven to the Iroquois Hotel. This was to be a day of rest for the candidate with no campaigning. At 11 a.m. Ansley Wilcox called at the hotel and escorted Taft to the First Presbyterian Church on the Circle. Afterward, the two men went for lunch to the home of Mr. Wilcox, where President Roosevelt had taken the oath of office in 1901. After lunch Taft returned to the hotel, where he spent the night. He thanked the city of Buffalo "for the enthusiastic demonstrations which greeted me on Friday night. They will survive in my memory during my term as president—I expect to be elected on Tuesday—and I will not forget them thereafter."[14]

Mrs. Taft arrived from New York City in the afternoon to be with her husband during the last days of the campaign. The couple left Buffalo at 7:30 Monday morning, their ultimate destination being their home town of Cincinnati, Ohio.

Taft made four more visits to Buffalo, two as president and two as former chief executive. The first was a short stop that lasted only a few minutes, but the second was an official presidential visit.

The president's train stopped at Buffalo's Exchange Street Station at two in the afternoon on Friday, March 18, 1910, to transfer it from the Lake Shore to the New York Central railroad tracks. Taft's car was at the rear of the train and he did not leave it. But he came out on the back platform and acknowledged the greetings of railroad workers. A group of about 200 men crowded around the rear of the car, dozens of whom were plainclothes and uniformed policemen. Two Secret Service men stood on either side of President Taft. Smiling to the crowd, he recognized the familiar face of Postmaster Fred Greiner.

"Hello there, Brother Greiner," he remarked as he extended his hand over the railing, "I'm glad to meet you."

W.C. Brown, president of New York Central, introduced Buffalo Mayor Louis P. Fuhrmann to the president. Fuhrmann was a Democrat but nevertheless took the time to courteously come out to the station to greet the Republican president.

In a testament to the condition of the depot, the president remarked. "Let me see, this station burned down, didn't it, Mr. Brown?"

"No such luck," replied the mayor. "It's just the same as it's always been."

"Well, it seems to me that I have heard that they are going to build you a new station," said Taft.

"We have a promise and a plan," replied Mayor Fuhrmann.[15]

Smiling and completely at ease, President Taft was introduced to scores of city officials and prominent citizens. The mayor of Rochester and a committee from that city were there to board the train and escort the president to their city. The Ad Club of Buffalo invited him to attend the Follies of 1910 later in the month and received a smile in return. But Mayor Fuhrmann got a promise that the president would attend a Chamber of Commerce dinner in Buffalo in April. A reporter asked the president about matters in Washington and Taft asked for a newspaper. As Taft glowered down at it, an "All aboard!" was heard and the train began to chug out of the station. The president lowered the paper, smiled and waved goodbye. The reporter never received an answer. The entire stop had lasted but ten minutes. There was not a bigger crowd at the station because the exact time of the arrival of the president's train was known to only a few.

President Taft returned to Buffalo on April 30, 1910. This was the first official visit by a U.S. president to the Queen City since the assassination of President William McKinley in 1901. His train pulled into the Exchange Street Station at 7:25 a.m. His main purpose was to attend a dinner celebrating the merger of Buffalo's Chamber of Commerce with the Manufacturers' Club. The train was greeted at the station platform by a reception committee from the Chamber of Commerce, and also Mayor Fuhrmann, Ansley Wilcox, and Police Commissioner Henry C. Zeller, who also happened to be the chairman of the entertainment committee which planned the arrangements for the president's day.

Once the train stopped the committee was allowed to enter the president's car to formally welcome him to Buffalo. Accompanying Taft on this visit were Secretary of State Philander Knox and the president's military aide, Captain Archibald W. Butt.[16] As the president emerged from the car and was escorted through the station he was cheered mightily by the crowd that had gathered. Coming out onto Exchange Street he was greeted by thousands more who let loose great cheers. Police pushed back at the crowd, which surged toward Mr. Taft.

Two Secret Service agents were at the president's side and the Buffalo Police, no doubt conscious of the legacy of the McKinley assassination, had dozens of uniformed and plainclothes men stationed both inside and outside the depot to safeguard the chief executive. A platoon of mounted police and a car full of police were located directly outside the exit. Protection of the president had advanced to a considerable degree since 1901.

President Taft and the others climbed into waiting automobiles, then the cars moved out, led by two patrolmen on motorcycles. Next came the mounted police followed by the car full of policemen. Then came the presidential automobile, a brand-new Pierce-Arrow, its top down.[17] Also in the president's car were W. E. Robertson of the Chamber of Commerce, Mrs. Fuhrmann and Captain Butt. A Secret Service man stood on the running board. The auto was surrounded by a phalanx of mounted police. Next came a car with yet more policemen and a Secret Service agent, followed by one with Secretary Knox and Buffalo Congressman DeAlva S. Alexander. Last in line were other cars containing members of the reception committee, including Ansley Wilcox, whose house was the motorcade's destination.

The morning sun shone brightly and the trees and bushes were beginning to show their spring buds. The route followed was down Exchange to Main through Niagara Square and up Delaware to the Wilcox mansion. As President Taft's car passed the McKinley Monument in Niagara Square he doffed his hat in salute to the memory of the martyred president. Shortly after the president arrived at the Wilcox home he and Secretary Knox had breakfast with the Wilcox family. He did some work in the library, the very room where President Roosevelt had taken the oath of office after President McKinley's death. Later in the morning he sat for an interview with newspaper reporters.

He discussed national issues but remarked that he would rather talk about matters of interest to Buffalo. When asked about the comments he made in March about the inadequacy of the rail station, he said there appeared to be room for improvement, then asked the reporters to tell him about plans for its future. He also inquired about ongoing improvements to the canal and harbor facilities in Buffalo and emphasized how important that work was.

"In this country, our river terminals are sadly neglected, and I think more attention should be paid to them in the future then has been paid in the past," opined the president.[18] This was said to be one of the first, if not the first, interviews conducted with a U.S. president from which reporters were allowed to directly quote him.

At around 11:30 Taft was taken for a short automobile ride through the streets and parks of Buffalo. At around 12:30 in the afternoon the president, along with Secretary Knox, Captain Butt and Police Commissioner Zeller, was driven to the Chamber of Commerce Building. That was a thirteen-story office building at 238 Main Street at the northwest corner of Seneca that wrapped around the smaller Bank of Buffalo that stood exactly at the corner of Main and Seneca.[19]

Thousands of people were gathered near the building, where the president was to hold a public reception. His car pulled around to the Seneca Street entrance and he was greeted with a great amount of cheering. He and the others entered the building and came around to the Main Street lobby, which was decorated with a profusion of American flags. The doors were opened and the public filed through to greet President Taft. A few hundred persons had the privilege of shaking his hand. Ever mindful of the McKinley tragedy, a Secret Service man and a large police force were present and the hands of each person in line were carefully scrutinized.

In short order the president and his guests exited the building onto Main Street and were driven to the Buffalo Club on Delaware for a luncheon sponsored by the Ad Club of Buffalo, an organization supporting local marketing, advertising and design businesses, which still operates today. The presidential party entered the clubrooms through the Trinity Street entrance and they were escorted upstairs to the main dining room. The entire club, as well as the dining room, was exquisitely decorated with roses, dogwoods and other blooms.

President Taft was presented with a gold pen, which he promised to use to sign his favorite bills into law. During the luncheon songs were sung, including "America" and lighthearted ditties about the president, with all members joining in. Afterward, the president was presented a resolution making him an honorary life member of the Ad Club. He made some comments and a few lighthearted quips and thanked the members for their welcome. Secretary Knox told a few stories, after which a toast was made to the president. Then Taft held a reception and shook hands with the many guests as well as Buffalo Club members who had not attended the Ad Club luncheon.

After this President Taft went to the University Club at 540 Delaware at the southwest corner of Allen Street.[20] He reached the building at 3:15 and was met by a rank of soldiers from Fort Porter at the entrance. Taft was the guest of honor at a reception held under the auspices of the Yale Alumni Association of Buffalo, which gave him the old Yale college yell, since Taft himself was a Yale graduate. He went to the library where another detail of soldiers stood. Almost all members of the club took advantage of the opportunity to meet the president.

At 4 p.m. Taft was driven to the Gratwick Cancer Laboratory on High and Elm Streets across from the current Buffalo General Hospital, and which was part of the Roswell Park Cancer Institute that had been founded in 1898. The president was given a tour conducted by institute President Dr. Harvey R. Gaylord. Mr. Taft then went back to the Wilcox home where he relaxed prior to the big event of the day, his speech at the Convention Hall.

The president and his party left for the hall in the early evening, arriving there a few minutes later for the 7 p.m. dinner. He entered to "Hail To The Chief" from the stage left entrance, crossed the stage and went down the center aisle to the Virginia Street entrance, up the dais to take his place at the speakers' table for the banquet. There was huge applause as the president smiled and bowed in appreciation.

Tables were set for 1,025 guests to share dinner with the president. Preparing the meal was no mean task. The Iroquois Hotel catered the affair. Most of the cooking was done in an improvised kitchen specially built in the alley outside the Convention Hall, with some preparation also done in some of the hall's side rooms. Scores of waiters were required and some thirty were drafted from out of town. Alcohol was not served, but champagne could be purchased separately.

Among others, Toastmaster Thomas Penney, Mayor Fuhrmann and Secretary Knox spoke, but the highlight was, naturally, President Taft's address, which began shortly after ten o'clock. In it, he discussed New York State affairs, barge canal improvements, and his administration's conservation policies, a topic of great interest at the time. He spoke of the beauty of the city of Buffalo and called nearby Niagara Falls an "embarrassment of grandeur." He said he hoped for closer trade ties with Canada, which would benefit Buffalo, remarking that "they are a rapidly growing nation, with resources and enterprise, and if we are sensible we shall rejoice in their prosperity."[21] After the speech, President Taft was driven directly to the train station and his train left the city in short order.

William Howard Taft's first visit to Buffalo as former president came on Friday, October 22, 1915, mainly to address a meeting of the New York State Bar Association. However, his twelve hours in the Queen City were filled with other activities. He was met at the train station at noon by a committee from the Yale Alumni Association of Buffalo. He was driven to the old Statler Hotel at Swan and Washington where the Yalies held a 1 p.m. luncheon in his honor.[22] Yale grad Taft spoke happily about the collegiate comradery.

The former president granted a short interview to some newspapermen. Asked whether he would accept a nomination for president in 1916, he laughingly said, "Now look here, young man, we just succeeded in decently interring the Progressive Party with appropriate ceremonies, and I don't propose to disinter the remains."[23] In other words, no. Asked about current economic maladies, he replied that we had gone too far in one direction and that it was time to halt attacks on capitalism. About the Great War, then raging in Europe, Taft voiced his support for American neutrality, which was then the official government policy.

After that the former president was driven to City Hall on Franklin Street. His appearance in the city council chamber interrupted a speech by Judge Alton B. Parker, who had been the losing Democratic presidential candidate in 1904. An outburst of applause greeted Taft, who was then voted an honorary member of the New York State Bar by the assembled members. From City Hall, at 4 p.m. Taft went to the Buffalo Consistory Hall of the Masons on Delaware Avenue between Mohawk and Huron Streets where he spoke briefly to a meeting of the Daughters of the American Revolution.[24] At that point it was time for a dinner break.

The highlight of Mr. Taft's visit took place that evening in the auditorium of Hutchinson High School on South Elmwood Avenue.[25] This was not a speech for students, but for members of the bar association, which had been given permission to use the school's facilities. Upon entering the auditorium, the former President was escorted on stage and greeted with three to four minutes of sustained cheering. He joined other distinguished lawyers and jurists, including Judge Parker and Henry L.

Stimson, who had been secretary of war in Theodore Roosevelt's cabinet.

Taft's speech addressed revisions to New York State's constitution, and he urged more appointment power for the governor, including the right to appoint state judges. He also called for changes that would result in more harmony between the executive and legislative branches. Touching on freedom of the press, he called for restrictions on newspapers' "reckless sensationalism" and penchant to try cases in the press to the detriment of accused persons. He believed this could be achieved without violating the First Amendment.

Following his address at the high school Taft was driven to the Buffalo Club on Delaware where he held an informal reception. He shook hands and chatted with bar association members and old acquaintances. He left town at midnight for Connecticut.

Mr. Taft made his last visit to Buffalo on January 4, 1917. He was here as a guest of the Buffalo Club in commemoration of its fiftieth anniversary Joining the former president at the dinner was former Buffalonian John G. Milburn, who was then a prominent New York City lawyer.

There was scant coverage of the event in the Buffalo newspapers, in large part because the club members did not wish to have the speakers' addresses published. Taft arrived late in the day and went directly to the club rooms on Delaware. An informal reception was held there before the dinner, which was attended by more than 200 members.

The former president left Buffalo immediately after the celebration. A reporter saw him at the Exchange Street Station waiting for a train that night.

"Have you anything to say?" the newspaperman asked.

"Yes. I have two reservations in the sleeping car for Pittsburgh," replied Mr. Taft.[26]

Woodrow Wilson's Four Visits To Buffalo

Woodrow Wilson made a total of four political visits to Buffalo. The first two came as he was seeking the presidency of the United States. On April 9, 1912 Wilson, then the governor of New Jersey, arrived by train at 2 p.m., probably at the Exchange Street Station. He was traveling from Syracuse on a pre-convention campaign tour. Presidential primary elections were not numerous in those days and the nomination for president, in Wilson's case the Democratic nomination, would largely be decided by party bigwigs meeting at a national convention in the summer.

Still, it was important for a man interested in the nomination to do a little campaigning, to meet and greet the people, to show his demeanor and style, and especially to meet with and convince party bosses in various cities that he should be their man. A committee of Buffalo citizens met the governor at the station. He was driven to the University Club at 540 Delaware at Allen for lunch, then taken for an automobile ride about the city. Back at the University Club, he held a reception from 5 to 6 p.m.

Afterward, Governor Wilson was driven to the Ellicott Square Building downtown where he was scheduled to give an after-dinner address at the Ellicott Club on the top floor. Prior to being seated, he held a reception for club members in the foyer of the clubrooms. Dinner was scheduled for 7:30 and the 250 to 300 men and women began to take their seats in the banquet hall. It was decorated for the occasion with large black and orange streamers strung from the walls to the center of the ceiling, where a huge Princeton banner was hung. Wilson had been president of Princeton University prior to assuming the governorship of New Jersey. Groups of American flags were arranged on the walls and arrangements of lilies graced the small dining tables throughout the hall where the diners sat. During the dinner, vocal solos by a female contralto and selections by an orchestra provided a pleasant backdrop.

After the tables had been cleared Governor Wilson, seated at the head table, was introduced and was warmly applauded. The theme of his speech was "The Present Situation." In it, he touched on some of the concerns of the American people. He blamed the discontent of the citizens on repeated disappointments and broken promises of elected officials, and said that people were suspicious that government was controlled by an inner circle whose influence was concealed. He predicted that the nation would be saved by the judgment of the average American. But it was Wilson's belief that the tariff would be the main issue of the upcoming presidential election. The governor's speaking style was described as pleasing, convincing and instructive. Governor Wilson remained in

Buffalo for the night and left for Pittsburgh the next morning.

After Governor Wilson had secured the Democratic nomination for president in July of 1912, he began his formal campaign for the White House on Labor Day, September 2, in Buffalo.[27] He chose Buffalo, the home of a strong working class, to begin his attack on Theodore Roosevelt, whom he rightly perceived to be his main rival.

Planning for the visit had begun several days earlier by the governor's host for the day, the United Trades and Labor Council of Buffalo. Wilson's train pulled into the Exchange Street Station on schedule at 10 a.m. from New York City. He and his campaign secretaries and agents were met on the platform by a labor committee and they were quickly escorted to waiting automobiles in Exchange Street. A few hundred persons lined both sides of the street and they let out a cheer as Wilson entered his car. He bowed gracefully to acknowledge the welcome. Many people rushed up to greet the candidate and he cheerfully shook hands with many of them.

A mounted police escort and several detectives accompanied the cars as they proceeded slowly westward on Exchange, up Main Street and right on Clinton to the entrance of the Lafayette Hotel at Clinton and Washington. Many people lined the curbs along the way and Governor Wilson tipped his hat to them. The dapper Wilson was dressed in a steel gray suit with a brown Fedora hat.

The governor was greeted by a packed room of well-wishers as he entered the hotel lobby and was pushed through to a ground floor reception room. Police formed the people into a line in the lobby which passed into one door of the room and out another. Several hundred men and women were able to shake hands with Mr. Wilson, who smilingly thanked them and traded the occasional quip. After several minutes the meet-and-greet was interrupted by a committee from the Catholic Young Men's National Union, which was meeting at the Broezel Hotel at 129 Seneca Street at Wells Street.[28] They extended an invitation for the governor to meet with the members there. He acceded at once and was driven to the Broezel where he gave a congenial five-minute talk aimed at the young audience, which was well received. Through a driving rain he was whisked back to the

Lafayette where he finished his reception, ending it as noon approached.

The governor was then taken upstairs to room 306 where one delegation of Polish Americans and another of Italian Americans were waiting to meet him. Prominent Polish American and Buffalo Health Commissioner Dr. Francis Fronczak questioned Mr. Wilson about a passage he had included in a book he had written some thirty years earlier that had criticized Polish, Italian and Hungarian immigrants. His explanation satisfied both groups. He then had a brief conversation with the labor committee that had met him at the station, after which he took a much-needed break.

At 1 p.m. Governor Wilson attended a luncheon at the hotel attended by about a hundred men, mostly powerful local Democrats such as Mayor Louis P. Fuhrmann, but also Buffalo Roman Catholic Bishop Charles Colton and Father Nelson Baker, as well as a handful of Republicans. It was a standing luncheon, but Wilson sat and chatted with newspapermen and others. And he did give a short impromptu speech.

After a fifteen minute rest the candidate was on the go again. He was driven up Genesee Street to Braun's Park near the city line.[29] In the car with him were Mayor Fuhrmann, Democratic national committeeman Norman E. Mack, and William J. ("Fingy") Conners, a notorious Buffalo businessman who was chairman of the New York State Democratic Committee and who, ironically on this Labor Day, was known for his anti-labor stance.

Arriving at the park at about 2:30, the governor's car was driven through the rain-soaked grounds to a speakers' platform, though the sun now tried to break through the low clouds after the late morning rain. A labor committee of 200 welcomed him and the park soon filled with about 3,000 cheering supporters. The Trades and Labor Council was the host organization for this event.

After brief remarks by the mayor, Governor Wilson began his speech at about three o'clock. As expected on this Labor Day, he mostly spoke in sympathy with the working man, but warned that labor must think of itself as part of the whole and not a separate class. After the half hour talk Wilson shook hands with hundreds of well-wishers for another thirty minutes. Then it was off to another venue. The governor's car hurried to Kenmore's Village Hall.[30] There, he was received by village president Matthew D. Young. It was the Kenmore Day celebration. Wilson delivered a short five-minute address to those assembled inside in which he advocated for a social center system of organized community opinion.

At 4:30 Governor Wilson and his party were off again, speeding down Delaware Avenue toward downtown Buffalo. Even with a slight detour through Delaware Park, his car arrived at the Prudential Building in fifteen minutes for his next appointment. He was now the guest of Erie County's Wilson and Marshall Club, the local booster club of the Democrats' presidential and vice presidential candidates. The club's headquarters was in room 110 and the chamber was packed to overflowing to meet its man and hear his remarks.

By five o'clock Governor Wilson was off again, back to the Lafayette Hotel for a reception that lasted about an hour, this one attended by many women. He then enjoyed a short rest in his room before he took dinner in the hotel's private dining room, attended also by leading Democrats of the county. He gave a few remarks, urging election of a Democratic Congress.

As 8 p.m. approached it was time for Wilson to depart for the Broadway Arsenal where he was to give the capstone speech of his day. He was driven to the building while his fellow diners marched as a body to the hall. Proceedings there began at 8:20 and a few minutes later Governor Wilson, escorted inside by a phalanx of twenty policemen, entered the building to ten minutes of thunderous cheers from the waiting audience of 5,000. Preliminary speeches lasted till almost nine o'clock before Wilson was introduced, at which time he received another ovation. To more applause, he opened with the line, "I must say in the circumstances that I am very glad they put me off at Buffalo, for certainly your greeting makes my heart very warm indeed."

He went on to emphasize that government must be improved to serve all classes equally. "I am much more interested in seeing government take care of the people who are not powerful than I am in seeing it take care of the people who are powerful," he said to great applause.[31] He declared that the Republicans were in debt to big money, and warned against voting Progressive, for that presidential candidate would have no

Congressional support to carry out a progressive agenda. As a progressive Democrat, he himself would be in a position to move forward such ideas. He also warned against Theodore Roosevelt's proposed legalization of monopolies under government control.

At around 10 p.m. Governor Wilson concluded his speech and was driven back to the Lafayette Hotel where he briefly bid goodbye to a few friends. Then it was on to the Exchange Street Station for a scheduled 10:35 journey to New York. Because the train expected to take his special car eastward was running an hour and a half late, another train was put together to take him away, and this left Buffalo at ten minutes after eleven.

Democrat Woodrow Wilson became our twenty-eighth president after he won the storied three-way presidential contest of 1912. He had defeated incumbent Republican President William Howard Taft and former President Theodore Roosevelt, the Progressive (Bull Moose) Party candidate.

Woodrow Wilson's fourth known visit to the Queen City came as president of the United States. As in 1912, he was campaigning for the presidency, albeit this time for reelection and at the tail end of the contest, just six days before the general election. The president arrived at the Lackawanna Station at the foot of Main Street via special train at 1:15 p.m. on Wednesday, November 1, 1916. He was greeted with a cacophony of automobile horns and boat whistles from the nearby harbor. Accompanying him were First Lady Edith Wilson, his daughter Margaret, his brother Joseph, niece Helen, his secretary Joseph Tumulty and his personal physician Dr. Cary T. Grayson.

The president and his party stepped off the rear platform of his rail car to the cheers of at least a thousand men and women, whom he acknowledged with a broad smile and a wave of his hands. Received by Mrs. William B. Hoyt and George C. Riley of the Ellicott Club, under whose auspices President Wilson was invited, the group got into waiting autos. They were driven through downtown, cutting through Perry from the station, up Washington to Exchange to the Terrace, where a large group of supporters cheered mightily. Firemen were in formation before their firehouse nearby.

The cars proceeded up Delaware to Virginia, then down Main Street.

Crowds were sparse until Lafayette Square where people were lined twenty deep around Democratic Party headquarters. Reaching the Ellicott Square Building, the little motorcade whirled around to the rear entrance on Washington. The party was then escorted to the Ellicott Club on the top floor of the building. President Wilson was warmly applauded as he entered the club's main hall. He was seated at the speakers' table with club president Knowlton Mixer and other ranking members. Flowers adorned that table and also the nearby table where the first lady sat with a group of women. The hall itself was simply decorated with large American flags.

A luncheon was served and afterward, close to three o'clock, the president was formally introduced to the hundreds of guests by Mr. Mixer. They stood and politely applauded. President Wilson proceeded to address the gathering for just over thirty minutes. He spoke about the tariff and briefly on the war in Europe, decrying partisanship in foreign affairs. "And I want to register my solemn protest here against the use of our foreign relationships for political advantage," he declared.

A considerable part of his speech concerned social problems. Concerning the courts he said, "Law too seldom has any heart in it, too seldom has any bowels of compassion, too seldom has any quick sympathies of perception.... Courts of law are sometimes not courts of justice."[32]

The president took his leave after his address for a driving tour of the city. A crowd cheered President and Mrs. Wilson as they entered their automobile. They were driven to Swan then up Main Street and left on Court to Niagara Square. There, the cars of the motorcade stopped, Mr. Wilson alighted and was handed a wreath by the first lady. Through a lane cleared by police, the bare-headed president stepped bearing the wreath, up to the McKinley Monument. From a large crowd, cheers rang out and car horns blared, drowning out an assembled band at Central High School directly across the square. President Wilson handed the wreath to a policeman who placed it at the monument.

After he returned to his car, the motorcade proceeded east on Court Street back to Main Street, to North, Porter, to the Front (now the Front Park-Peace Bridge area) where two khaki-clad soldiers fired a twenty-one-gun salute. From there it was on to Massachusetts Avenue to Front Avenue, Porter, North, Delaware, Chapin, Lincoln, through Delaware Park to Humboldt Parkway, looping south of the Humboldt Park wading pool to Fillmore. From there it was south to Broadway, turning west toward downtown and then north onto Johnson Street, down Genesee to Main to the Iroquois Hotel at Eagle Street.

Newspaper reporters who had been accompanying President Wilson on this campaign remarked that his reception in Buffalo was the coolest and least enthusiastic of any of his stops throughout the country. Wilson faced a formidable Republican challenger in Charles Evans Hughes of New York, and did not carry the state, but he commanded considerable support in the Buffalo area. Hughes did, however, win Erie County.

The weather was not a factor in deterring people. However, the fact that it was a Wednesday kept most working men away. All along his automobile ride through the city, crowds were thin with only sporadic clusters of larger crowds at certain points. Schools had closed early and on the tour of the city pupils and their teachers stood along the curbs near their schools if they happened to be near the route. The children waved flags and cheered as the president rode by. On narrow residential Johnson Street, bedecked with flags, housewives were thrilled to see the president of the United States and the first lady motor past their modest homes.

Security was tight throughout this visit. In addition to the Secret Service agents who never got far from the president, Buffalo policemen and department detectives provided additional security. Fifty-four of them were present when Wilson arrived at the train depot and 200 were detailed for his evening speech at the Broadway Auditorium. At the Iroquois Hotel, President and Mrs. Wilson and their party retired to a third-floor suite to rest and have a private dinner. The main event of the president's visit was coming up, his campaign speech at the Broadway Auditorium, the renamed Broadway Arsenal. A crowd of 14,000 packed the hall, waiting for Wilson's arrival. He left the Iroquois shortly before 8 p.m.

The streets along the way were filled with people. From the cars accompanying the president's auto, men held out large sparklers. The way to the auditorium was described as "a lane of red fire all the way," presumably from flares or torches displayed on the street that illuminated the night.³³ This was the enthusiasm on display that had earlier been lacking. Three times the audience at the auditorium became excited that the president was arriving, but they were false alarms. Finally, to the strains of "Hail To The Chief," he and Mrs. Wilson entered the hall. The people burst forth with shouts and clapping and flag waving that lasted for seventeen minutes as the couple sat on the speakers' stage. Some young men and boys climbed up on girders to get a better view. Standees jammed the aisles, blocking the view of those seated behind.

During the introduction of the president, the unruly audience paid little attention, and shouts of "Sit down! Sit down!" were aimed at those standing and obstructing a clear view of the stage. A bugler's fanfare failed to quiet the crowd. Police attempted to move the standees, but only aggravated the situation. Once President Wilson began his oration the continuing shouts of "Sit down!" caused him to pause and interject with a smile, "There is nothing to see." This drew some laughter and seemed to calm the audience.

Though the address was billed as non-partisan, it was nevertheless a campaign speech. In it, the president highlighted unity and fairness, talking about America's place in the world in light of the ongoing European war. He also spoke of the plight of the working man. Wilson drew a great round of applause when he mentioned the laborers. "I say it is high time that we should organize the assistance of the nation for the education and advancement of the working people of this country of every caste and grade," he intoned.

Continuing on he said, "We have heard a good deal recently about the eight-hour day. One of the things that interests me about the eight-hour day is not merely justice to the men who work. Men have asked me: 'How far do you go? How far are you in favor of the eight-hour day?' And I say, wherever it can possibly be made to work."³⁴ President Wilson also elicited great cheers toward the end of his address when he spoke of war and peace, saying "America is not afraid to fight. America would not be disinclined to fight when it found something as big as the American ideal to fight for."³⁵

This remark foreshadowed the U.S. entry into World War I a few months later, as Wilson declared at that time that we were entering the war to make the world "safe for democracy," something indeed as big as the American ideal. When he ended his forty-five minute speech, the president gave a wave of his hand and a smile, acknowledging the cheers of the audience, which rushed for the exits. Wilson and his party were then escorted to their cars and whisked to the Exchange Street Station where they entered his private rail car, the "Mayflower." There was no crowd at the depot. The special train pulled out for New York City at 10:35 p.m.

Woodrow Wilson's final visit to Buffalo came on Monday, November 12, 1917 as the United States was fully involved in the World War. The president's specific purpose for the journey was to address the thirty-seventh annual national convention of the American Federation of Labor (AFL), at whose direct invitation he came. It was being held at the Broadway Auditorium.

The president's special train pulled into the Exchange Street Station at precisely 9:33 a.m. directly from Washington, D.C. Accompanying him were First Lady Edith Wilson, his secretary Joseph Tumulty and physician Dr. Cary W. Grayson.

Long before the train arrived the station and surrounding streets were jammed with people. Security arrangements were very stringent for this war time president. A contingent of 1,200 soldiers from Fort Niagara, and Buffalo police, both uniformed and plainclothes, were present to provide protection, as was, of course, the Secret Service.

AFL President Samuel Gompers and several other of the organization's officials entered President Wilson's private car to welcome him to Buffalo. One of the reasons Wilson was so willing to come to Buffalo was to show his support for Gompers' reelection as head of the AFL against a socialist challenge. Gompers was a staunch Wilson supporter, and the president needed organized labor's backing in his war mobilization efforts. He did not want to deal with labor strikes or slowdowns.

After a few minutes the president, flanked by Secret Service men, along with his party and the labor leaders, emerged from the rear of the car to tumultuous applause. He wore a top hat and dark winter coat and smiled broadly. A cordon of soldiers guarded a path straight from the rail car through the station to waiting automobiles. President and Mrs. Wilson were surrounded by police and the military and followed by the Secret Service. No member of the public was allowed to get within fifteen feet of them. A large crowd was gathered outside but was kept a distance away. Once everyone was in the cars a slow motorcade left the station for the auditorium.

The route was west on Exchange to Main and then east on Broadway, and it was lined by cheering crowds. A platoon of mounted police led the parade followed by a hundred-man band that played "Stars And Stripes Forever" along the entire way. A double file of soldiers marched on each side of the cars, toting rifles on their shoulders, with eight Secret Service men following directly behind the president's closed car. Motorcycle policemen rode alongside, and police on foot also strode along.

The president and his party reached the auditorium at ten o'clock. The cars swung around to the rear entrance on Potter Street. President and Mrs. Wilson were escorted by the police to the rear of the stage directly in front of the entrance at the south end of the hall. They waited there for Mr. Gompers to introduce the president. A delegation of 400 AFL members had also just arrived from their headquarters at the old Statler Hotel at Swan and Washington. Thousands of members of the public were also seated within the building in floor seats and in the balcony gallery.

The inside of the hall was decorated with American flags. The stage was a mass of red, white and blue banners with a tall vase of yellow chrysanthemums and potted palms. On each side of the platform large colored portraits of President Wilson and President Gompers were displayed. At a quarter past ten the band struck up the opening notes of "The Star-Spangled Banner," bringing the audience to its feet with a waving of flags. At exactly this moment President Wilson emerged from back of the stage to a mighty roar.

After a short introduction by Mr. Gompers, the president stepped up to the speakers' podium to another ovation. With a wave of his right hand he motioned for quiet. The theme which would run throughout President Wilson's speech was that of the American war effort. He began by asking his listeners to regard him as a fellow citizen, there to counsel them, not as a figure of authority. He proceeded to excoriate men of peace. "What I am opposed to is not the feeling of the pacifists, but their stupidity. My heart is with them, but my mind has a contempt for them. I want peace, but I know how to get it and they do not," he exclaimed.

He praised Mr. Gompers and voiced support for improved working conditions, but urged cooperation between labor and management during the war. He seemed to issue a veiled threat against work disruptions when he said, "If we are true friends of freedom, our own or anybody else's, we will see that the power of this country and the productivity of this country is raised to its absolute maximum, and that absolutely nobody is allowed to stand in the way of it. When I say that nobody is allowed to stand in the way I do not mean that they shall be prevented by the power of the government but by the power of the American spirit."

A good part of the president's address was a condemnation of the enemy nation of Germany, but he also included a criticism of Russia, which had dropped out of the Allied war coalition and adopted a communist system. He called that country ill-informed. He included a lighter note, saying he "came away from Washington because I get lonely down there…I have to come away and get reminded of the rest of the country." In his closing line, he said that he wanted the people to think of him "as the expression for the time being of the power and dignity and hope of the United States," in direct contrast to his opening lines when he asked that he be regarded as merely a fellow citizen.[36]

At the conclusion of the forty-five-minute speech, interrupted several times by applause, President Gompers called for three cheers for President and Mrs. Wilson. The first lady was presented with two huge bouquets of roses. The couple stood and chatted for a couple of minutes with a few people onstage, then left the auditorium through the same doors behind the stage through which they had earlier entered. The street was closed off and soldiers stood by as the Wilsons and the others reentered their automobiles. The cars moved down Broadway to Ellicott back to the Exchange Street Station with the same security escort as had been used on the way to the auditorium. Motorcycle police cleared the way, making sure onlookers were kept back. This time the Wilsons rode in an open car, as opposed to the closed car in which they had earlier ridden.

The motorcade quickly arrived at the station. The president and his party walked through a lane of soldiers and climbed back aboard the presidential rail car. In a few minutes the special train pulled out, headed back to Washington. The visit had lasted less than three hours.

Rowland B. Mahany

In the last years of his presidency Woodrow Wilson appointed Buffalo lawyer and former Congressman Rowland B. Mahany to several different posts in the federal government. He had previously served as U.S. Envoy to Ecuador under President Benjamin Harrison. In the Wilson administration, Mahany served on the War Labor Board and Foreign Trade Commission and was the U.S. Representative to the International Commission on Immigration and Emigration. He was also the assistant to the secretary of labor from 1918 to 1919, and acting secretary of labor from 1920 to 1921 when the secretary of labor took an extended leave of absence.

Warren G. Harding, Calvin Coolidge and Herbert Hoover

Warren G. Harding, Calvin Coolidge and Herbert Hoover each visited Buffalo before they became president. None of them came to the city while he was chief executive, but Hoover visited once as former president.

Herbert Hoover came to Buffalo on Wednesday, November 12, 1919 to deliver an address at the invitation of the All-Polish Convention, a meeting of a thousand Polish Americans from throughout the country. They were in the Queen City to discuss concerns of Polish Americans and the situation in the newly reconstituted nation of Poland. At the time, Mr. Hoover was the former head of the U.S. Food Administration during World War I and the current director general of the American Relief Administration, which he founded. He was working hard to help the people of the new Polish state recover from the devastation of the World War.

He arrived by train around nine in the morning, saying that he had originally intended to stay in Buffalo for three days, but other invitations from elsewhere precluded him from visiting for more than a few hours. He dismissed a question about a possible run for president, saying he would retire to private life after finishing his present work. Mr. Hoover first went to the Dom Polski Hall at 1081 Broadway in the heart of the city's Polish American community, arriving at 11 a.m.[37] He went to the upstairs auditorium, which was packed with conventioneers, both on the main floor and in the balcony, and he was greeted with a fifteen-minute ovation. Accompanying Hoover was Polish Ambassador to the United States, Prince Casimir Lubomirski, and Polish diplomat Count Francis Pulaski.

Hoover began his address by reporting on the progress of the new Polish state. He lauded its leadership and commitment to democracy. He praised Polish Americans but made a plea for Americanism and warned against foreign agitators in the United States. His talk was followed by a few remarks by Prince Lubomirski. After these speeches, Hoover and Lubomirski were rushed downtown to the old Statler Hotel to speak before a luncheon hosted by 400 businessmen of the Chamber of Commerce.

The luncheon began before noon and Mr. Hoover was immediately introduced when he came into the dining room, which had been tastefully decorated with Polish and American flags. He began his talk by thanking the citizens of Buffalo, especially its women, for their support for Belgian relief during the late war and current European relief efforts. He noted ongoing economic and social difficulties both here and abroad but expressed confidence that Americans would overcome them. Hoover also criticized Europe's class system while praising America's equality of opportunity and warned against socialism and nationalization of industry.

Prince Lubomirski then spoke briefly and Hoover made his exit, as he had to board a 1 p.m. train for New York City to keep another commitment. He had been scheduled to be a guest of honor at an evening banquet at the Hotel Lafayette, but his early departure, of course, prevented his attendance.

During Senator Warren G. Harding's successful run for the presidency in 1920, he operated a modified front porch campaign. Front porch campaigning was popular in the late nineteenth century, whereby a candidate for public office would literally do his electioneering from his front porch, giving speeches to reporters and others who gathered on the front lawn of his home. The people came to him, rather than the other way around. However, Harding's campaign manager decided that the modern candidate had to do at least some campaigning on the road. As a result Senator Harding made a few trips away from his Marion, Ohio home to get out among the people. One of his journeys took him into New York State, and one of his stops was in Buffalo.

At 8:50 a.m. on Thursday, October 21, 1920. Harding's train stopped in Buffalo, but only long enough to change engines. The senator did not make an appearance and in a few minutes the train was off eastward to Rochester, where he was scheduled to attend a rally. Later that afternoon Harding was back in Buffalo, when his train pulled into the Exchange Street Station at 4:30. Senator Harding and his wife Florence came out onto the rear platform of their car, waving and bowing to the cheers of the crowd of supporters that had gathered round. A reception committee of area Republicans was there to greet them. After posing for a few photographs, the Hardings were escorted to a waiting automobile, the senator shaking the hands of railroad workers.

Honking horns mixed in with cheers as the Hardings made their way through the station to their car, which was decorated in American flags. Led by a contingent of motorcycle police, they were rushed through Exchange and Main Streets to the Iroquois Hotel, whose lobby was filled with men and women anxious to meet the candidate at a planned five o'clock reception. Harding shook the hands of several hundred people and around 6 p.m. took dinner at the hotel. Joining the Hardings at the meal was Nathan Miller, the Republican candidate for New York governor.

Around 7:30 two marching bands escorted the automobile of Mr. Miller to the Broadway Auditorium, where the evening's rally was to take place. He was enthusiastically greeted when he entered the hall and took his place on the speakers' stage on the west side, which was crowded with several hundred VIPs. The auditorium was decorated in red, white and blue streamers and American flags. Back of the stage large pictures of Theodore Roosevelt, William McKinley and Senator Harding were displayed. Estimates of the crowd ranged from 7,000 all the way up to 16,000, but the hall was generally reported to be full.

Miller addressed the audience for about thirty minutes. Then Senator and Mrs. Harding made their entrance. The crowd let loose with the waving of hats and handkerchiefs and loud cheering. A wedge of police had to force an opening from doorway to stage down the center aisle for the Hardings. The two bands that had escorted them from the hotel entered the hall, music blaring, as the couple waved, bowed and smiled from the stage.

After several minutes the master of ceremonies was able to gavel the place into some semblance of order. Senator Harding began his speech after a brief introduction. Still in the days before microphones, his voice strained and husky from numerous campaign speeches, Harding began by saying, "You will have to bear with me for a moment until my voice returns to me." At first unable to be heard in the back, the senator's voice got stronger as he went along. He attacked the proposed League of Nations, and in a dig at President Wilson he said, "I'm not the sort of a candidate who believes he can run the world. I'll want a lot of help in the United States alone."[38]

Harding touched on education, social justice, immigration and America's role in the world. During the speech the candidate was constantly interrupted by applause. He spoke for one hour and twenty-five minutes. At the conclusion, the crowd leapt to its feet and the band struck up "The Star-Spangled Banner." The senator started to shake hands with some of the people who had rushed forward, but his handlers interfered, reminding him that he had to be at the station for his train by midnight, which was fast approaching. He left by a door at the rear of the stage and after several minutes he and his wife were aboard the train for Marion.

Herbert Hoover's second visit to Buffalo was on Saturday, January 8, 1921. He was in the city as national chairman of the European Relief Council, which was raising money to feed the destitute children of France, Germany, Austria, Poland and Czechoslovakia, which were still reeling from the aftereffects of the First World War. At the time, he was considered one of the greatest humanitarians in the world.

Mr. Hoover was met at the Exchange Street Station by A. Conger Goodyear, chairman of the local Relief Council, Buffalo Health Commissioner Dr. Francis Fronczak and Colonel William J. Donovan. Hoover posed for photographers, then went to Mr. Goodyear's office at the Marine Bank Building, now known as the Main Seneca Building. There he gave an interview outlining the purpose of the relief campaign. He emphasized that it was an emergency action until the people of Europe were able to look after themselves and said that the U.S. had a surplus of food and clothing.

"About $33 million is needed. That makes out to about ten dollars a youngster. Ten dollars is not a very large price to pay to save the life of a boy or girl until next harvest," he said as he puffed on a cigar. He rejected charges that relief money had gone to the Polish military in its war with the USSR.[39] Afterward, accompanied by Mr. Goodyear and Dr. Fronczak, Hoover called on Buffalo Mayor George S. Buck in the old City Hall, but the mayor was out of town.

Noon found Hoover at the Hotel Lafayette for a luncheon held in the ballroom under the auspices of several women's groups. Lunch was served on tin plates, a double ration of what was to be fed to a European child once a day. Hoover opened a plea for aid by appealing to "Buffalo's accustomed generosity."[40] After the luncheon Hoover was driven to Dom Polski Hall on Broadway where he addressed a packed auditorium of Polish Americans. His appearance was sponsored by the Polish Committee of Buffalo, headed by Dr. Fronczak. Mr. Hoover received a great welcome. He informed the audience of conditions in Poland and neighboring lands and asked his listeners to support the saving of lives of Polish children.

At 8 p.m. Hoover appeared at the Elmwood Music Hall at Elmwood and Virginia. He was greeted with a great ovation when he entered the building, filled with invited guests and the general public. He received another when he was introduced to speak. In his speech, he emphasized that it was "against the conscience of America" to let children of Europe starve, and that helping them was the necessary thing to do, lest those children someday fill the prisons of Europe and America.

"If these children are allowed to starve, the world will face anarchy, Bolshevism and kindred evils and the very foundation of our civilization will be shattered," he declared.[41] Reverend C. Wallace Petty of Brooklyn spoke briefly after Mr. Hoover. At the conclusion, people rushed forward to pledge donations to the cause, and an estimated $100,000 was raised within several minutes.

The man who would become the thirtieth president of the United States upon the death of Warren G. Harding, Vice President Calvin Coolidge, paid a visit to Buffalo on Tuesday, July 11, 1922. He came at the invitation of the Buffalo Chamber of Commerce to deliver an address to its members.

He arrived in the city at 8:10 a.m. and was met at the train station by Walter P. Cooke, a Buffalo lawyer and University of Buffalo administrator, and by a reception committee of Chamber of Commerce and Ellicott Club members. He was promptly driven to Mr. Cooke's home at 155 Summer Street, then to breakfast at the Buffalo Club on Delaware Avenue.[42] The vice president was then taken on an automobile tour through some of the streets and parks of Buffalo and a visit to the new Main Street (now south) campus of the University of Buffalo, then still under development.

Back at the Cooke home, Mr. Coolidge commented, "It was a very delightful trip Mr. Cooke gave us through the parks. Buffalo can pride herself on some wonderful streets and some wonderful trees. We've got some elms in my home city of Northampton, but not in such profusion as you have here."[43] Coolidge also met a few old friends he knew from his earlier days in New England.

The vice president consented to be interviewed by newspaper reporters in the library of the Cooke home. He addressed the tariff, ship subsidy legislation and a World War I bonus. He also explained how difficult it was to get away from Washington while still carrying out his constitutional duty to preside over the Senate. He said that the position was one of honor and dignity, but was no comparison to his previous position of governor of Massachusetts.

Coolidge was driven to the Ellicott Square Building downtown for a noon luncheon at the Ellicott Club with 500 members of the Chamber of Commerce. Attendees at the speakers' table besides the vice president included Walter Cooke; Buffalo Mayor Francis X. Schwab; William J. Donovan, future developer of the Central Intelligence Agency but at the time the U.S. Attorney for Western New York; Judge John R. Hazel, who twenty-one years earlier had administered the presidential oath of office to Theodore Roosevelt at the Ansley Wilcox mansion; and Mr. Ansley Wilcox himself.

After the meal, tables were cleared form the hall and another 500 businessmen and Ellicott Club members came in to hear Coolidge's speech. Mayor Schwab extended a welcome to the vice president, who was given the keys to the city. Then Mr. Cooke, as master of ceremonies, formally introduced the guest of honor, saying he was "noted as an exponent of adequate brevity." He praised Vice President Coolidge's handling of the Boston Police strike as governor of Massachusetts, which received a standing ovation. And he reminded Mr. Coolidge that Buffalo had furnished two presidents and that Theodore Roosevelt took the oath of office in the city.

After a round of applause the vice president opened his speech with compliments about Buffalo. He said the country should look to businessmen for leadership. "The voice of those who are trying to tear down are always strident. You who want to build and endure must be equally active," he urged. Coolidge also praised business for its remarkable job in readjusting the country back to a peacetime economy following the late war. He touched on problems in Mexico, unemployment, the tariff, the merchant marine and the veterans' bonus. He praised the peace treaties with our World War I adversaries, explaining that "we have escaped all of the obligations and perils that might have been ours as a member of the League of Nations."[44]

He closed with an appeal to businessmen to take the lead in American affairs. Vice President Coolidge then left for Rochester by automobile where he was scheduled to address that city's Chamber of Commerce.

Herbert Hoover's third visit to Buffalo was on Saturday, June 14, 1924 as he was serving as secretary of commerce under President Coolidge. As commerce secretary, he was a member of the United States St. Lawrence Commission, which was looking into improvements of the Great Lakes-St. Lawrence River system in cooperation with Canada.

Secretary Hoover's train arrived in Buffalo at about 9 a.m. He was accompanied only by his secretary and they were met at the station by the president of the Niagara Falls Power Company and an army engineer. They left immediately in an automobile for Niagara Falls, arriving there a little after ten o'clock. Mr. Hoover was to have arrived in Buffalo the previous morning. But developments at the Republican National Convention, specifically that his name was entered as a vice presidential nominee, kept him in Washington an extra day.

Secretary Hoover briefly inspected the Niagara Falls power situation and the problem of erosion of the Horseshoe Falls. He and his party then went to Canada to observe the ongoing enlargement of the Welland Canal, then on to Toronto eastward toward the St. Lawrence River before returning to Washington from Quebec. Mr. Hoover acknowledged that improvements to the Welland Canal would mean a loss of commerce for Buffalo, since its necessity as a lake vessel-to-rail center would be lessened, but said that improvements to electric power production on the Niagara would negate that effect.

CHAPTER 10

FDR, DEPRESSION, WAR AND RECOVERY

In 1907 at the age of twenty-five, Franklin Delano Roosevelt was admitted to the New York State bar. He quickly secured a position with the New York City law firm of Carter, Ledyard and Milburn, one of the most prestigious in the city. And therein lies the story of an FDR-Buffalo connection.

Carter, Ledyard and Milburn was formed when John G. Milburn joined a law firm headed by James C. Carter and Lewis C. Ledyard in New York City in 1904. Milburn had been a Buffalo attorney and was a friend of Grover Cleveland.[1] He represented the interests of former President Cleveland in 1890 in a Buffalo libel trial filed by a political enemy of the former president against the *New York Evening Post*. Milburn was successful in the Post's defense, which may have saved Cleveland's political career. Milburn, of course, had been the president of Buffalo's Pan-American Exposition in 1901, and the gravely wounded President McKinley had died in his house on September 14 of that year. Three years later Milburn abandoned Buffalo for Manhattan.

Young FDR did not seem to be particularly interested in the law, though he performed rather routine tasks at the firm well enough to be retained. And he did have actual personal interactions with Mr. Milburn on the job.[2] Roosevelt left his position in 1910 when he decided to run for the New York State Senate. Ironically, Carter, Ledyard and Milburn specialized in defending large corporations against government anti-trust actions. The anti-trust laws had been enthusiastically enforced by Franklin's cousin, Theodore Roosevelt, when he was president, and FDR himself, when he became president, was a huge thorn in the side of big business.

Today the firm retains its reputation as one of the most distinguished Wall Street law firms, still operating under the name of Carter, Ledyard and Milburn.

Roosevelt's First Visit To Buffalo

As his fifth cousin Theodore Roosevelt had done, Franklin D. Roosevelt made several trips to Buffalo during his life. As a native New Yorker with strong political ambitions, FDR did not hesitate to travel throughout the state to make himself well known to the public.

Roosevelt's first recorded visit to the Queen City occurred in 1911, a few months after attaining his first political office, that of New York State senator representing his home district of Duchess County just north of New York City. The twenty-nine-year old senator was in town to address a meeting of the Saturn Club at 417 Delaware Avenue. He arrived by train on the morning of Saturday, December 23.

He was driven to the Lafayette Hotel where he registered, though he did not spend the night. While there, he met with reporters and talked about his proposals to wrest control of the Democratic Party's political apparatus from the corrupt men who held a tight rein on state party affairs. He called for primary elections, changes in the balloting process, and a new state Democratic Party leader. Already attracting attention simply because of his family name, young Roosevelt had proceeded to build on that notoriety by positioning himself as a reformer and leading insurgent within his own Democratic Party as well as in state politics in general. At the hotel, he also met with local Democratic insurgents.

In his talk at the Saturn Club following dinner that evening, Senator Roosevelt expanded on what he had earlier said to the reporters that day, boldly naming party bosses who should be replaced. He was confident that the decent people would prevail and construct a fairer party system, and he closed with the following: "The American citizen is again fighting for his freedom. He is confronted by oligarchies and tyrannies on the one hand and by anarchy on the other, and those of us who have the old abiding faith believe that the American citizen will triumph again as he has done in the past."[3]

At the close of the address an unscheduled reception was held, after which Senator Roosevelt was driven to the railroad depot for a late train back east.

More Trips to Buffalo

On February 3, 1912 Senator Roosevelt was back at the Saturn Club to attend a dinner and make a speech at a gathering of local Harvard graduates. FDR was a Harvard alumnus, Class of 1904. The senator's address was strictly non-partisan, and only political in that he urged appointment of a Harvard grad to the state's Public Service Commission and urged all Harvard men to be participants in the political world. It was an enthusiastic speech that was received and applauded in true old school comradery.

Among his comments, he declared, "I am glad to see what Harvard men of Buffalo have done in our national and civic life." He also noted the international aspect of Harvard, rather ironically stating, "The captain of our next season's baseball team is a Jap. This shows that every nation in the world has equal privilege and rights in Harvard and it is the survival of the fittest."[4]

On Tuesday, September 22, 1914 FDR, now assistant secretary of the navy in the Woodrow Wilson administration, arrived in Buffalo once again. Democrat Roosevelt was here to attend a luncheon and hear the speech of Harvey D. Hinman, candidate for the Republican nomination for governor of New York, who was Theodore Roosevelt's choice. The luncheon was held at the

Ellicott Club in the Ellicott Square Building.

On July 7, 1917 Roosevelt was at the Chautauqua Institution where he gave a Liberty Loan address and warned about the dangers facing America if Germany were allowed to win the ongoing World War.

Two years later FDR was once again in Buffalo. He arrived at 6 a.m. on August 6, 1919 to attend the national peace convention of the Knights of Columbus, a Roman Catholic fraternal organization, along with Secretary of War Newton D. Baker. Roosevelt still held the position of assistant secretary of the navy. Among the day's activities, Supreme Knight James A. Flaherty, the national leader of the Knights, accepted the French Cross of War and U.S. Distinguished Service Medal on behalf of the organization at a ceremony in Lafayette Square. It was attended by both Secretary Baker and Assistant Secretary Roosevelt.

Both men delivered addresses to the convention delegates at the old Statler Hotel that afternoon. Roosevelt spoke of the unrest that existed in the post-World War I world, noting that progress toward peace and prosperity must be made, but that law and order must be maintained.

That evening the Boston, Massachusetts delegation of the Knights called on FDR to ask him to use his influence in bettering conditions at the Boston Navy Yard, where thousands of employees were being laid off. Assistant Secretary Roosevelt informed them that he had already sent a special request to Congress to provide funding for improvements.

Vice Presidential Candidate Roosevelt in Buffalo

In 1920 thirty-eight year-old Franklin D. Roosevelt was the Democrats' vice presidential candidate, running on the national ticket with James M. Cox of Ohio for president. They were opposed by the Republican combination of Warren G. Harding and Calvin Coolidge.

On October 21, 1920 Mr. Roosevelt made a campaign stop in North Tonawanda on the very same day that Republican presidential candidate Harding was in Buffalo for a rousing election rally. In a stump speech, FDR appealed to voters to elect the Democrats, who would have America join the League of Nations, which he contended was the right thing to do to keep the United States engaged in the world.

At the conclusion of his talk he was taken to Niagara Falls where he delivered another speech. He left from Buffalo early the next morning for Elmira. His appearances drew scant attention from the Buffalo newspapers, most likely due to the coincidence of the Harding appearance.

Roosevelt and the Governorship

In 1921 Roosevelt was stricken by poliomyelitis, the disease which would leave him unable to walk for the rest of his life. This kept him out of politics for a few years, but proved to be only a temporary setback on the way to his ultimate goal, which was obviously the White House. He and his advisers first set their sights on the New York State governor's mansion. And FDR was able to secure the Democratic nomination for the governorship in 1928.

His statewide campaign brought him to Buffalo on Saturday, October 20, 1928. Roosevelt was crossing the state, and in his own automobile he drove into Buffalo from Dunkirk, arriving at the Lafayette Hotel at 4 p.m. In accordance with his wishes, his arrival was kept low key; few guests at the hotel even noticed it. Mr. Roosevelt met with a few Democratic party officials, then worked on his evening speech. In his suite, he was guest of honor at a small dinner party.

At 8:15 p.m. in the Broadway Auditorium, filled with legions of Democratic party loyalists, the lights were dimmed. As "The Star-Spangled Banner" played, a spotlight shone on a portrait of outgoing Governor Alfred E. Smith above the speakers' platform, and the audience rose to its feet and cheered. Smith was now running for president. Preliminary speeches from a host of candidates followed, but at 9:25 the speakers were interrupted by the chairman. FDR had arrived and took a standing place at the speakers' table on stage. To wild cheers, he waved and smiled broadly. After he was formally introduced more loud cheers rang throughout the hall.

Roosevelt then began his address. In it, he heavily criticized the Republicans' labor record, calling it a "dirty envelope of broken promises." Beyond the typical political rhetoric, including attacks on his opponent, he concluded with an appeal for the elimination of the religious issue from political campaigns. Governor Smith was the first major party presidential nominee to be Roman Catholic, and many people would not vote for him based on that fact alone. Of the religious bigot, FDR intoned, "May God have mercy on his miserable soul."[5]

Mr. and Mrs. Roosevelt spent the night at the Lafayette. They attended services on Sunday morning at Trinity Episcopal Church at 371 Delaware Avenue. From 5 to 6 p.m. they held a reception at the hotel. They left on Monday morning for Rochester.

Franklin D. Roosevelt won the 1928 election. As governor, he took a trip to Western New York in the summer of 1929. After a night at Jamestown, he arrived at the Chautauqua Institution about noon on Friday, July 12, with his wife and their son Elliott. After lunch at a private home, they spent the rest of the day and overnight at Chautauqua. On Saturday afternoon, the governor went to the amphitheater where he delivered a 2:30 speech to 3,000 people. The governor urged his audience to join in an effort to have the government help the seriously mentally and physically infirm. "This is a problem which demands a crusade," he said.[6]

Following his address FDR was escorted in a wheelchair to the porch of the Atheneum Hotel where for more than a half an hour he received members of the Chautauqua Women's Club, their relatives and friends. Shortly afterward, the Roosevelts were driven by car to Buffalo, where he received cheers from onlookers along Main Street, and as the automobile pulled up in front of the Lafayette Hotel at 7 p.m.

Inside, Governor Roosevelt delivered a campaign speech in support of James W. Higgins for Erie County Sheriff. The dinner crowd consisted of some Republicans as well as members of his own Democratic Party. FDR then held a reception.

After spending the night at the hotel, the next day Roosevelt went to the home of Oliver Cabana Jr. in Elma for lunch. Cabana was a millionaire

Buffalo businessman and Democratic Party operative. The governor then was driven to Niagara Falls by way of River Road, returned to the Lafayette Hotel and left by train the next morning, July 14, for Albany.

Now running for reelection as governor of New York, Roosevelt visited the Queen City on Wednesday, August 27, 1930. He and Mrs. Roosevelt arrived that morning at the new Central Terminal on Paderewski Drive on Buffalo's east side. They were greeted by a large crowd and personally welcomed by Buffalo Mayor Charles E. Roesch. A state police detail was present, which was assigned to protect the governor throughout his stay.

He was driven to the Hotel Statler on Niagara Square where he addressed the morning session of the New York State Federation of Labor. He was preceded by Frances Perkins, the state industrial commissioner. In his talk, the governor stressed the need for an unemployment insurance program in the United States, at the time beset by the economic upheaval of the Great Depression. He also voiced support for a program of old age financial security and protective labor laws for women and children.

At noon FDR was in Niagara Square for the laying of the cornerstone of the new state office building on the site of the former Central High School, a parcel bounded by Court, Franklin and West Genesee Streets.[7] Surrounded by an array of state and local politicians and a huge crowd of 2,000, the governor was introduced by Mayor Roesch. Mr. Roosevelt then took silver trowel in hand and spread mortar over the stone. He remarked: "Your mayor and council are to be congratulated on creating a civic center here which, in a few years, will be rivaled by no other city in the country."[8] Directly across Niagara Square on its western side, the new city hall building stood three-quarters complete. It would open the following year.

The governor then went back to the Statler Hotel for a luncheon sponsored by the Rotary and Exchange Clubs. Roosevelt delivered a short speech in which he defended the efficiency of state government under his watch. Seated at the speakers' table with him were Mrs. Roosevelt, Lieutenant Governor Herbert Lehman, Mayor Roesch, Frances Perkins and various other officials.

At 2 p.m. Governor Roosevelt was off on a tour of the Niagara

Frontier. He and his party were driven to the Grand Island ferry crossing where they took the boat across the Niagara River to the island. He stopped at the home of Democratic Committeeman Frank J. Offerman, inspected the sites of the proposed Grand Island bridges and visited the new Beaver Island State Park and a girls' camp.

The ferry on the north side of the island carried him to the city of Niagara Falls where he made a short stop to pick up his wife, who had motored there earlier in the day. They drove back down Niagara Falls Boulevard and returned to the Lafayette Hotel late in the afternoon. The governor dined privately with a few Democratic Party leaders. After that, he attended a reception with Mrs. Roosevelt at the Lafayette, sponsored by the Democratic Women of Erie County. Just before the Roosevelts left Buffalo at 9:30 the next morning, they met with their Buffalo cousins, Mr. and Mrs. Thomas R. Punnett, at the hotel.

Well into his reelection campaign, Governor Roosevelt was once again in Buffalo, on Monday, October 20, 1930, a cold fall day. He traveled into the city by car from Elmira via Batavia, pulling up at the Lafayette Hotel at a quarter past five in the late afternoon. The governor looked trim and dapper. After a rest in his room FDR was the guest of honor at a dinner given by the local Democratic organization in the Mahogany Room of the hotel. He was given a rousing standing ovation as he took his place at the main table. In attendance were the other Democratic candidates for the top state offices on the November ballot. The room was filled with scores of party officials. After dinner, each person passed by the governor's table and shook hands with him and the other candidates. The main event of the day was a campaign rally at Elmwood Music Hall. It got under way at 8:30 at night with preliminary speeches and introductions of various local candidates. Most of the evening's activities were broadcast live locally on radio.

At 9:45 Governor Roosevelt entered the hall behind a police escort, on the arm of his personal bodyguard. He was given a standing ovation from the crowd of 2,500 as he got on stage and took a seat. Once he was introduced, the governor launched into a scathing indictment of the Republican Party for its alleged failed record on the economy.

Roosevelt all but ignored his Republican gubernatorial opponent in favor of attacking the national administration of President Herbert Hoover, although he did mention important local issues. Using his typical charismatic and energetic speaking style, the governor, in the midst of a partisan political rally excoriating Republicans and urging the election of Democrats, amazingly disavowed partisanship. "This is not the time to inject party and politics or campaign propaganda into the situation in any shape, manner or form," he claimed.[9]

FDR's speech lasted about forty-five minutes and ended at 11 p.m. He was driven back to the Lafayette Hotel where he spent the night. He left Buffalo at ten o'clock the next morning. His little auto caravan headed to Batavia, Geneseo and Rochester.

On to the White House for Roosevelt

Governor Roosevelt was reelected and by 1932 he was the most popular politician in America. He easily won the Democratic nomination for president of the United States that summer. Breaking with precedent, he planned to accept his party's nomination in person at the national convention that had just chosen him. In order to do so, he had to travel from the state capital in Albany to the convention site in Chicago in less than twenty-four hours. Though this could have been accomplished by special express train, FDR chose to fly.

Airline service was in its infancy in 1932. The governor's airplane was typical for passenger travel of the time. It was a Ford Tri-motor fifteen passenger ship, noisy, cramped and small, though huge for its era. It was supplied by American Airways, a predecessor company of today's American Airlines. The governor's flight was not non-stop. The plane had to land for refueling in Buffalo and Cleveland. And so it was that the plane landed at Buffalo Municipal Airport (now Buffalo Niagara International Airport) in Cheektowaga at 11:05 a.m. on Saturday, July 2, 1932.

It had been previously announced that the plane would be refueling in Cheektowaga, so a contingent of a thousand supporters had gathered behind a fence near the expected refueling spot at the American Airways hangar. It was a pleasant, somewhat breezy day as the plane touched down on schedule. A shout went up from the crowd as the plane taxied up to the hangar. Mrs. Roosevelt emerged first and was greeted by a group of local politicians. She and the other passengers accompanying the governor strolled into the hangar's office for a snack of coffee and sandwiches.

Much to the dismay of the assembled crowd, Governor Roosevelt remained aboard the plane. Ostensibly, the reason was that he was working on his nomination acceptance speech. But the real reason was probably the great time and effort that he would have spent getting up for a few minutes, given the fact that he did not have use of his legs.

A few politicians, friends and newspapermen were allowed to board the airplane for a few minutes to talk to the governor. He was asked about his acceptance speech and his potential vice presidential running mate. He expressed his regret about his inability to attend Buffalo's centennial festivities the day before, which included the unveiling of the Fillmore and Cleveland statues at City Hall. "But of course, you understand why I couldn't be here," he said with a smile.[10]

He also voiced his appreciation for the support he received from Buffalo for the presidential nomination. He said he would be back in the summer, but that turned out to be October. No news about a vice president. After about thirty-five minutes, the passengers all back on board, the plane taxied away and took off for Cleveland. The publicity surrounding FDR's flight was considered to be a big boost for the airline passenger business in general, and for American Airways in particular.

The Roosevelt for President campaign was in full swing when the governor rode into Buffalo for his only 1932 campaign stop in the Queen City. His train rolled into the Central Terminal at 5:30 p.m. on Tuesday, October 18. His large group of family, friends and aides was greeted by party officials and they piled into several Lincoln limousines. They were driven down Broadway "between banks of red fire" to Main Street, to North, then down Delaware to the Statler Hotel on Niagara Square.[11] He was treated to a sumptuous dinner there.

After resting and schmoozing with local Democrats, Roosevelt and his entourage were taken to Elmwood Music Hall. Already filled to capacity by 7:30 for the scheduled eight o'clock start of the rally, it was standing room only as the standees lined the side aisles and rear of the auditorium. Preliminary speeches were made. Governor Roosevelt entered the hall at nine o'clock, steadied by the arm of his son James. The crowd unleashed a tremendous standing cheer as the governor was helped to the flag draped rostrum on the stage, which was filled with 250 seated VIPs. The band had burst out with "Anchors Aweigh," supposedly Roosevelt's favorite song. The candidate was dressed in a double-breasted slate blue suit with white shirt and blue tie.

The governor launched into his speech in typical FDR style. But rather then talk about national issues, he confined himself to state issues, and stumped for the Democratic gubernatorial candidate, his Lieutenant Governor Herbert Lehman. He expressed his admiration for Buffalo in his opening lines. "Mr. Chairman, and my old friends of Buffalo and Erie County, and the western part of my state: The last time I was here in waking hours was on a certain second of July when I entered Buffalo from the air on my way to Chicago, and I shall never forget either that splendid flying field of yours out there, or that devoted group of my old friends of Buffalo who came to wish me godspeed on the rest of a very bumpy journey."[12]

Roosevelt concentrated on state fiscal concerns such as bond issues, spending and the budget, and state debt. While touting the attributes of Democratic gubernatorial candidate Lehman and defending his own record as governor, he criticized the proposals of the Republican nominee, William J. Donovan. Yet he seemed to go easier on Donovan in Buffalo than he had in other parts of the state. It was quite probable that he lightened up on Mr. Donovan because the Republican was from Buffalo, and he did not want to risk raising the ire of Buffalonians with too sharp an attack on one of their most respected fellow citizens.[13]

As to why Roosevelt concentrated on state issues rather than his own national campaign, it is probably because he sensed an easy win in the presidential contest in New York State, and so could afford the luxury of sidetracking into purely state politics.

By midnight Governor Roosevelt and his party were back at the Central Terminal where they boarded their train. After a few minutes, it pulled out, headed for Pittsburgh.

Franklin D. Roosevelt's first visit to Buffalo as president of the United States less than spectacular. Very few people knew about it and he himself probably never remembered it because he was asleep. The president was traveling westward by rail across New York State from his Hyde Park home, on his way to Chicago to address the American Legion convention.

The special train carrying FDR rolled into the Central Terminal at 12:30 a.m. on Monday, October 2, 1933. He was asleep in his Pullman car, having retired for the night a couple of hours before, near Syracuse. Railroad employees checked and serviced the train during its stop, which lasted only a few minutes. A group of railroad policemen, on board since Hyde Park, was relieved by a fresh squad.

The arrival of the presidential train had been kept strictly secret. Only the railroad police, a few station officials and employees, and some reporters were aware of it. No one was allowed to disturb the president. People at the station went about their business as usual, waiting for trains or alighting from them, unaware of the important visitor just a few tracks away. A few Secret Service men moved discreetly among them. In short order, its servicing complete, the presidential special was on its way to the Windy City.

President Roosevelt visited the Chautauqua Institution on Friday, August 14, 1936. He arrived by train at Mayville at 7:30 p.m. where he was greeted not only by residents and local officials, but by a large group of Erie County politicians, including Buffalo Mayor George T. Zimmerman. The president was transported by automobile the four miles to Chautauqua, the route lined with cheering spectators, many of their homes decorated with flags.

The reason for FDR's trip was to deliver an address on foreign relations and the deteriorating situation confronting world peace, his famous "I Hate War" speech. He took to the stage at the Chautauqua amphitheater upon his arrival to a rousing welcome of applause, waving handkerchiefs and "Hail To The Chief." Acknowledging the enthusiastic greeting in the filled venue, he began his address. Already running for reelection, it might have been construed as a campaign speech, but the content seemed to be decidedly apolitical.

Roosevelt used the first several minutes of the speech praising the good relations between the United States, Canada and Latin America, the so-called "Good Neighbor Policy." He chided nations that violated international agreements, saying that there should be "scrupulous respect for the pledged word." Concerning the attitude of the United States toward the world, he declared, "We are not isolationists except insofar as we seek to isolate ourselves from war. Yet we must remember that so long as war exists on earth there will be some danger that even the nation which most ardently desires peace may be drawn into war. I have seen war. I have seen war on land and sea…I hate war."[14]

The president pledged that American neutrality would continue, despite ongoing troubles on other continents. He then proceeded to blame American business for exacerbating the danger of war by seeking to profit from it. He closed with a plea to other nations for peaceful relations with America. After the speech, Roosevelt held an hour-long reception at a private home. He was then driven back to his train in Mayville. It left around midnight for Binghamton.

President Roosevelt's next visit to Buffalo came in the midst of his 1936 reelection campaign. He was accompanied by his wife. Shortly before 11 p.m. on Friday, October 16 FDR's twelve car train rolled through the Central Terminal from Cleveland, but did not stop at the station. It proceeded slowly through the depot and came to a halt about a half mile down on a side track near the south end of Person Street, where it remained overnight.

The president retired for the night in his special rail car shortly after the train was parked. Railroad police and Secret Service agents were on guard around it throughout the night and would let no one near it. The train pulled out of the Buffalo yards the next morning at 7:30 and headed for Niagara Falls. Ninety minutes later President Roosevelt emerged from his private car in the Cataract City.

The thousands of persons gathered near the station gave him a hearty greeting and he waved and smiled broadly in response. Formally welcomed by a reception committee, the president was surrounded by state troopers and Secret Service men. President and Mrs. Roosevelt and Democratic Party national chairman James A. Farley got into an open automobile. Led by a detail of state police, a twenty-six-car procession rode over a six mile route lined with cheering spectators, with soldiers stationed at key points along the way. An early morning rain had stopped, but had left things in a damp, soggy state. The destination of the president was the newly built Hyde Park Stadium, which he was scheduled to formally dedicate.[15] As the car entered the grounds a band played the national anthem. All 4,000 seats in the facility were filled with another thousand or more people standing on the soaking wet grass of the field.

The president's car stopped directly in front of the spectator stands. A microphone was brought to him, and he delivered a short dedicatory address from his seat in the car, which was amplified through the stadium's public address system. He lauded the value of such a project as Hyde Park Stadium, which was built with the federal funds provided by one of FDR's pet agencies, the Works Progress Administration (WPA). He also praised the peaceful Niagara international border, which brought great applause from the crowd.

With the ceremony concluded in just a few minutes, the presidential motorcade rode out of the stadium, its ultimate destination being downtown Buffalo. A drizzle began to fall and the president, in the open car, firmed up his hat and topcoat against the elements. The cars crossed the North Grand Island Bridge and stopped at the Civilian Conservation Corps camp at Buckhorn Island where a Buffalo reception committee joined the procession.

Over the South Grand Island Bridge and onto Sheridan Drive the motorcade came, crowds of spectators cheering from the side of the road as the president smiled and waved, though the rainy weather kept down the numbers. The long line of cars turned southward onto Delaware Avenue, took a short detour through Delaware Park, and passed by the Ansley Wilcox mansion where the president's cousin had been sworn in as the twenty-sixth president. FDR arrived at Niagara Square at 10:45 a.m. to dedicate the new nine story federal court house.[16]

By now the rain had stopped. The piercing sirens of a fire boat in the Buffalo harbor heralded the president's arrival. The square was packed with spectators on this Saturday morning, a day off for many workers. Stopping at the east end of the square at Court Street, Roosevelt was helped out of his car and onto a temporary stage that had been erected in front of the McKinley Monument. It faced east, with the new federal building at the southeast corner of Court and the square, directly across Court Street from the state office building for which Governor Roosevelt had laid the cornerstone a few years earlier.

The crowd was estimated at 30,000 and it filled much of the east end of the square and extended out to radial streets, especially Court. Yet more gazed down from the windows of nearby buildings. The president sat on a chair once used by Mayor Grover Cleveland, next to Mrs. Roosevelt. About a hundred other officials were seated behind them. Police were in evidence everywhere. Plainclothesmen and Secret Service agents were out in force. Near the stage was a contingent of Coast Guardsmen, a thousand uniformed mailmen, naval militiamen, an army band playing lively tunes, and veterans' groups.

The president's speech was carried over local radio. After brief introductory remarks, he was introduced and the crowd loudly cheered. His address lasted perhaps fifteen minutes. He praised the government programs that made the building of such structures as the new court house possible, saying they brought money into the hands of workers and into local communities, helping to assuage the effects of the Depression. In closing, Roosevelt said, "I am always glad to get back to my state. I wish the city of Buffalo and for these communities in the western end of our state every success. May we grow not only in material wealth, but also in good citizenship for which we all strive. I hope to come back here many times in the days to come and perhaps there will be another building to dedicate."[17]

Immediately after the dedication the president and Mrs. Roosevelt and their party reentered their automobiles and were driven up Court Street and east on Broadway. The curbs were thinly lined with spectators until the Broadway-Fillmore area, where they grew thicker. Several hundred soldiers and police lined the entire route. Turning down Lindbergh Drive (now Memorial Drive) to Curtiss Street, the president and his contingent entered their waiting train at the Curtiss Street siding.

A few thousand people were crowded around. President Roosevelt stood on the rear platform of the train waving his hat and smiling as the train pulled out at 11:30 for Rochester. After a few minutes, he went inside and Mrs. Roosevelt stepped out as the train disappeared into the distance.

Franklin D. Roosevelt's final visit to the Buffalo area came during his winning reelection campaign for an unprecedented third term as president of the United States. At 11:10 on the morning of Saturday, November 2, 1940, just three days before election day, the twelve-car presidential special arrived at the Central Terminal. A team of men immediately rushed to service the train. The engines were changed and the train was switched to the Niagara Falls track. By noon it reached the Woodward Avenue crossing in the Town of Tonawanda, where FDR alighted and was applauded by a few thousand onlookers and welcomed by local Democrats. The president entered a waiting open-top automobile. His train returned to the Central Terminal for further maintenance and servicing. Led by a Secret Service car, the president's vehicle and others headed for the Bell Aircraft plant about two miles south, at 2050 Elmwood Avenue in Buffalo.[18]

Cheering crowds lined the sidewalks along the way. A morning rain had stopped, but the sky was overcast. The presidential motorcade of twenty cars reached the plant and drove through it, riding up and down the aisles as workers continued busily working on the assembly line, building aircraft for the national defense, as well as for Britain through the Lend-Lease program. The entire visit lasted twenty minutes.

The motorcade was out the entrance on its way to its next stop, an inspection tour of the Curtiss Aeroplane plant at 2303 Kenmore Avenue at the corner of Vulcan in the Town of Tonawanda, two miles to the northwest.[19] As at the Bell plant, the motorcade entered the interior of the huge eighteen-acre factory, up one aisle and down another. The president was clearly impressed by the operation, the workers displaying their efficiency as hardly a head turned to glance at the distinguished visitor.

Leaving the plant after a few minutes, the president's car stopped at the guardhouse at the main gate where he took a microphone and gave a short pep talk over the plant's loudspeakers. "God bless you...and hurry up the work," he said.[20]

Then the motorcade took off southward toward downtown. Around ten o'clock in the morning people had begun to gather in Niagara Square for a scheduled address by the president. Traffic was cut off and several hundred policemen and the Secret Service were on duty in the area. By noon several bands had assembled and kept the crowd entertained with various tunes. A huge American flag was draped over the City Hall entrance and the Democratic Party distributed thousands of small flags to the spectators, estimated at 30,000 total.

Around one o'clock the president's motorcade was spotted coming down Niagara Street and a great cheer built as the Roosevelts' car turned into Niagara Square in front of City Hall and drove up on the sidewalk in front of the entrance. After a brief introduction by Mayor Thomas L. Holling, a microphone was handed to the president so that he did not have to leave the automobile.

He gave a brief talk lasting but several minutes. In it he praised united labor, pledged to do more for it, and commented on the peaceful Niagara border with Canada. He noted America's intense preparations for defense while working to avoid war. He said,"[O]ur eyes are on the goal of peace and this administration will continue an eight year record of peace in the next four years."[21]

Immediately after the speech the motorcade was off again. Motorcycle police led thirty cars, the first of which was occupied by Secret Service agents, and followed by President's Roosevelt's car, with Mayor Holling seated next to him. The line of cars swung out of the square south on Delaware, east on Eagle Street then north on Main and through Lafayette Square to Broadway. The entire way was lined with spectators, particularly at the Soldiers and Sailors Monument at Lafayette Square. The cars zipped eastward on Broadway with both sides of the street lined with onlookers. Reaching Broadway-Fillmore, where the motorcade turned south, a huge crowd cheered the president.

Down Fillmore to Smith to South Park to Ridge Road the motorcade progressed. At one point, President Roosevelt remarked, "So this is the famed South Buffalo." Mayor Holling simply replied, "It is." Now at the Buffalo-Lackawanna city line, the crowds lining the route were thicker in some spots than others, but all happily cheered the president. Finally reaching Route 5, the motorcade turned into Gate No. 1 of the

Bethlehem Steel complex. Hurriedly shown through the huge place by the general manager, the presidential motorcade departed through Gate No. 4 to Lake Avenue eastward into Blasdell.

Less than a mile later the cars stopped at the Lake Avenue railroad crossing where the president's train was waiting. President Roosevelt and his traveling companions alighted from their automobiles. An American Legion veterans' group formed a guard of honor. The president said his goodbyes, waved his hat to the crowd and was helped onto the rear platform of his special car. In very short order the train pulled away, at about two o'clock. His whirlwind visit to the Buffalo area had lasted less than three hours.

Robert H. Jackson

One of President Roosevelt's significant appointees was Robert H. Jackson. Jackson was born in Pennsylvania but was raised in Frewsburg, New York near Jamestown in the Southern Tier. Though he did not graduate from college, he became a member of the bar. He entered federal service in 1934 with the Bureau of Internal Revenue, was appointed solicitor general by the president, then attorney general, a post in which he served from 1940 until 1941 when he was appointed an associate justice of the Supreme Court. One of his law clerks was the future Chief Justice William Rehnquist, who in turn had as one of his clerks the future Chief Justice John Roberts, who was born in Buffalo. President Harry S. Truman appointed Jackson to be part of the U.S. team at the Nuremberg War Crimes Trial of Nazi leaders in 1945. Jackson was the chief American prosecutor while retaining his Supreme Court seat.

In 1917 Jackson had worked for the Buffalo law firm Penney, Killeen and Nye in the Ellicott Square Building. He lived in an apartment at 49 Johnson Park and supposedly walked to work past the site of the federal courthouse on Niagara Square that now bears his name.

By the following year, he was in Jamestown serving as corporation counsel, and continued to live there for many years before going to Washington. Jackson died in 1954 and is buried in Frewsburg. The Robert H. Jackson Center in Jamestown honors his memory and accomplishments.

Harry S Truman's Forays Into Buffalo

President Roosevelt's sudden death on April 12, 1945 thrust Vice President Harry S Truman into the White House. Truman had been a rather obscure U.S. senator from Missouri before he became chairman of a special Senate committee in 1941 formed to investigate defense contract fraud. This raised his profile such that the Democrats chose him as their vice presidential nominee in 1944, despite the fact that Roosevelt and Truman were not particularly enamored of each other.

Truman had a connection to Buffalo going back to the 1920s, according to his own recollections. He had been elected to a judgeship in Jackson County, Missouri in 1922 with the help of Democratic Party operative T. J. Pendergast, who was suspected of being a crooked politician who used illegal means to elect men whom he could control for his own personal gain. Though accused of being a lackey of Pendergast, Truman always denied this and never was seriously accused of doing anything illegal. Awarding government contracts was one of Judge Truman's duties, and he explained in a 1952 memorandum how he went about deciding how to award a building contract authorized by a bond issue in 1928:

> The county had a bond issue carried by a three fourths majority instead of the required two thirds. I appointed the engineers and the local architects. Then I took my private car – not a county one – and drove to Shreveport, Denver, Houston, Racine, Milwaukee, Buffalo, Brooklyn, Lincoln, Baton Rouge and several other places and looked at the new public buildings, met the architects and contractors, inspected the buildings and finally decided to employ the architect of the Court House at Shreveport as consulting architect for our county building.[22]

Apparently, Truman was not in Buffalo again until after he became vice president. He came to the Queen City for a two day visit in the spring of 1945. His train arrived at the Central Terminal on Saturday, April 7 at 8 p.m., where he was met by a contingent of local Democrats.

He was taken to the Statler Hotel where he enjoyed a breakfast.

Mr. Truman held a brief press conference with reporters, and then attended a meeting of Democratic Party leaders. He was driven to the Buffalo Hotel where he was guest of honor at a luncheon.[23] Afterward, the vice president went back to the Statler where he rested in his room for the remainder of the afternoon. At 5 p.m. he attended a dinner sponsored by the Royal Order of Jesters Buffalo chapter at the Buffalo Athletic Club at 69 Delaware Avenue. The Jesters is the fraternal organization affiliated with the Masons, and Truman was a member of the Kansas City chapter.

That evening at the Statler the vice president was the featured speaker at the Grover Cleveland Dinner, an event held to honor the esteemed Democrat, Buffalo mayor, New York governor and U.S. president. After the meal, brief talks were made by Buffalo Mayor Joseph J. Kelly and a few other area Democrats. Truman's address began at around 10:30. It centered on the economy and returning World War II veterans. "You people of Buffalo, situated at the western gate of the Empire State, already have performed a gigantic task for America," he declared, referring to the area's defense industries. He stressed the importance of the hard work ahead needed for a smooth transition from a wartime to a peacetime economy, and emphasized the debt everyone owed to returning veterans. He predicted no surge in unemployment, because those veterans would take the places of others who would willingly leave the workforce, especially women, and boys going back to school.

Vice President Truman stayed overnight at the Statler. On Sunday morning he attended services at the Church of the Good Shepherd on Jewett Parkway, a short distance from the Darwin Martin House. He was then the guest of Buffalo businessman Walter A. Yates for lunch at Mr. Yates' house on Chapin Parkway. In the afternoon Truman took a tour of the Bell Aircraft factory in Wheatfield where he viewed test flights of a helicopter and jet airplanes. He then had dinner at the Country Club of Buffalo in Williamsville. That night he was back at the Central Terminal and left for Washington. Four days later he became president of the United States after the sudden death of Franklin D. Roosevelt.

Harry S Truman's first visit to Buffalo as president came at the tail end of a three day rail trip through Canada, on Friday, June 13, 1947. His last stop in Canada was Niagara Falls, Ontario that morning. He left his train and was driven to the Table Rock area near the brink of the Horseshoe Falls where he observed the thundering water for several minutes.

Back aboard his train, he headed back to the United States, most likely crossing the International Railroad Bridge into Buffalo. The eleven-car train rolled slowly past the Terrace west of Main Street where hundreds of flag-waving school children and others greeted him. The president waved to them as he stood on the rear platform of his car.

The train arrived at the Central Terminal at 11 a.m. where it stopped for servicing and a track switch. Workers washed windows, checked the brakes and undercarriages and loaded tons of ice aboard for the air conditioning system. President Truman came out on the rear platform and welcomed State Democratic Chairman Paul E. Fitzpatrick and his daughter aboard. The two men chatted amiably for fifteen minutes on the platform as the daughter went inside to chat with Mrs. Truman. The president also bantered with reporters from his perch.

Security was tight. Dozens of plainclothes and uniformed police kept onlookers back. The Secret Service, of course, was present. All rail traffic through the terminal had been halted during the president's layover. Five Royal Canadian Mounted Policemen in full dress uniform shook hands with the president and he thanked them. They had been part of his security detail in Canada. At 11:35 the servicing was complete and the presidential train was switched to another track for its journey back to Washington, D.C.

President Truman's second visit to Buffalo was a more formal affair and came during his presidential election campaign of 1948. He arrived in the city on Friday, October 8, 1948 at the end of a day-long whistlestop campaign run, making twelve stops between Albany and Buffalo. Mr. Truman's sixteen car train rolled into the Central Terminal at 8:20 p.m. An estimated 5,000 people were at the station to greet President and Mrs. Truman. Most of them were kept behind a roped-off area.

Several local Democratic Party leaders boarded the train and posed for a few photographs with Truman. After a few minutes a loud cheer rang out through the depot as the first couple stepped out of the train onto the station platform. A color guard and drum and bugle corps led the way for the Trumans and other officials through the concourse and outside to waiting automobiles with the cheering of the crowd adding to a cacophony of noises. The president acknowledged the enthusiastic welcome with waves of his gray Fedora.

Police with sirens blaring led a motorcade of fifty cars down Paderewski Drive to Fillmore, then west on Broadway to Court Street to the Statler Hotel on Niagara Square. About 10,000 people watched the cars whiz along the route, most of them in the Broadway-Fillmore neighborhood.

A thousand more spectators were gathered at the hotel entrance as President and Mrs. Truman emerged from their car and were escorted inside, where the chief executive gave a brief talk to a large group of local politicians and labor leaders in the Georgian Room. He briefly discussed his campaign tour and expressed his feeling of optimism about the race against his Republican opponent, New York Governor Thomas Dewey.

In a lighthearted vein, he excused himself from shaking hands, saying he had shaken so many hands in the previous days, about 40,000. "I want you to go along with me and decide that you've already shaken hands with me. It doesn't do any good to elect a man president if you're going to pull him apart before he gets there," he joked.[24]

After the brief meeting, Truman and his party left the hotel and were driven to the Eagles Auditorium at the southwest corner of Pearl and Tupper Streets for a campaign rally.[25] It had originally been scheduled for outdoors at the old Offerman Stadium at Michigan Avenue at East Ferry but was moved because of rainy weather, which had dogged the Truman train all the way across the state, but had let up in Buffalo.[26]

When the president arrived at the auditorium it was surrounded by a crowd estimated at 10,000 persons. They were held back by police barricades as the Trumans entered the theater, which was packed to the rafters with 2,000 raucous partisans who cheered at the top of their lungs. Once on stage, the president was introduced by Democratic County Chairman William B. Mahoney. Truman laid into the Republicans and his opponent, Governor Dewey. He was in an energetic and jocular mood, responding to the enthusiasm of the audience and chuckling at many of their remarks and shouts. He lambasted the "do-nothing Congress," controlled by the Republicans.

He briefly dwelt on the topic of war and peace, saying that he would rather have world peace than be president. But the bulk of his speech concerned the economy. He accused the Republicans of supporting policies that would fail to control inflation, favoring special interests, dallying on the housing shortage, and said they were putting the country at risk of another depression. At the conclusion of the rally President and Mrs. Truman were escorted back to their limousines and driven directly back to the Central Terminal. The president thanked local officials for their splendid job and climbed aboard his train, which departed at 11 p.m. for Washington.

The protection afforded to President Truman was typical of presidential visits to Buffalo and other cities in the first half of the twentieth century. The main mode of transportation for our chief executives at that time was by rail. It was the most comfortable and efficient way for them to travel around the country. The rail network reached into every corner of the United States.

Security started with the president's personal rail car, which by Truman's time was heavily armored. An experienced and trustworthy crew was chosen to man the train and all systems were meticulously checked before, during and after the journey. Of course, the Secret Service was always aboard. Along the route of travel, all railroad crossings, overpasses and underpasses were under the surveillance of either the Secret Service, local police or the railroad police. All rail traffic was stopped for several minutes in each direction before and after the president's train passed any given point. A pilot engine typically preceded his train by a few minutes to make sure the tracks were clear.

When the special train arrived at a station like the Central Terminal, unauthorized persons were kept away from it and a special detail of police guarded it for as long as it remained there. If the president alighted from the train, he was surrounded by Secret Service agents and local and railroad police handled crowd control as he made his way through the station. Harry S. Truman's last visit to Buffalo as president of the United States occurred in the fall of 1952. He was retiring from the presidency but was on a coast to coast whistlestop campaign for the Democrats' nominee as the next president, Adlai E. Stevenson of Illinois.

The president's train pulled into the Central Terminal on October 9, 1952 at seven o'clock in the evening. About 3,000 supporters cheered his arrival. A group of 200 local Democrats was on hand to formally welcome him. But only one, Herbert Lehman, went aboard to escort Mr. Truman out of his car.

The smiling president was followed by his daughter, twenty-eight-year-old Margaret, to whom the local newspapers seemed to pay much attention. The first lady was not making this trip. President Truman entered the rear seat of a convertible, top down, and led by screaming police sirens, the long motorcade proceeded down Paderewski to Fillmore to Broadway to the Statler Hotel. Red torches were displayed at Broadway and Fillmore, Lafayette Square and the McKinley Monument. Firecrackers exploded. Tens of thousands of people lined the curbs to see the cars pass by and Secret Service agents trotted alongside the presidential limo.

A brass band greeted the president as he stepped out of his car at the Delaware Avenue entrance of the Statler. He and his daughter dined privately, after which they rested for a while. At nine o'clock Truman emerged from an elevator to the applause of a crowd gathered in the lobby. Mixed in with the cheers seemed to be a few boos and "I like Ike" shouts. "I like Ike" was a popular campaign slogan used by the campaign of Governor Stevenson's Republican opponent for the presidency, General Dwight D. Eisenhower.

The president climbed into a car and was whisked away to Memorial Auditorium for a scheduled Stevenson rally.[27] When he and his daughter took places onstage, already filled with politicians, he received a stirring welcome from the audience. To the disappointment of local Democrats, only about 5,000 persons were in attendance in the facility, which could have held perhaps three times as many at the time. But that was made up by the enthusiasm of the crowd in the flag-draped "Aud."

Introduced by Democratic County Chairman Mahoney, President Truman got a loud ovation. He immediately tore into the Republicans and Eisenhower. Interrupted many times by applause and shouts such as

"Give 'em hell, Harry!" he warned that the election of a military general would threaten the Bill of Rights. He accused Eisenhower of encouraging Eastern Europeans to sacrifice themselves in a futile uprising against their communist masters, yet defended the expenditure of American lives in the Korean War.

Truman warned to be careful that constitutional rights were not violated in the hunt for communists in the United States. He railed against restrictive immigration policies and racial and ethnic discrimination. Governor Stevenson, he maintained, would defend civil rights and civil liberties and was the best man for the job of president of the United States.

Immediately after his speech, the president and Miss Truman were driven back to the Statler. After a brief rest, Mr. Truman appeared in the hotel's Georgian Room for a reception with area labor leaders. The Trumans stayed at the hotel overnight and were driven back to the Central Terminal the next morning. At 10 a.m. their train headed east as the president readied himself for another day of campaigning.

Buffalo Liked Ike, Too

Two weeks after President Truman's campaign stop in Buffalo on behalf of Adlai Stevenson, Republican presidential nominee Dwight D. Eisenhower came to town to make his own appeal for votes. His appearance was just one day after Stevenson himself had appeared in Buffalo. All three men spoke at Memorial Auditorium.

Just before 4:30 p.m. on Thursday, October 23, 1952 Ike's eighteen-car campaign train reached the Central Terminal. Traveling with him was his wife Mamie. Booming cannons and firecrackers signaled his arrival.

The 5,000 persons crowded in and around the depot went wild when the general stepped off the rear platform of his car. He was preceded by a group of Republican dignitaries. They included Buffalo Mayor Joseph Mruk, New York Senator Irving Ives and New York Governor Thomas Dewey, the GOP's unsuccessful candidate for the presidency in 1944 and 1948.

Eisenhower was quickly escorted through the cheering throng and was seated in a light blue convertible that led a fifteen car motorcade down Broadway to Jefferson then William to the Statler Hotel. All along the route the smiling candidate was applauded by onlookers who came out to see him. Ike entered the Statler through the Delaware Avenue entrance, received by a crowd of more than a thousand supporters in the lobby who let loose a deafening roar. "I Like Ike" buttons were everywhere. The cheers were acknowledged with a smile and a wave. Eisenhower, Ives and Dewey entered an elevator for an upstairs suite.

The general returned downstairs for a reception held in his honor by the Citizens for Eisenhower Committee, met with various ethnic groups and then returned to his suite for a short rest before delivering his campaign speech at the auditorium. General Eisenhower arrived at the auditorium with his wife, who had left the train separately, a little past 9 p.m. They appeared on stage during a preliminary speech by Governor Dewey and the crowd went wild. Fully 20,000 supporters were packed into the arena, with every nook and cranny occupied. It was called a record turnout for any event at that venue.

Grinning and waving, Ike looked happy and confident. Mayor Mruk introduced him and after the cheering died down the general launched into his speech. He attacked the Truman administration and said that America would get more of the same with Stevenson. He brought up the Korean War quagmire, and countered Democrats' claims of discrimination on the part of the GOP, accusing the opposition of running a low-level campaign, "setting group against group, special interest against special interest, section against section."[28]

He attacked bossism and corruption in Washington, promising to launch a crusade to clean things up, which would start a new era of peace and prosperity. Eisenhower also called for the election of local GOP Congressional candidates, including William E. Miller of Niagara County, who would one day be the Republicans' vice presidential nominee.

Following the rally Ike and his party were quickly driven back to the Central Terminal. They re-boarded their train and in short order it pulled out for Detroit and yet another day of campaign stops.

Former President Hoover Dedicates a School

A former president had not visited the Buffalo area in thirty-four years when Herbert Hoover came to dedicate the Herbert C. Hoover School in the Town of Tonawanda on Thorncliff Road on October 10, 1951. It is now known as Herbert Hoover Middle School.

Mr. Hoover was first the guest of honor at a luncheon at the Buffalo Club on Delaware Avenue. His speech at the school's dedication ceremony began around 2:30 p.m. The seventy-seven-year-old former president looked healthy and sounded strong as he delivered his talk outdoors before the new school's auditorium. In it, he warned against federal interference in the education of American children. "If we surrender the welfare of our children and the independence of our higher education to a Washington bureaucracy, we abandon the first obligation of parenthood, the foundation of local government and we endanger an essential defense of freedom," said Hoover.[29]

He spoke on a breezy and somewhat cool day before about 5,000 students and 2,000 adults. He also gave an interview to a newspaper in his Statler Hotel suite, and it is assumed he spent the night there.

A New Generation of Politicians

By the 1950s a generational change was beginning to take place in American society and politics. That demographic group often called the Greatest Generation, which had come of age during the Great Depression and sacrificed for us in World War II, was starting to assert itself.

In national politics its rising stars were people such as John F. Kennedy, Richard Nixon, Barry Goldwater and Hubert Humphrey. These were men born in the twentieth century, in contrast to those then holding the reins of power. When the White House changed hands in 1953, outgoing President Truman was sixty-eight years old. Incoming President Eisenhower was sixty-two. By comparison, Kennedy and Nixon were thirty-five and forty years old, respectively. Both of these future presidents would visit Buffalo more than once in the coming years.

John F. Kennedy's First Visit

Newly elected Senator John F. Kennedy of Massachusetts came to the Queen City on April 30, 1953 to deliver an address at the Grover Cleveland Dinner in the Statler Hotel. The event was not given much press coverage, but noted that Senator Kennedy was a rising star in the Democratic Party due to his upset election victory in the decidedly Republican year of 1952.

Local Democrats who spoke dwelt on corruption in the Republican City Hall. Senator Kennedy, who was billed as the principal speaker, warned that on the national scene, Democrats needed to be vigilant to make sure that the Eisenhower administration did not go too far in cutting defense spending so as to endanger the security of the United States.

It is not known if Kennedy stayed overnight in Buffalo.

Richard Nixon's First Visit

Richard Nixon's first visit to Buffalo came as he was running for reelection as vice president of the United States. He arrived at the Buffalo airport in Cheektowaga at 7:10 p.m. on Tuesday, October 16, 1956 in the chartered airplane that was carrying him around the country in the campaign.[30]

Several hundred persons welcomed Nixon and his wife at the airport and he was quickly driven to the Hotel Statler in a small motorcade led by motorcycle police, probably straight down Genesee Street.

In short order Vice President and Mrs. Nixon were driven to Memorial Auditorium, arriving there at 9:30 to an enthusiastic welcome from an audience of 11,000. Already a controversial politician who often seemed cold, distant and disingenuous, he appeared to have no problem connecting with the assembled supporters.

In his talk, he centered his attack on the Democratic presidential nominee, once again Adlai Stevenson, by asserting that Stevenson's proposals to stop atomic bomb testing and end the military draft would endanger American security, calling them policies of military weakness. Concerning domestic issues, Nixon said that "for the great majority of Americans, the Eisenhower years have been the greatest four years in our lives."[31]

Given a rousing ovation at the conclusion of his talk, he and Mrs.

Nixon were driven back to the hotel, where they spent the night. The next morning, they departed on their plane for Rochester.

John F. Kennedy's Second Visit

John F. Kennedy was back in Buffalo on May 21, 1959, once again as the principal speaker at the Grover Cleveland Dinner at the Statler Hilton Hotel.[32] Now, six years after his first visit, the young senator was regarded as a serious contender for the Democratic nomination for president in 1960.

Senator Kennedy and his wife were greeted by some 200 supporters at the Buffalo airport shortly after 1 p.m. The official welcoming group included Buffalo Mayor Frank A. Sedita. Kennedy discussed current affairs with area leaders, gave interviews for local television, and visited the *Buffalo Courier Express* where he conferred with the daily's editor and publisher. He also talked to the Frontier Press Club, an informal organization of Buffalo area journalists.

Kennedy said that he was not yet a candidate for the presidency and that he would probably not make a decision until the following year. But he described his visit as a political one. At his talk at the dinner before a thousand attendees, the senator said the future of the nation relied on its youth and new ideas. He talked at length about what was wrong with both the domestic and foreign policies of the Eisenhower administration. He also pointed out that he had learned that Grover Cleveland had been president in his early forties, obviously drawing a comparison to his forty-one-year-old self.[33] Kennedy was given a standing ovation at the conclusion of his address.

Thirty-five Democratic county leaders from all over New York were present at the dinner, and Kennedy had breakfast with them the next morning. He and his wife stayed overnight at the Statler Hilton.

Richard Nixon's Second Visit

Vice President Richard Nixon, the presumptive Republican nominee for president in 1960, visited Buffalo twice that year. The first time was on

Wednesday, May 18, part of an effort to reach out to the electorate before formal campaigning would begin in September.

Vice President and Mrs. Nixon landed at the Buffalo airport in the late morning and a crowd of about a thousand supporters was there to greet them. They were taken to the Hotel Lafayette where hundreds of people waited outside the entrance to catch a glimpse of the couple as they arrived at 12:30.

A luncheon was served inside the hotel and the Nixons held a reception for the general public. It was estimated that as many as 10,000 people streamed into the packed ballroom, and the smiling Nixons shook hands with as many as they could. The size of the crowd and the enthusiasm shown far exceeded what was expected, so the Nixon team was very pleased. At 2:30 the vice president and his wife went to Memorial Auditorium where he spoke briefly to a convention of the African Methodist Episcopal Zion Church. In the late afternoon, Nixon held a press conference at the Statler Hilton Hotel in which he addressed the U2 spy plane incident, racial integration, and the upcoming presidential election.

Vice President Nixon's main event in Buffalo was an after-dinner speech to the National Sales Executives International convention at the hotel. He received a huge ovation from the 1,100 sales executives. In his talk, Nixon heavily criticized Soviet leader Nikita Khrushchev over the Berlin issue, the U2 incident, and for wrecking a summit meeting. He also touched on government spending. In a lighter vein he remarked, "I don't think any city can exceed Buffalo in hospitality. I understand they vote here, too."[34]

Vice President and Mrs. Nixon left Buffalo immediately after the address.

JFK Campaigns in Buffalo

Democrat John F. Kennedy, popularly referred to as JFK, and Republican Richard Nixon both had their sights set on the White House throughout the 1950s, and they secured their respective parties' nominations for the presidency in 1960, setting the stage for one of the closest and most exciting presidential elections in American history.

Each man campaigned in Buffalo that year in the general election; the first to do so was Senator Kennedy. An energetic, charismatic campaigner, the forty-three-year-old blitzed Western New York with several campaign stops in one day. Kennedy and his team descended upon Niagara Falls airport in three planes, including the senator's family-owned plane. It was Wednesday, September 28, 1960, just two days after the first historic Kennedy-Nixon debate.

This presidential campaign truly was a break from the past. Not only were two candidates from the new generation opposing each other, it was the first genuine national television campaign, what with the debates and heavy use of television advertising. For transportation, use of trains was gone, now replaced by air travel. This allowed Kennedy and Nixon to travel around the country much faster, so that they could include visits to more population centers in a shorter period of time. Modern campaigning had been born.

JFK was greeted at the Falls airport by a crowd of about 600 persons. Official greeters included Mayor Robert Wagner of New York and State Comptroller Arthur Levitt. Kennedy climbed into an open convertible and made a few remarks from it to the onlookers. He was driven to North Tonawanda in a ten-car motorcade where he gave a five-minute noontime speech to an outdoor rally of about 4,000 in front of the city hall. He emphasized that the Democratic Party was one of greater service to the people.

The motorcade continued on to the Bell Aerospace plant in Wheatfield where Kennedy gave a brief address to some 500 employees, answering questions about defense contracts and advocating for civil rights and medical care for the aged. He invoked the name of Grover Cleveland, quoting his adage, "What good is a man unless he stands for something?"[35]

"The next stop was the Treadway Inn in Niagara Falls for lunch with 250 party operatives.[36] An estimated 7,000 persons were surrounding the place when he arrived. JFK was presented the key to the city by the mayor. After the luncheon, he was driven to the brink of the American Falls for a brief look at nature's wonder, which he had never before seen in person. Then it was off to downtown Lockport where he stopped to give a short talk to a gathering of 4,000 in front of a bowling center. He told the crowd that the Democrats believed that government should help the people. "We believed it in the New Freedom of Woodrow Wilson, the New Deal of Franklin Roosevelt, and the Fair Deal of Harry Truman. And we believe it today as we stand on the New Frontier," he said.[37]

Kennedy's motorcade sped back to the Falls airport and he was flown to Rochester where he made a few appearances. He returned to the Niagara Frontier that night, his plane landing at the Buffalo airport at 8:30. About 2,000 people were gathered there to shout an enthusiastic welcome. He made a few remarks, then the motorcade was off to Kleinhans Music Hall via the Thruway.

The senator strode into the hall around nine o'clock. The audience was made up primarily of senior citizens, there to attend a dinner dance to celebrate the twenty-fifth anniversary of the Social Security Act. He was given a standing ovation by the 3,000 attendees. Naturally, he emphasized Democrats' efforts to pass a bill for medical care for the elderly. He called out his opponent Nixon, citing him as a leader of the opposition to such a program, and criticized Republicans for opposing "every effort to bring help to our senior citizens."[38]

His speech concluded, JFK was now off to deliver his highlight speech of the day at Memorial Auditorium. A jam-packed hall of 20,000 rabid supporters awaited him. Even outside many thousands more were anticipating his arrival. Shortly before ten o'clock Kennedy made his entrance from the rear of the auditorium directly opposite the stage and walked down the center aisle. A spotlight shone on him as he made his way to the front, protected by a phalanx of policemen. The crowd was now in an absolute frenzy, clapping, shouting, screaming, waving hands and placards, and jumping up and down.

The term "rock star" is one of the most overused phrases of the twenty-first century, but if any politician could ever be called a rock star, it was John F. Kennedy. Young, handsome, tanned and seemingly fit and full of energy, he was adored by young women and girls. Even young men could admire certain of his traits: he was witty, intelligent, a war hero, and someone closer to their age to whom they could relate. And he possessed that certain unteachable quality called charisma. People just wanted to literally reach out and touch him.

Confetti floated through the air and spotlight beams swept around the auditorium as the senator climbed on stage, joining a large group of politicians already assembled there.

After ten minutes, Buffalo Mayor Frank A. Sedita was able to start his introductory speech. Too long-winded for the crowd, the mayor was repeatedly interrupted by shouts for JFK. Finally, he relented, and Senator Kennedy took to the podium to another loud demonstration. He started out by saying, "I told them in Rochester their rally was the largest of the campaign. I'm sorry to have to amend it, but Buffalo just beat it."[39]

That set off another wild outburst. Kennedy then launched into his attack on the GOP and Richard Nixon. He accused the Republicans of opposing programs to help the elderly and to alleviate poverty. He hit back at Nixon for saying that he, Kennedy, was spreading "untruths," and asserted that the Republican Party was indifferent to progress.

JFK's speech lasted only twenty minutes and was completely unrehearsed, with no notes or text used. He appeared to be in fine form despite a head cold. When he was done, he quickly exited by a door to the rear of the stage, protected by police lest he be mobbed. His car reached the airport shortly before midnight, where his plane took off for yet another round of appearances elsewhere.

Richard Nixon Returns To Campaign

Richard Nixon returned to Buffalo on Monday, October 17, 1960, this time in full campaign mode as the Republican candidate for the presidency. Two and a half weeks after John F. Kennedy's visit, Nixon's airplane touched down at the Buffalo airport at 5 p.m. Just like Kennedy, his entourage was traveling in three planes.

A crowd of about 2,000, including a high school band, greeted the candidate, who was traveling with his wife Pat. They were officially welcomed by Governor Nelson Rockefeller and Senator Kenneth Keating. Vice President Nixon said a few words to the crowd, and then was driven away in a fifteen-car motorcade for his first stop, a rally at the Polish Union Hall on Fillmore Avenue on Buffalo's east side.[40]

At 5:45 the Nixons arrived in their open convertible. A crowd of 2,000 lined both sides of the street. Ignoring many pro-Kennedy signs, they entered the building's auditorium, jammed with 1,500 supporters. The vice president received a great ovation as he was introduced. Naturally, his talk centered on Poland and its subjugation under communism. "Those who have believed in freedom have brought down tyrants, and it will happen in Poland," he presciently declared to thunderous applause.[41]

At the conclusion of his remarks, the entourage was driven downtown to the Statler Hilton Hotel, during which a false bomb threat against Nixon was called in. After resting in his hotel suite for a while, the vice president was driven to Memorial Auditorium for the big rally of the day. Arriving at 9:30 Nixon received a huge welcome when he appeared on stage. The arena was just as packed as it had been for Kennedy, with 20,000 people shouting and waving placards in a noisy five-minute demonstration.

Nixon shook hands with the group of politicians on the platform and waved at the audience with his arms above his head in "V" for victory signs, a pose that would become all too familiar to Americans in future years. Governor Rockefeller introduced the candidate, who began by attacking his rival Kennedy and the Democrats' foreign policy position. His talk centered exclusively on foreign affairs, principally the communist threat. Nixon accused Kennedy of being inexperienced and a man who spoke before he thought, and of being inconsistent and weak in his policy toward Red China and the USSR.

Vice President Nixon spoke for thirty minutes before exiting. He had planned to speak from his car to the 2,000 or so people standing outside the main entrance to the auditorium afterward. However, a loud shouting match had developed between Nixon and Kennedy supporters in the crowd, so that plan was scuttled after a brief stop.

Nixon headed back to the Statler Hilton, where he and his wife spent the night. They left the next morning for an appearance in Niagara Falls, then they were off to Miami, Florida.

Former President Truman In Buffalo

Harry S Truman's airplane touched down at the Buffalo airport shortly before 7 p.m. on Sunday, March 25, 1962. He came in on a commercial flight from Chicago with his friend and aide, Kansas City Mayor Pro Tempore Thomas Gavin, and was greeted by a crowd of 500.

The former president came to Buffalo to accept an honorary degree from Canisius College and to inaugurate its William H. Fitzpatrick Chair of Political Science. Those welcoming Mr. Truman at the airport were the Republican mayor of Buffalo Chester Kowal, and Paul and Walter Fitzpatrick, sons of the late William Fitzpatrick, a longtime Democratic Party operative. Mayor Kowal presented the former president a key to the city.

A fast ten-minute press conference was held at the airport and Truman was as sharp-tongued as ever, giving terse, no-nonsense answers to questions ranging from nuclear testing to Richard Nixon to the John Birch Society. Asked how he felt, the seventy-seven-year-old replied, appearing obviously healthy, "How do I look?"

A police escort whizzed Mr. Truman downtown to the Statler Hilton where he held a private reception in his twelfth-floor suite. The former president was up early the next morning. At 7:30 he stepped out of the hotel onto Delaware Avenue accompanied by two Buffalo police detectives and a few reporters. He wore a gray hat, top coat, suit and tie. Truman was known for his brisk daily morning walks.

Walking straight up the east side of Delaware, he crossed to the other side at Edward Street and returned to the hotel by eight o'clock. All along the route people stopped to say "Good morning," and he greeted them with a smile. At one point, he stopped to chat briefly with a few students from nearby Hutchinson Central Technical High School.

Back at the Statler, Mr. Truman attended a breakfast with a hundred invited current and retired politicians and area VIPs. In brief remarks, he said how he would like to get the younger generation to "continue the greatest republic in the world."

Around noon the former president arrived at Canisius College. He reviewed the school's ROTC drill team, accompanied by the college president and cadet officers. He then enjoyed a private lunch in the faculty hall. Afterward, he held a quick fifteen-minute press conference addressing the Cold War and Niagara River power, among other topics.

Mr. Truman spoke to a meeting of 300 students in the college lounge, which was telecast via closed circuit television to other rooms. He held a question and answer session, during which he gave his opinion of a few other presidents, including Buffalonians Fillmore and Cleveland.

Late in the day the former president was presented with an honorary doctor of law degree in the same student lounge. He lectured the assembled students, again carried to other rooms by closed circuit television. In his talk, he defended his use of the atomic bomb on Japan and recalled his ascendancy to the White House.

Truman's visit received heavy coverage in the local news. He was considered the elder statesman of America, more popular in retirement than he had ever been as president.

CHAPTER 11

THE MODERN ERA

President Kennedy's Famous Visit

President John F. Kennedy visited Buffalo and the Niagara Frontier on Sunday, October 14, 1962, just as the Cuban Missile Crisis was coming to a head. He was making a swing through the northeast campaigning for Democratic candidates, but his remarks in Western New York were completely apolitical. He came to Buffalo to participate in its annual Pulaski Day Parade at the invitation of the Central Council of Polish Organizations and Buffalo Congressman Thaddeus J. Dulski.

Kennedy's plane, a DC-8, not the Air Force One with which we are familiar today specifically designated to fly the president, landed at the Niagara Falls Air Force Base around 2 p.m. President Kennedy was greeted by about a thousand airmen and their family members as he stepped out of the plane. He was driven across the airfield to the administration building of the Niagara Falls airport.[1]

Upon his arrival there, he was welcomed by a crowd of more than 15,000. He was formally greeted by a score of Niagara County Democratic politicians, including E. Dent Lackey, who was trying to unseat Congressman William E. Miller. Congressman Dulski of Buffalo was also among the greeters. From a platform erected outside the building, Kennedy addressed the crowd for fifteen minutes. He thanked Niagara

County for supporting him and said that the hope of the free world rested upon Americans to prevent enslavement of the world by communism.

The president's motorcade then took off for Buffalo. It consisted of three police cruisers, twenty-five police motorcycles, twenty automobiles and three buses. JFK rode in an open convertible limousine. all along the route to the North Grand Island Bridge the streets were lined with cheering, waving spectators, an estimated 30,000 of them to the see the president.

While the cars crossed the Grand Island Bridges, all watercraft were kept a half mile away by U.S. Coast Guard vessels. Along the Thruway on the island and into Tonawanda were thousands of cars illegally parked on the roadside, their occupants there to see the president pass by. This continued into Buffalo. Cabin cruisers on the Niagara River saluted JFK with blasts of their horns. Spectators were atop railroad cars and rooftops and leaning out of windows along the way.

When the Smith Street exit was reached, the motorcade left the Thruway and that is where the crowds now became thick along the curbsides. Near St. Stanislaus Church at Fillmore and Peckham stood a group of some thirty nuns, and President Kennedy ordered his car stopped. He got out to greet the sisters personally.

Reaching its destination of the intersection of Broadway and Fillmore at 2:30, the motorcade fell into the Pulaski Day Parade, which had begun from that location an hour earlier. The people at curbside were now five, ten, twenty deep along Broadway as the president's limo headed slowly downtown. They were hollering, screaming, waving and applauding. The young president waved and smiled, the sunlight playing off his shock of red hair on a beautiful warm fall day. It was estimated that 200,000 spectators lined Broadway.

At several points the people surged so close to Kennedy's car that Secret Service men leapt out of their cars to keep the way clear. After reaching Main Street, the parade route veered left toward Shelton Square, but because the throng of spectators there was so thick, the president's car detoured before reaching it and soon pulled up at the back entrance to City Hall on Elmwood Avenue, its ultimate destination.

The president was met there by Robert M. Morgenthau, the

Democratic candidate for governor of New York, Republican Buffalo Mayor Charles Kowal and others. He was escorted upstairs to the front entrance of the building where he paused inside. Already preliminary speeches had been made. A specially constructed stage on the City Hall steps was filled with scores of politicians. Niagara Square was packed with a sea of humanity 100,000 strong. The Secret Service was vigilant, having checked out vantage points from buildings ringing the square, although many heads were spotted peeking out from some windows.

Finally, JFK was introduced by Henry J. Osinski, president of the Central Council of Polish Organizations. A passage from one of the Buffalo newspapers seemed to capture the essence of the moment:

> Kennedy stood alone inside the front entrance. He shuffled gently from foot to foot. He coughed. His face reddened briefly. As he leafed through his text, he became almost grim. None of the thirty people near him spoke to him. No one spoke above a whisper. It was almost still. Then an aide said softly, "We're ready Mr. President." Kennedy straightened, folded his text in his left hand, smiled, then strode out to the platform. The square exploded in cheers, a band played "Hail to the Chief," and the program began.[2]

The president started his speech by linking General Pulaski, who fought and died in the American Revolution, to the cause of freedom around the world. He called communist domination of Poland temporary, asserted that the Poles were free in their hearts, and said Pulaski's sacrifice for America was relevant to today's Poles and Polish Americans.

> My own belief and observation shows me, and all of us, that there is no stronger reservoir of freedom in the world today than imprisoned   Poland. They know the meaning of freedom as no one else can.[3]

Kennedy called for increased ties to the people of Poland and called for free elections. He delighted Polish Americans by quoting Poland's national anthem, "Jeszcze Polska nie zginęła," meaning "Poland is not yet lost."

The president's speech lasted all of nine minutes. At its conclusion, he left through City Hall's rear entrance and was driven back to the Falls airport, passing by substantial but thinner crowds. He said his goodbyes, climbed aboard his plane and was off for New York City at 5:25 p.m. His visit to the Niagara Frontier had lasted only three and one half hours, but was one the area would never forget.

President Kennedy drew the largest crowd ever to turn out to see any person in the history of the city of Buffalo or of the county of Erie, at least 300,000 in the city and another 100,000 on the route to and from Niagara Falls.

A New Era of Presidential Travel

Just as the Kennedy-Nixon contest of 1960 ushered in the modern era of presidential campaigning, a new era of presidential travel began with the Kennedy administration.

President Eisenhower had traveled extensively by air, but the use of a designated aircraft as Air Force One with its familiar markings began in November 1962 when a Boeing jet airliner was put into service for use by President Kennedy. Rail travel by the president was by now abandoned completely, except as a novelty. Traveling by airplane meant the president need not schedule his visits to Buffalo or other places as one stop on a long tour. He could now, if he wished, visit different places far from one another in a single day. It was possible, if he so chose, to have breakfast in the White House, be in Buffalo by late morning, spend three or four hours there, and be back in Washington for dinner.

And air travel was safer from a security standpoint. It was no longer necessary to inspect and guard thousands of miles of railroad track each time the president traveled.

Perhaps over time this has made a presidential visit less special, this ability to flit in and out of Washington so easily, especially combined with the extensive face time the president receives on television and other media. Nevertheless, these appearances are still quite notable to the communities visited.

President Johnson Campaigns in Buffalo

Following the tragic assassination of John F. Kennedy in 1963, Lyndon B. Johnson became the thirty-sixth president of the United States. A year later he was running for election to the presidency in his own right.

President Johnson campaigned in Buffalo on Thursday, October 15, 1964. His DC-8 landed at the Buffalo airport at noon. Accompanying him were Robert F. Kennedy and his wife Ethel, Congressman Thaddeus Dulski, New York Mayor Robert Wagner and Undersecretary of State Averell Harriman. Kennedy was the late president's younger brother and was running for the U.S. Senate from New York.

Wearing a gray suit with western-style gray hat, Texan Johnson waved to a crowd of about 2,000 and was welcomed by a group of local politicians. He walked to a barricade and shook hands with some of the people standing in back of it. He met an old school friend whom he took into his limousine for the ride downtown. The president's motorcade of two dozen vehicles headed down Genesee Street, but stopped in front of a restaurant near Dick Road to shake hands with a group of fifty nuns. Moving north on Cayuga to Maryvale Drive, crowds lined the curbsides. The motorcade stopped at Maryvale Elementary School where the pupils and teachers stood waiting to greet Johnson. The cars then headed onto the Thruway to downtown Buffalo and arrived at the rear entrance of City Hall.

In Niagara Square were gathered some 50,000 people to hear the president and Robert Kennedy speak. Preliminary speeches were made, Kennedy spoke, effusively praising Johnson, and he then introduced the president. To the strains of "Hail to the Chief," and the roar of the crowd, he strode out onto the platform on the City Hall steps.

He proceeded to deliver a thirty-minute-long campaign speech in which he in turn praised Robert Kennedy and urged his election. Speaking of his own race, he emphasized the difference between himself and Republican candidate Barry Goldwater, asking which man would be more trustworthy dealing with Moscow and being in charge of America's nuclear arsenal. Following his speech, the president and his party were sped back to the airport, and his plane took off at 2:30 p.m. Due to time constraints, planned visits to Grand Island and Niagara Falls had to be canceled.

Coming less than a year after the Kennedy assassination, security for Johnson was the tightest it had ever been for a presidential visit to the area. The Secret Service presence was obvious, and they coordinated their activities with local and state police, who were out in force. Rooftops and windows all around Niagara Square were checked out and access restricted. Traffic all along the motorcade's route was halted for several minutes before it passed any given point. Bridges were kept clear by the police. And police detectives arrested a man with a rifle in a warehouse near the president's scheduled route.

William E. Miller

The Lyndon B. Johnson-Hubert H. Humphrey Democratic presidential ticket won the 1964 election by a landslide over the Republican team of Barry Goldwater and William E. Miller. With Miller, the Niagara Frontier had another connection to the presidency. He was the Congressman representing New York's fortieth district, covering all of Niagara County and a small portion of Erie County.

William E. Miller was born in Lockport on March 22, 1914 and that city remained his hometown throughout his life. He received a law degree from the Albany School of Law and served in the U.S. Army during World War II. Following the war, Miller was appointed to be a prosecutor of Nazi criminals at the Nuremberg war crimes trials. After that, he was appointed district attorney of Niagara County in 1948. Miller's political career began in earnest when he was elected to the U.S. House of Representatives in 1950. He at first represented New York's forty-second district, but from 1953 he represented the fortieth.

Congressman Miller became well respected enough by his fellow Republicans to be chosen the chairman of the Republican National Committee in 1961, in name the national leader of the Republican Party. Still, Miller was practically unknown nationally when Republican presidential candidate Barry Goldwater chose him to be his vice presidential running mate at the Republican National Convention in the summer of 1964. Goldwater, when asked why he picked Congressman Miller, replied, "Because he drives [President] Johnson nuts."

Miller was in fact extremely disliked by Johnson. As a practical matter, Miller offered geographic balance to the ticket, with Goldwater being from Arizona. Also, though both men were very conservative, Miller may have been perceived as having broader appeal, since he was Republican Party chairman. The two men appeared at a rally at the Niagara County fairgrounds in Lockport on September 5 of that year.

After his defeat in the 1964 election, Miller went back home to Lockport and resumed his law practice. A little burst of fame came his way when he appeared in the American Express Company's first "Do You Know Me?" television commercial, a series which appeared in the early 1980s.

William E. Miller died on June 24, 1983 and is buried in Arlington National Cemetery. Goldwater attended the funeral mass for Miller in Lockport and delivered a eulogy.

President Johnson in Buffalo for a Second Time

President Johnson was back in Buffalo on Friday, August 19, 1966 to address a Niagara Square crowd about lake pollution. His Boeing Air Force One with the presidential seal, the first time that famous airplane had landed at the Buffalo airport, touched down at 1:20 p.m. This was the same plane that had carried the slain President Kennedy's body from Dallas to Washington in 1963.

As the president and Mrs. Johnson stepped from the plane, they were greeted by a group of sixty politicians, including Republican Governor Nelson Rockefeller, Buffalo Mayor Frank Sedita, area Congressmen Thaddeus Dulski and Richard McCarthy. A thousand members of the public were behind a nearby fence and Johnson went over to shake hands with many of them.

The presidential motorcade of some twenty vehicles took off for downtown along Genesee to Dick Road to Walden Avenue to the

Thruway, and arrived at the rear entrance of City Hall at two o'clock. A crowd estimated at 65,000 was gathered in Niagara Square. They heard preliminary speeches, then President Johnson took the podium. He spoke for twenty minutes on the themes of cleaning up the Buffalo River and Lake Erie, and the newly passed Medicare and Higher Education laws.

After the address, President and Mrs. Johnson and other politicians were driven to the Buffalo River where they boarded the Coast Guard cutter *Ojibwa* for a ten minute excursion, taking off from the mouth of the river for a quick look at the harbor area. On board, they examined polluted water samples. By 3:30 the Johnsons' limousine was back at the airport and Air Force One took off a few minutes later.

The Return of Richard Nixon

Declared politically dead after losing a race for California governor in 1962, the resurrected former Vice President Richard Nixon brought his election campaign for the presidency to Buffalo on Monday, October 7, 1968. In a remarkable comeback, he had secured the Republican presidential nomination that summer.

The year 1968 was one of great turmoil in this country. American involvement in the Vietnam War was at the height of its unpopularity, inner cities had broken out in race riots for the second summer in a row, and a few months earlier the prominent civil rights leader Martin Luther King, Jr. and Democratic presidential contender Robert F. Kennedy had been shot to death. The United States was the most divided it had been since the Civil War. Into the middle of all this stepped Richard Nixon, perhaps appropriately, for he was one of the most divisive characters in American history.

Nixon's plane landed at the Buffalo airport at 6:45 p.m. He was greeted by a crowd of a hundred supporters and an equal number of news reporters. He was driven to the Statler Hilton on Niagara Square. At 8:30 he was at Memorial Auditorium for a large campaign rally. Some 20,000 supporters filled the arena, thought to be a record crowd. It was a raucous audience in the auditorium filled with balloons, placards and banners, and the crowd was jovial. Entertainers Lionel

Hampton and Frank Fontaine warmed up the crowd.

Sharing the stage with Mr. Nixon were, among many others, Buffalo football star Jack Kemp, Senator Jacob Javits and Governor Nelson Rockefeller, all of whom gave preliminary speeches. Nixon received great cheers when he was introduced, and was interrupted many times by applause during his speech, during which he tore into the Democrats and his major opponent, Vice President Hubert Humphrey. He all but ignored the third-party candidate, Alabama Governor George Wallace.

After his address, Nixon went back to the Statler Hilton where he spent the night. He flew out of the airport at about nine o'clock the next morning.

Shirley Chisholm

It would be remiss not to mention Shirley Chisholm, who drew nationwide attention in 1972. Chisholm was a native of Brooklyn who in 1969 became the first African American Congresswoman in American history. In 1972 she declared her candidacy for the Democratic Party's nomination for president of the United States. She thus became the first African American as well as the first female African American to seek a major party's nomination for president. Chisholm gained little support for her run and won only a minimal amount of delegates for the nomination. But she had made history.

In 1977 she married her second husband, Arthur Hardwick Jr., a Buffalo store owner and former New York State assemblyman. After leaving Congress in 1983 she made her home in Williamsville, New York with her husband. After his death in 1986 she moved to Florida where she died in 2005. Shirley Chisholm is interred in Forest Lawn Cemetery's Birchwood Mausoleum in Buffalo next to Mr. Hardwick. Her epitaph reads, "Unbought and Unbossed."

Vice President Gerald R. Ford in Buffalo

Gerald R. Ford, as vice president of the United States, was in Buffalo on Friday, May 10, 1974 for a political fundraising visit. He arrived at 12:35

p.m. at the facilities of Prior Aviation, an airplane service company on North Airport Road off Wehrle Drive on the north side of the Buffalo airport. Fifty persons greeted him, including Congressman Jack Kemp, County Executive Edward V. Regan and the county GOP chairman.

The vice president was sped to the Statler Hilton Hotel downtown. As he alighted from his limousine on Delaware Avenue, some 150 protesters in Niagara Square were shouting, "Jail Nixon!" Ford's visit was at the height of the Nixon administration's Watergate scandal. Throughout the day, the protesters were at times allowed to gather in front of the hotel or directly across Delaware Avenue from it, at all times under the watchful eyes of the police.

Ford held a Republican Party reception in the hotel followed by a news conference. He said that President Nixon would not resign and that he would not face impeachment because he had committed no impeachable offenses. He was obliquely critical of the president's handling of the scandal, yet defended him.

The vice president attended a mid-afternoon luncheon at the Statler sponsored by the Buffalo Building and Construction Trades Council. Also speaking was Secretary of Labor Peter J. Brennan. Ford visited his former House colleague John R. Pillion at Brothers of Mercy Home on Ransom Road in Clarence and attended a reception at the Buffalo Club on Delaware at 5 p.m.

By six o'clock he was back at the Statler where he was the featured speaker at a Republican fundraising dinner. He of course urged election of Republicans to Congress. Mr. Kemp and Mr. Regan also spoke to the 1,000 guests.

Vice President Ford was then driven back to the airport where his plane departed at 10 p.m.

Jimmy Carter Runs For President

Former Georgia Governor James E. "Jimmy" Carter won the Democrats' nomination to become their presidential candidate in 1976. His opponent on the Republican side was incumbent President Gerald R. Ford, who had succeeded to the presidency upon the resignation of President Nixon in August 1974.

Carter made a visit to Buffalo on November 20, 1975. He spoke at Norton Hall on the University of Buffalo Main Street campus while vying for the nomination, and was well received by the students assembled there. He gave some introductory remarks and conducted a question and answer session. He expressed his opposition to direct federal aid to New York City, then in the throes of a deep fiscal crisis, said welfare costs should not be borne by local governments, and called the Department of Defense the most wasteful agency in the federal government.

In the general election, Mr. Carter came to the Queen City on Thursday, September 30, 1976 for a brief stop. Flying directly from Georgia, his plane arrived at Prior Aviation at the airport shortly before 9 a.m. He was greeted by New York Senator Daniel P. Moynihan, local Congressman John J. LaFalce and Erie County Democratic Chairman Joseph Crangle. He was also welcomed by a crowd of 300 members of the public, to whom he directed a short campaign speech.

He was driven to a diner on Kenmore Avenue, the Chat and Chew Restaurant, where he spent twenty-five minutes talking to Western Electric employees who were about to be laid off due to their plant closing. Carter then went across the street to the parking lot of the plant at Vulcan and Kenmore in the Town of Tonawanda where he addressed a group of about 500 persons.[4] He was highly critical of President Ford, charging him with not caring about the unemployed.

On his way back to the airport Mr. Carter was interviewed by a reporter. He addressed public employee strikes, welfare and his recent debate performance. At around 11:30 a.m. his plane took off for his next campaign stop in Boston, Massachusetts.

His audiences in Buffalo were described as attentive but unenthusiastic.

President Ford Pays a Campaign Visit to Buffalo

As the Republican nominee for president in 1976, incumbent President Gerald R. Ford made a campaign stop in Buffalo. Air Force One landed at the Buffalo airport at Prior Aviation shortly before 11 p.m. on October 30, 1976 and a few minutes later the president emerged, wearing a blue raincoat against the wet weather. He was greeted by local GOP dignitaries including the county chairman and Representative Jack Kemp. And about 200 of the general public stood behind a fence to welcome the president at that late hour, including about twenty anti-Ford hecklers.

Ford was driven to the Statler Hilton downtown. As he entered the hotel he was cheered by about 500 supporters who chanted, "We want Ford!" Traveling with the president were Senator Jacob Javits and sportscaster Joe Garagiola, who had become Ford's chief cheerleader in the campaign. After ten minutes of shaking hands and exchanging pleasantries, the president took an elevator to his twelfth-floor suite. A hundred twenty-two rooms had been reserved, many of them for the 160 strong press corps following Mr. Ford.

The next day, Sunday, the president attended an early morning rally in the hotel's Golden Ballroom. Ford spoke for ten minutes and shook hands with many of the 1,500 supporters in the room. It was a gloomy, rainy Sunday as he left the hotel for a ride to St. Stanislaus Roman Catholic parish on Townsend Street near Fillmore on the city's east side. Though he was an Episcopalian, he had decided to attend the 9 a.m. Mass at the Polish American Catholic Church. A thousand people greeted him outside the church in the rain, including children from the parish's Polish Saturday School in Polish folk costumes. Another thousand parishioners were inside the church to worship with the president. The priest who celebrated the Mass welcomed President Ford during his homily and all but endorsed him for the presidency. Upon leaving the church, the president was warmly applauded and shook hands with many of the people who lingered nearby.

By 10 a.m. Ford was back at the Statler Hilton where he attended a fundraising breakfast with 450 GOP faithful. By 11:30 he was at the airport where he shook hands with several people gathered nearby. In parting remarks he said, "I am grateful to the people of Buffalo and Erie County. It's been a wonderful experience."[5]

Carter as President on the Niagara Frontier

Jimmy Carter defeated President Ford in the 1976 election. As president, he made two trips to the Buffalo area. He arrived at the Buffalo airport on Saturday, October 28, 1978, with Air Force One pulling up to Prior Aviation at 10:30 a.m. Local Congressmen John LaFalce and Henry Nowak accompanied him.

The president was welcomed by a group of Democratic Party officials. In a light rain, he was ushered to a portable stage occupied by about seventy others, including Senator Moynihan, Buffalo Mayor James Griffin, Cheektowaga Supervisor Kenneth Meyers, and New York Governor Hugh Carey. It was to campaign for the governor that Carter had come.

Moynihan, Meyers and Carey spoke, then it was the president's turn. He proceeded to deliver a twenty-minute speech during which he gave an update on Egypt-Israel peace negotiations, praised Governor Carey and touted his own accomplishments.

A few sign-carrying demonstrators were present, but Carter nevertheless shook hands with many in the crowd of 5,000 after he finished speaking. By 11:25 Air Force One was airborne, ending the extremely brief stopover, one of a series of campaign stops for the president.

Carter's second visit to the Niagara Frontier as president came on Wednesday, October 1, 1980 during his reelection campaign. His plane landed at the Niagara Falls Air Force Base at 5:30 p.m. He was greeted by a crowd of about 200 politicians and invited guests, including Buffalo Mayor James Griffin.

A thirty-vehicle motorcade took the president to the Niagara Falls Convention Center, now the Seneca Niagara Casino. In a room at the center, Carter signed into law a bill to provide federal money to relocate families from the contaminated Love Canal area of Niagara Falls, and another to provide federal funds for the clean-up of the West Valley nuclear waste site.

The president then entered the main hall to address 1,400 delegates attending the Civil Service Employees Association state convention. On his fifty-sixth birthday, Carter was serenaded by the conventioneers with "Happy Birthday." Sharing the dais with President Carter were Republican New York Senator Jacob Javits, Governor Hugh Carey, Senator Moynihan and Representative John LaFalce. In his speech Carter rolled out a litany of criticisms against his Republican opponent, Ronald Reagan, charging that Reagan was an enemy of labor. He also tried to justify his opposition to Reagan's proposal for a large federal tax cut, a very popular proposal among Americans.

Upon exiting the convention center Carter was met by a group of about 400 people. In the darkness, illuminated by television lights, he climbed atop the roof of his limousine and smiled and waved at the crowd for about thirty seconds. He was then driven back to the air base and Air Force One took off for Washington at 8 p.m.

Ronald Reagan

Ronald Reagan, the actor turned politician, had kept his eye focused on the presidency for many years. His name was first put forth for the office at the Republican National Convention in 1968 while he was governor of California, and he was a serious competitor for the GOP nomination in 1976.

After being bested by Gerald Ford that year, he embarked on a heavy schedule of speaking dates throughout the country. His objective: to get his name, face and ideas before the American public. His goal: the 1980 Republican nomination, then the presidency itself. Reagan may have visited Buffalo in 1977 or 1978. On Saturday, October 6, 1979, he was in the city to speak at the Buffalo Convention Center. Reagan shared the speakers' spotlight with Erie County Executive Edward J. Rutkowski and U.S. Representative Jack F. Kemp. Congressman Kemp and Mr. Reagan were no strangers to each other.

Well known to Western New Yorkers and nationally to American football fans, Kemp was the star quarterback of the American Football League champion Buffalo Bills teams of the 1960s. A native of California, he became involved in politics by becoming a volunteer in Republican Barry Goldwater's failed 1964 presidential bid. In 1966 he worked on Ronald Reagan's successful California gubernatorial campaign. The following year he was appointed to a staff position in Governor Reagan's office. Two years later he was an assistant to the Republican National Committee chairman. It was during these years that Kemp and Reagan developed a lasting political comradery.

The two men saw eye-to-eye on economic and fiscal issues and by 1979 Reagan had become a strong supporter of the Congressman's Kemp-Roth tax cut legislation. Kemp first ran for Congress at the end of his football career in 1970, parlaying his popularity in the Buffalo area into an easy win. He went on to represent the Southtowns in Congress for eighteen years, though his critics pointed out that he never lived in the house he owned in the district at 45 South Lake in Hamburg, but in Maryland.

Though not yet an official candidate for the GOP nomination at the time, Reagan, for all practical purposes, was already running. The former governor first held a news conference in Buffalo during that 1979 visit, in which he harshly criticized President Jimmy Carter's handling of U.S. relations with the Soviet Union and communist Cuba. He also said it was too early to consider Representative Kemp as a possible vice presidential running mate, but considered him qualified for the job.

Repeating many of the same themes during his thirty-five-minute speech at the convention center before 800 enthusiastic Republican supporters, Reagan lambasted the Soviets, called for deep federal tax cuts and declared himself against expansion of the federal government. Mr. Reagan left for New York City immediately after his speech.

During the 1980 Republican primary contest Reagan made a quick stop in Cheektowaga on primary day itself, March 25. His plane landed at the Buffalo airport at ten in the morning and taxied over to the Prior Aviation building. Congressman Kemp was the first one to greet Reagan. Reagan stepped off the plane smiling and shook hands with many of the 200 or so well-wishers who stood behind a fence to cheer him.

He hurried into the lobby of the Prior Aviation office where a fifteen-minute news conference was held before reporters, aides, local Republican leaders and security agents. Introduced by Kemp, Reagan wasted no time criticizing incumbent President Carter's presidency, railing against his fiscal policies and his handling of the Iran Hostage Crisis. Asked about Congressman Kemp as his possible running mate, he replied that he had not yet thought that far ahead. His remarks concluded, Reagan climbed back aboard his plane and left for Dallas. In a hard fought primary campaign, Reagan wound up losing New York that day to Texan George H. W. Bush, a former Congressman, director of the Central Intelligence Agency and ambassador to China.

Ronald Reagan won the GOP presidential nomination. Despite the hopes of Western New York Republicans, however, he bypassed Jack Kemp as his running mate and instead chose Bush for the position.

Reagan's only stop in Buffalo during the general election campaign came in early September. His plane landed at the Buffalo airport on Wednesday night, September 10, 1980. He was in the area to speak to labor union leaders. He and his wife Nancy were greeted at Prior Aviation by area Republican officials. The Reagans were driven to the Buffalo Hilton Hotel at 120 Church Street at Lower Terrace, now Adams Mark Hotel, where they were greeted by a thousand noisy supporters and a band.

The next morning Mrs. Reagan made a visit to Children's Hospital. Meanwhile, Mr. Reagan was driven to Armando's Restaurant on Lake Shore Drive in Blasdell for a breakfast meeting with fourteen officers of the International Longshoremen's Association (ILA) labor union, including its president.[6] Accompanying Reagan was Congressman Kemp.

When the ILA men arrived at the restaurant they were met by some eighty picketers who were members of other unions that had endorsed incumbent President Carter for reelection. When Reagan and Kemp's limousine pulled up, police moved the picketers away from the building entrance. The two men were met by jeers, catcalls and insults from the demonstrators, who carried anti-Reagan placards.

When Reagan, Kemp and the ILA men left the restaurant forty minutes later they were again jeered by the picketers. They drove a few miles north to the Port of Buffalo terminal off Fuhrmann Boulevard where Mr. Reagan gave an outdoor speech with the windy waterfront as a backdrop. He promised to expand the navy if elected president, increase business for U.S. flagships and reinvigorate the shipbuilding industry.

Speaking before a hundred persons, including many port workers, Reagan cited the economy, military and energy fields as areas that were in crisis under the Carter administration. An anti-Reagan union member interrupted ILA president Teddy Gleason's remarks with catcalls. The Reagans departed from Buffalo at 11:30 a.m.

The next day Mr. Gleason heavily criticized the union demonstrators, saying that they did a disservice to the labor movement with their antics, and that as ILA president, he was legitimately interested in hearing Reagan's ideas relating to the shipping industry, and that there was nothing wrong with conferring with a major party presidential candidate.

President Reagan Campaigns for Reelection in Buffalo

Victorious over Jimmy Carter in the 1980 presidential election, Ronald Reagan made only one visit to Buffalo during his eight years as president of the United States. That happened on Wednesday, September 12, 1984 during his reelection campaign.

Air Force One touched down at the Buffalo airport just before 11 a.m. On the airplane with the president were Congressman Kemp and U.S. Senator Alfonse D'Amato of New York. As Reagan came off the plane he was greeted by a crowd of local officials, all Republicans, with one glaring exception. That was Buffalo Mayor James Griffin, nominally a Democrat, who was the first to shake the president's hand.

President Reagan was whisked down the Niagara Thruway in a multi-car motorcade to Connecticut Street on Buffalo's west side. His visit to the Queen City was jointly sponsored by the Federation of Italian American Societies and the Polish St. Stanislaus Community Association. Its purpose was to garner support from Buffalo's ethnic groups for the Reagan reelection effort and to dedicate a housing project.

The president and other dignitaries emerged from their vehicles at Connecticut and Fargo Avenue under the watchful eye of the Secret Service. At the corner stood the brand-new Santa Maria Towers apartment building for senior citizens and the handicapped. It was built with federal funds and was being administered by the Roman Catholic Diocese of Buffalo. Outside the building were 10,000 spectators out to see the president, variously described as enthusiastic or merely polite. Far away down Fargo were a hundred or so protesters.

President Reagan was given a brief tour of one of the Towers' apartments then headed back outside where he addressed the crowd with a campaign speech. He hit on his favorite themes, deftly working Buffalo into each point. He thanked the Italian group for their support of the new building, and the Polish group for its efforts to establish the Monsignor Adamski village on the east side.

At the conclusion of his remarks the president cut a ceremonial ribbon to open the Towers, then was escorted a short distance down Fargo Avenue into D'Youville College where he attended a luncheon held at the school's dining hall. The school had been closed for the day., and the sidewalks were lined with hundreds of people during Mr. Reagan's short walk.

At the hall, Reagan was seated at the head table between Mayor Griffin and Senator D'Amato. Also at the table were Representative Kemp, County Executive Edward Rutkowski, County Comptroller Alfreda Slominski, Sheriff Kenneth J. Braun, State Comptroller Edward Regan and Buffalo Roman Catholic Bishop Edward Head. Around 600 guests in all attended.

The president was serenaded with Polish songs and he was served traditional Italian and Polish dishes for lunch. Polish and Italian ethnic touches were everywhere, on buttons and flags. In remarks, President Reagan called Buffalo "a real melting pot town," and praised hard-working immigrants, emphasizing how his programs had helped America's working class.[7] He urged passage of Kemp's enterprise zone legislation and called for tax simplification.

By 2 p.m. the president was back at the airport and it was wheels up for Air Force One, destination Binghamton.

Jack F. Kemp

Jack Kemp remained a close political ally of President Ronald Reagan throughout Reagan's eight-year presidency. Kemp was the president's point man in the House of Representatives, especially concerning fiscal matters, on which the two men saw eye to eye.

Many Republicans viewed Kemp as the president's heir apparent. Reagan's more obvious successor, Vice President George H.W. Bush, was looked upon by a considerable amount of Reaganites as a faux conservative. They could not forget Bush's campaign in 1980 to take the Republican presidential nomination, in which he called opponent Reagan's tax cut plan "voodoo economics," and saw Reagan's choice of Bush for vice president as mere political expediency.

In the 1988 Republican presidential primaries, Vice President Bush's main opponent was Congressman Kemp. In the end, Kemp could not overcome the advantage of the vice presidency that Bush enjoyed and his campaign lost steam. The man with Buffalo ties was not to become a major party presidential candidate. Jack Kemp decided not to seek reelection to his Congressional seat in 1988 and officially changed his legal residence to Bethesda, Maryland from Hamburg, New York at the end of his final term. He then served as Secretary of Housing and Urban Development for the entire four years of the Bush administration. If Reagan had chosen Kemp to be his running mate in 1980, however, chances are good that Buffalo would have had yet a third man in the White House to go along with Fillmore and Cleveland.

George H. W. Bush Before the Presidency

George H.W. Bush would go on to win the presidency in the 1988 general election. He was a resident of Texas but a native of Connecticut and a World War II naval aviator who nearly lost his life in the conflict. After the war, he attended Yale University. One of his classmates there was Seymour Knox III of the Knox family of East Aurora. While a student, young George Bush visited the Knox Estate, now Knox Farm State Park in East Aurora, and slept in the main house.[8]

As vice president of the United States, Bush had spoken at Genesee Community College in Batavia, forty miles east of Buffalo, on May 30, 1981, in conjunction with a trip to Rochester.

On Wednesday, April 13, 1988 the vice president brought his Republican primary campaign to Buffalo. After his plane landed at the airport in the early afternoon, his motorcade took him to the Ellicott Square Building where he entered the lobby for a rally just before one o'clock.

A friendly crowd of about 500 supporters was there to greet him. The vice president was introduced by Congressman Kemp, who had dropped out of the presidential contest a few weeks earlier. Bush spoke for about ten minutes, pledging to keep the Reagan years of prosperity going as he touched on all the main campaign talking points. Afterward, he and his group, surrounded by security, walked across the street for a quick tour of Buffalo's new downtown baseball stadium, set to open the following day. Bush was a baseball aficionado and had been captain for the Yale baseball team when he attended the school.

After the stadium tour the vice president reentered his limousine and quickly returned to the airport, and left for a campaign stop in Rochester.

George W. Bush

In March or April of 1988 George H.W. Bush's son, George W. Bush, made a stop in the Buffalo area to campaign for his father. His escort for the day was Thomas A. Loughran of Amherst, who was active in the Republican Party at the time.

The two men drove to the old Memorial Auditorium in downtown Buffalo and met Buffalo Sabres owner Seymour Knox III and went to a reception at Mr. Loughran's business, Loughran's Bar and Restaurant, then located at 2067 Kensington Avenue, now Snyder Bar and Grill. There, Mr. Bush mingled with invited guests and bar patrons before leaving town.[9]

Former President Ford at UB

During the general election of 1988 former President Gerald R. Ford came to the Buffalo area to give a talk at the State University of New York at Buffalo's Alumni Arena on the north campus in Amherst. He was there on Monday, September 26, 1988 to participate in a "Power and the Presidency" lecture series.

At a news conference before a fundraiser at the Airport Holiday Inn in Cheektowaga, Ford predicted that George Bush would win the presidential election, which he did, and made several other comments on the race. Speaking before about 2,000 people at UB, the former president also opined that too much power had been taken from the president in favor of the Congress, while at the same time saying that he did not want an imperial presidency.

Former President Carter at UB and Niagara

On May 5, 1989, former President Jimmy Carter was also at UB to give a talk as part of the lecture series. His plane landed at Niagara Falls that afternoon. Before his speech at Alumni Arena, Carter held a news conference during which he mainly fielded questions about the Iran-Contra Scandal. During his forty-five-minute talk that evening before an audience of 3,000 the former president was highly critical of the late Reagan administration, but less so of the new Bush presidency. He also defended his own legacy.

Carter and his wife Rosalynn were again in the Niagara Region from Tuesday July 9 to Thursday July 11, 1996 on a combined fiftieth wedding anniversary–business trip to Canada. The couple stayed at a hotel on the Canadian side of the falls. On Wednesday, they took a boat ride on the *Maid of the Mist* and attended a play at Niagara-on-the-Lake. They also unexpectedly ran into former Canadian Prime Minister Pierre Trudeau in a hotel lobby in Niagara Falls.

On Thursday, the Carters walked across the Rainbow Bridge to the American side, which included a stroll onto Goat Island. It was the only time the couple had visited the actual falls. Everyone who met them was impressed with their friendliness. The former president and first lady left for Toronto that day. It is assumed they flew in and out of Toronto.

The First of the Clinton Visits

George H.W. Bush failed to win reelection to the presidency in 1992. His Democratic opponent, William J. "Bill" Clinton, was the victor. Clinton, then the governor of Arkansas, came to Buffalo on Saturday, March 21, 1992 for the first time, while campaigning in the Democratic primary election. He was in the city to participate in a forum of presidential candidates at Shea's Buffalo Theater sponsored by the Erie County Democratic Committee. Joining Clinton on stage were three other Democratic hopefuls: former Governor Jerry Brown of California, former

Senator Eugene McCarthy of Minnesota, and little known Lawrence Agran, former mayor of Irvine, California.

Before a capacity crowd of 3,000 the four men were questioned by ten panelists for ninety minutes beginning at 3 p.m. It was Buffalo's turn in the national spotlight, though the debate was not carried live on national television, only on local radio. Afterward the candidates dispersed. Clinton visited the Olivencia Community Center on Swan Street and the Masten Avenue Block Club Coalition on Humboldt Parkway. He also attended a $300 a plate fundraiser at the Radisson Hotel in Cheektowaga across from the airport.

Clinton campaigned in the general election in Buffalo on August 23, 1992. President Bush did not visit the area that year. Clinton came into town via bus as part of a "Lake Erie Bus Tour." Accompanying him were vice presidential candidate Albert Gore, Mrs. Clinton and Mrs. Gore. The bus had earlier in the day stopped at the main square at the Chautauqua Institution where Governor Clinton and the others addressed a crowd of 5,000. After short stops in Westfield and Fredonia the campaign bus rolled onto the campus of Buffalo's Canisius College at eight in the evening, two hours late. After preliminary speeches, Gore took the microphone, then Clinton addressed the crowd of 8,000 noisy supporters. The candidates were scheduled to plant a tree in Delaware Park after the rally.

While running for reelection as president, Clinton visited the area again in 1996. Air Force One landed at the Buffalo airport in Cheektowaga near noon on Thursday, October 3. Welcomed by a horde of local Democratic officials, the president was immediately driven to nearby Sierra Research adjacent to the airport where he was greeted by blaring rock music rather than the more traditional "Hail To The Chief."

In cold forty degree weather he gave his stump speech on a makeshift outdoor stage and shook hands with many in the crowd of a thousand, which included many school children. The president then boarded his helicopter, Marine One, which had to be specially flown in on a separate airplane. His destination was the Chautauqua Institution.

There, he holed up at the Atheneum Hotel to practice for his upcoming campaign debate against the Republican presidential candidate. Three days later Clinton quietly returned via Marine One to the Buffalo airport and was flown to the debate city of Hartford, Connecticut.

Vice Presidential Candidate Jack Kemp

President Clinton easily won reelection to a second term in 1996 in one of the dullest presidential campaigns in American history. Clinton's Republican opponent was the long time Kansas Senator Robert Dole. Dole's running mate was former Housing and Urban Development Secretary Jack Kemp.

Why was Kemp chosen by Dole as the vice presidential nominee? Kemp had not been in public office for over three years, though he was a founder and director of Empower America, a fiscally conservative think tank. He also was serving on several corporate and advisory boards and on a tax reform commission. Kemp had declined to run for the 1996 Republican nomination for president, saying he was out of step with then-current party thinking. The fiscal policies of Dole and Kemp differed slightly but were generally conservative. Kemp was seen as someone who might attract racial minority voters and was considered attractive to the former Reagan supporters, with whom he had worked on supply side policies and tax cut legislation.

After his unsuccessful vice presidential run, Kemp continued to be an advocate for his conservative fiscal views. In 2008 he endorsed John McCain for president early in the Republican primary campaign. He died in 2009 at age seventy-three.

President Clinton Again

Bill Clinton made a second visit to the Buffalo area as president in early 1999, the day after delivering his State of the Union address. He had been impeached by the House of Representatives on December 19, 1998 for lying to a grand jury. In fact, he was on trial in the U.S. Senate on the very day he was in Buffalo.[10]

Though chances of him being removed from office appeared to be slim, the president wanted to salvage the remaining years of his presidency and protect his legacy. With these purposes in mind, he embarked on the trip to Buffalo, a reliably Democratic city with plenty of enthusiastic Clinton supporters and a sympathetic news media, a story that would play well nationally.

Accompanying President Clinton were his wife and Vice President and Mrs. Albert Gore. Air Force One and Air Force Two touched down at the Buffalo airport on the morning of Wednesday, January 20, 1999. The Clintons and the Gores and their entourage were driven in sport utility vehicles to the new hockey arena downtown, then known as the Marine Midland Arena. When they entered the auditorium they were amazed at the wildly cheering crowd of almost 22,000 who packed the place.

At 11 a.m. preliminary speeches were made by local officials, followed by Mrs. Gore, Mrs. Clinton and the vice president. Then it was the main event, the talk by President Clinton. He spoke for about half an hour about the main themes from his State of the Union address. Afterward, the Clintons, Gores and eight others, including Buffalo Mayor Anthony Masiello and Erie County Executive Dennis Gorski, ate lunch at the Radisson Hotel across from the airport. Shortly before 5 p.m. the president's and the vice president's planes took off for a rally in Norristown, Pennsylvania.

Former President George H. W. Bush at UB

As did former Presidents Ford and Carter, former President George H. W. Bush made a visit to UB's north campus in Amherst to speak. On Wednesday evening, September 29, 1999, he addressed a crowd of about 5,000 as part of the college's Distinguished Speakers series.

Speaking and answering questions for more than an hour, he expressed his thoughts on current events. And he iterated not-so-veiled references to the Clinton presidency's moral shortcomings, saying, "I made plenty of mistakes, but I think I served with honor." He later called the presidency a "resilient office" that can "bounce back no matter who is elected."

Texas Governor George W. Bush Campaigns in Buffalo

Just four days later Bush's son, Texas Governor George W. Bush, arrived at the Buffalo airport with his wife Laura. Already the odds-on favorite to capture the Republican nomination for president in 2000, he was greeted at Prior Aviation on Sunday, October 3, 1999 by several local GOP officials and an excited group of supporters, to whom he made a few remarks. The Bushes spent the night in the area.

The next morning, they were guests at a 9 a.m. political fundraising breakfast at Rich Renaissance Atrium on Niagara Street in the Queen City. Governor George Pataki of New York spent a half hour introducing Governor Bush to movers and shakers of the Western New York Republican Party present in the room. In his talk to the audience, Bush outlined his vision for leading America, a philosophy that had come to be called "compassionate conservatism."

After leaving the fundraiser, Governor Bush was driven to Mount Olive Baptist Church on East Delavan Avenue. This was part of his outreach to the African American community. He and Mrs. Bush attended a morning service during which he made general remarks emphasizing how his brand of conservative values could uplift all Americans.

Candidate George W. Bush was back in the Buffalo area on Friday, March 3, 2000. Then the solid frontrunner in the contest for the Republican presidential nomination, he stopped at the Buffalo airport just four days before the New York State primary election. Accompanying him were former cabinet member Elizabeth Dole and New York Governor George Pataki.

In a short ten-minute speech under a canopy on the airport tarmac, Bush touted tax cuts and an end to federal control over schools. Afterward, he talked to local reporters, denying charges that had surfaced that he was anti-Catholic. He stayed in the area overnight, but just where is not known.

CHAPTER 12

THE TWENTY-FIRST CENTURY

A new century, a new president. George W. Bush took the oath of office on January 20, 2001 to become the forty-third president of the United States, the second president's son to become president himself.

Former President Clinton in Buffalo

Not out of office for even a year, former President Bill Clinton made his way to Buffalo on November 2, 2001 to address a meeting of the Civil Service Employees Association at the Buffalo Convention Center. He spoke to an audience of about a thousand, speaking about the recent terrorist attacks of September 11 and defending the actions of his own administration.

The former president voiced his support for current President George W. Bush in the fight on terror, advocating increased security and defense, and argued for a need to emphasize and increase the amount of social aid given to foreign nations to demonstrate America's force for good in the world.

Afterward, he shook hands with hundreds of those in the audience and took a few questions from reporters. He then went to City Hall and met with Mayor Anthony Masiello for about half an hour.

Clinton was back in the area on April 10, 2002 to talk at UB's Alumni Arena in Amherst. The Wednesday afternoon speech drew 7,500 mostly young college people to the auditorium. The former president was the guest at a small reception before his speech, during which he met with student leaders and university officials.

Clinton's talk covered various topics and was slanted to appeal to his youthful audience. He praised his wife's work as U.S. senator from New York and defended his own record as president. Clinton answered questions that had been submitted in advance and which were filtered out to avoid any embarrassing questions such as his extra-marital affairs and his impeachment. At the close he shook hands with many of the UB students.

President George W. Bush Visits Buffalo

George W. Bush made his first and only appearance in Buffalo as president of the United States on Tuesday, April 20, 2004. His plane, the iconic Boeing 747 Air Force One, landed at the Buffalo airport shortly after 9 a.m. It was the first time a 747 had landed there. Regular commercial versions of the jumbo jet were not allowed to serve the airport due to the short runways combined with the heavier weight of those aircraft.

The president was met at the airport by New York Governor George Pataki and local Republican officials. He was quickly driven in a twenty-five-car motorcade to Kleinhan's Music Hall on Buffalo's west side. There he was escorted into the Mary Seaton Room to deliver a speech centered on homeland security.

When President Bush entered the room, he was greeted with sustained, enthusiastic applause. The 540 people in the audience consisted mostly of local uniformed law enforcement and emergency personnel. Reporters were assigned to bleachers at the back. A large television provided a backdrop for the stage, and the president sat on a stool along with five local officials, including U.S. Attorney Michael A. Battle and Buffalo FBI Agent-in-Charge Peter J. Ahearn.

Bush was described as funny and witty while acting like a jovial talk show host as he bantered with the men on stage, all the while defending the USA Patriot Act, a far-reaching anti-terrorism statute that was increasingly coming under fire in the country for its intrusion of civil liberties.[1] The president's event lasted about forty-five minutes, after which he headed directly back to the airport for a flight to New York City.

About 400 protesters had stood outside Kleinhans, but had been kept about 200 yards away with their vitriolic anti-Bush signs and rhetoric. Buffalo's Democratic Mayor Anthony Masiello was criticized for not greeting President Bush at the airport or at the Music Hall. He defended himself by saying he had not been invited to the event, but added that he would have snubbed the president and not attended even if an invitation had been extended.

John G. Roberts Jr.

On July 19, 2005 President George W. Bush appointed John G. Roberts Jr. to replace retiring Associate Justice of the United States Sandra Day O'Connor. In September he instead reappointed Roberts to fill the chief justice vacancy created by the death of William Rehnquist. He was confirmed by the Senate and became the nation's seventeenth chief justice on September 29, 2005.

Roberts was born in Buffalo in 1955, the son of a Bethlehem Steel executive. He attended St. Bernadette Elementary School in Orchard Park. When he was eight years old the family moved to Indiana. Roberts went on to earn a law degree from Harvard, clerk for the Supreme Court and serve in the Reagan and first Bush administrations. He was on the District of Columbia Circuit Court of Appeals before taking his seat on the high court.

Former President Clinton Again and Again. And Again

Former President Bill Clinton was in Buffalo again on December 14, 2005. He had been invited to the city by billionaire Rochester businessman B. Thomas Golisano, the owner of the Buffalo Sabres professional hockey team. The two had become friendly because Golisano was a multimillion-dollar donor to the Clinton Foundation, a controversial charity.

Clinton gave an address to 600 Democrats at the Buffalo Convention Center during which he lambasted the presidential administration of George W. Bush. The speech was attended by outgoing Buffalo Mayor Anthony Masiello and Mayor-elect Byron Brown. Later, Clinton went to the hockey arena, met with Sabres players and sat with Mr. Golisano in the owner's box for the game. He left after the second of the game's three periods.

Once more into the city came Mr. Clinton, on May 31, 2006, this time with his wife, Senator Hillary Clinton, to attend the New York State Democratic Convention. The Clintons had lived in Chappaqua in downstate Westchester County, New York since the former president had left office.

The convention was held at the Hyatt Regency Hotel at Main and Huron Streets downtown. The meeting attracted 1,200 delegates from throughout the state, and the former president sat in the audience that morning during his wife's acceptance speech of her automatic endorsement for reelection to her U.S. Senate seat. The Clintons later had lunch at Chef's Restaurant on Seneca Street where they shook hands with many of the patrons.

On October 1, 2006 Bill Clinton and his wife attended a Buffalo Bills football game at the stadium in Orchard Park. They sat in team owner Ralph Wilson's private suite and enthusiastically cheered on the Bills. The former president's stepfather, Richard Kelley, had been a Bills fan and had become friendly with Mr. Wilson. Kelley was a food distribution company executive in Arkansas. Before the game, Hillary Clinton made an appearance at the University of Buffalo's Amherst campus to announce a grant to the school as part of her reelection campaign for the U.S. Senate.

The Queen City was again the former president's destination on August 27, 2007. He was in Buffalo to highlight fundraisers for his wife's presidential bid. He spoke at a gathering of 200 at attorney Robert Siegel's home on Soldiers Place in Buffalo, with each person donating in excess of a thousand dollars to attend. Clinton's voice could be heard over a microphone in the neighborhood that evening. He later attended another fundraiser at The Church at Delaware and Tupper, now known as Babeville, that charged fifty dollars per person. All told, Bill Clinton raised about $200,000 for Hillary Clinton's campaign.

The fundraiser-in-chief was back in town on Sunday, January 20, 2008 to speak at a $100,000 event at the offices of the Phillips Lytle law firm on the thirty-fourth floor of the HSBC Tower, now One Seneca Tower. About 200 Democrats attended the evening affair, which was held to raise more money for his wife's presidential campaign. The former president then went to a rally in the lobby of the Ellicott Square Building. A couple of hundred were in attendance for that event.

Once again Mr. Clinton came to Buffalo, on Wednesday, December 10, 2008 to meet with B. Thomas Golisano and attend a Sabres hockey game. He had dinner with Mr. Golisano and other invited guests, including Buffalo Mayor Byron Brown, in the owner's suite at the hockey arena. Clinton said hello to Sabres players and their opponents before the game. The entire visit was strictly a private affair.

President Obama Comes to Buffalo

President Barack Obama made two visits to the Buffalo area while he was in office, but none before his presidency. The first came on Thursday, May 13, 2010. Air Force One landed at the Buffalo airport at 12:35 p.m. and Obama was met there by several local dignitaries.

He was driven a short distance to the airport's emergency rescue unit building where he met with ten loved ones of victims of the Flight 3407 air disaster that had occurred over Clarence, New York a year earlier. He assured them that he was doing all he could to advance an agenda of enhanced training for commercial pilots.[2]

The president was then driven to Duff's Famous Chicken Wings on Dick Road at the Dick-Urban Plaza in Cheektowaga. He entered a packed restaurant, people obviously having been tipped off about his stop. Mr. Obama ordered ten wings, french fries and onion rings, then shook hands and joked with the hundred or so customers and staff.

Then it was back into his limousine as his twenty-car motorcade headed to Buffalo's east side. His destination was Industrial Support

Incorporated on Depot Street near William and Lewis Streets. Many hundreds of onlookers stood along William near Lewis as the cars approached. The president was escorted inside the plant where he was greeted by the company's seventy employees. He watched demonstrations of various company products as he toured the workplace and bantered with the workers, in an obviously jovial mood.

Mr. Obama then held a forty-minute-long meeting with the employees. He touted the government's latest job growth numbers and insisted that the government had to do more to create jobs. He answered only four questions, to which he gave lengthy answers, as he was usually wont to do. The president then left for the airport and re-boarded Air Force One. The entire trip had lasted about three hours.

President Obama's second visit to the Buffalo area was on Thursday, August 22, 2013. He landed at the airport at 10:15 in the morning. He was greeted by New York Governor Andrew Cuomo, Buffalo Mayor Byron Brown and Congressman Brian Higgins. With Obama was Secretary of Education Arne Duncan.

The president was in the area to start a bus tour across New York State to highlight the problems of higher education. He and the others boarded a bus and were driven to Amherst, to Alumni Arena on the UB north campus. He entered the building at 11:15 with his entourage. A group of less than a hundred protesters had been kept some distance away.

Dressed casually in khaki pants, blue shirt, dark blue blazer and tieless, the president was cheered by the mostly young crowd of about 7,000. In a thirty-minute speech he outlined his plans to make college more affordable to middle class families. Afterward, he shook hands with many in the audience and in short order re-boarded his bus, which headed east to Auburn where the president was to spend the night.

Thomas E. Perez

Amherst (Snyder), New York native Thomas E. Perez became Barack Obama's Secretary of Labor in July of 2013. He was schooled at Christ the King Elementary School in Snyder and Canisius High School in Buffalo. He went on to earn a law degree from Harvard and held various government posts before becoming labor secretary. He currently lives in Maryland. The news media gave him an outside chance to be selected as Hillary Clinton's vice presidential running mate in 2016. In 2017, he was elected to be chairman of the Democratic National Committee, the titular head of the Democratic Party in America.

Former President Clinton Yet Again

After an absence of almost eight years, Bill Clinton was back in Western New York in 2016. An inveterate campaigner and glad-hander, he was no doubt happy to be back at it, campaigning for his wife Hillary's bid for the Democratic presidential nomination. For the first time since 1988, the votes of New York State's late primary election actually mattered in a close contest between Mrs. Clinton and Vermont Senator Bernard "Bernie" Sanders. Interestingly, the Republicans also featured a close presidential primary contest in which New York mattered.

At around two in the afternoon of April 5, 2016 the former president's private plane landed at the Buffalo airport and a few minutes later he was at Grapevine Banquets at 333 Dick Road in Cheektowaga. A few dozen protesters picketed outside the hall as Clinton entered to a lively welcome from an audience of 850 supporters. He was greeted by Buffalo Mayor Byron Brown, Erie County Executive Mark Poloncarz and Niagara Falls Mayor Paul Dyster. Looking and sounding much older than his sixty-nine years, Clinton proceeded to deliver a forty-five-minute speech in which he praised his wife's record as senator from New York and stressed the importance of the primary election.

By four o'clock Clinton had left the banquet hall, re-boarded his plane and headed for Rochester.

Clinton was back in the area just a couple of weeks later, on the eve of the primary election, to do more stumping for his wife. On the morning of April 18, 2016, he landed at the Buffalo airport. From there he was driven to Democratic Party headquarters on Seneca Street in the city, where he greeted and encouraged campaign volunteers.

He then went to St. John Tower assisted living center on Michigan Avenue where he said a few words to the residents assembled for a bingo game. Then he and his party stopped at Spot Coffee on Delaware and

West Chippewa where he ordered a cup of tea. The motorcade next headed to Alton's Restaurant on Walden Avenue just east of Union Road in Cheektowaga where he talked to and shook hands with many of the diner's patrons. He had the Secret Service stop traffic on Walden so he could walk across the street to give a few words of encouragement to striking workers manning a picket line in front of a telephone company store.

After that, it was back to the airport for a flight to Rochester. Clinton had been accompanied on his meanderings through the area by Buffalo Mayor Brown, County Executive Poloncarz and New York Governor Andrew Cuomo.

Donald J. Trump

Donald J. Trump made a campaign stop in Buffalo during the New York State Republican presidential primary on his way to a stunning victory in the general election that propelled him into the White House. On Monday, April 18, 2016, the day before the primary election, he flew into the airport and was whisked to the hockey arena downtown. At 7:30 p.m. he was introduced by Buffalo Bills football coach Rex Ryan and was greeted by a noisy, boisterous crowd that filled about two-thirds of the 18,000 seat auditorium.

Trump lambasted his primary opponents with his usual caustic and somewhat insulting rhetoric, which his supporters ate up. He also heavily criticized the likely Democratic presidential nominee, Hillary Rodham Clinton, blaming her and husband Bill Clinton's fiscal policies for ruining the economy of Buffalo and Western New York. And he delivered his famous catch-phrase, promising to "make America great again."

During that 2016 visit, Mr. Trump said he had been to Buffalo "many times," but as a private businessman, he likely came into town unannounced and without fanfare. But it is known that Trump was in Buffalo on June 7, 1992 to attend the Jim Kelly Shootout and Carnival of Stars at the baseball stadium downtown. It was a charity event that featured Bills' quarterback Kelly and many former football players. Trump was accompanied by his girlfriend Marla Maples, who knew Kelly.

EPILOGUE

It should be kept in mind that the subject of Buffalo and the presidents is an active one, and based on that fact alone, a book such as this can never be considered to be complete. Presidents of the United States will visit the area in the future, and future presidents may have set foot in the city already. Some day another local politician will again be a prominent figure in national politics.

Note the recent national publicity received by local U.S. Representative Christopher Collins of Clarence. Congressman Collins represents New York's twenty-seventh Congressional District, which includes most of Erie and Niagara Counties and stretches eastward to the far suburbs of Rochester. He was the first member of Congress to endorse the candidacy of Donald Trump for president of the United States in the 2016 race.

Though Collins has not yet been rewarded with an administration appointment by President Trump, he serves as an important liaison between the White House and the rank and file members of the House of Representatives. He also has been interviewed hundreds of times by the national news media in which he has defended the president and his policies.

Buffalo area native Thomas Perez served as secretary of labor under President Obama and in 2017 was elected to head the Democratic National Committee, joining William E. Miller of Lockport as the only persons from the Buffalo-Niagara area ever to lead a national political party. In 2016 Perez had been considered as a vice presidential candidate by Democratic presidential nominee Hillary Clinton.

Perhaps Buffalo Mayor Byron Brown should not be ignored. He was chosen to head the New York State Democratic Party in 2016 upon the recommendation of New York Governor Andrew Cuomo, who has long been considered to be a potential presidential candidate in the future. Should he attain the presidency, he may very well retain his close political relationship with Mayor Brown.

Based on Buffalo's history, the city and its residents will continue to play an important role in our national political pageant. That little child you see frolicking on local playgrounds or peering out of the window of the school bus may one day walk the halls of power in Washington, D.C. in a most vaunted position. It has happened before, and there is no reason to believe that it will not happen again.

APPENDIX

The following is a chronological list of presidents who have visited Buffalo before, during and after their terms of office. The periods during which Millard Fillmore and Grover Cleveland lived or visited here before their presidencies, or after as in the case of Fillmore, are excluded from this list. Normal roman type identifies presidents who visited before their terms of office, upper case those who came as incumbent presidents, and italics those who visited as former presidents.

William Henry Harrison – October 24-27, 1813
JAMES MONROE – August 9, 1817
Rutherford B. Hayes – June 9-11, 1834
Martin Van Buren – September 1-2, 1835
MARTIN VAN BUREN – September 2-3-, 1839
Zachary Taylor - August 10, 1840★
John Quincy Adams – July 26-27, 1843
Rutherford B. Hayes – August 1843##
John Quincy Adams – October 29-30, 1843
Rutherford B. Hayes – July 24, 1847
Abraham Lincoln – September 25-26, 1848
ZACHARY TAYLOR – September 1, 1849★★
MILLARD FILLMORE – May 15-20, 1850
John Tyler – September 21, 1851###
Rutherford B. Hayes – August 1853##
James A. Garfield – November 17, 1853
     June 30-July 1, 1854
     August 13, 1856

APPENDIX

Abraham Lincoln – July 24, 26, 1857
James A. Garfield – January 8, 12, 1858
Abraham Lincoln – February 16-18, 1861
Ulysses S. Grant – June 2, 1866
                September 3, 1866
ANDREW JOHNSON – September 3, 1866
James A. Garfield – October 31- November 1, 1866
                October 20-21, 1868
Benjamin Harrison – September 1870★
Rutherford B. Hayes – June 10, 1871
James A. Garfield – October 1871##
ULYSSES S. GRANT – August 15-16, 1875
James A. Garfield – November 3, 1876
                August 9-10, 1877
                July 28, 1878
                August 1-2, 1878
                September 1879##
                October 30-31, 1879
                August 3-4, 1880
Benjamin Harrison – August 3-4, 1880
William McKinley – August 3-4, 1880
Ulysses S. Grant – October 28, 1880
                November 16-17, 1883
Theodore Roosevelt – November 19-20, 1883
Rutherford B. Hayes – September 17, 1884
GROVER CLEVELAND – November 3, 1885
Rutherford B. Hayes – September 1887##
                September 9, 1887
Grover Cleveland – May 11-13, 1891★★★
William McKinley - September 15, 1892
Theodore Roosevelt – January 26-27, 1893
William McKinley – October 25-26, 1894
Theodore Roosevelt – September 10-11, 1895
WILLIAM MCKINLEY – Augist 24-26, 1897
Theodore Roosevelt – October 25-26, 1898

286

APPENDIX

                  May 15, 1899
                  August 16-17, 1899
                  February 22-23, 1900
                  October 31-November 1, 1900
                  May 19-22, 1901
WILLIAM MCKINLEY – September 4-14, 1901
Theodore Roosevelt – September 7-10, 1901
THEODORE ROOSEVELT – September 14-16, 1901
Woodrow Wilson – September 15, 1901
Grover Cleveland – October 9, 1903
William Howard Taft – October 30, 1908
                  November 1-2, 1908
WILLIAM HOWARD TAFT – March 18, 1910
                  April 30, 1910
Theodore Roosevelt – August 25, 1910
                  November 1, 1910
Franklin D, Roosevelt – December 23, 1911
                  February 3, 1912
Woodrow Wilson – April 9-10, 1912
                  September 2, 1912
Theodore Roosevelt – June 10-11, 1913
Franklin D. Roosevelt – September 22, 1914
Theodore Roosevelt – August 2, 1915
William Howard Taft – October 22, 1915
WOODROW WILSON – November 1, 1916
William Howard Taft – January 4, 1917
WOODROW WILSON – November 12, 1917
Franklin D. Roosevelt – August 6, 1919
Herbert Hoover – November 12, 1919
Warren G. Harding – October 21, 1920
Franklin D. Roosevelt – October 21-22, 1920
Herbert Hoover – January 8, 1921
Calvin Coolidge – July 11, 1922
Herbert Hoover – June 14, 1924
Franklin D. Roosevelt – October 20-22, 1928

APPENDIX

Harry S Truman – 1928 or 1929##
Franklin D. Roosevelt – July 12-14, 1929
                October 20-21, 1930
                August 27-28, 1930
                July 2, 1932#
                October 18, 1932
FRANKLIN D. ROOSEVELT – October 2, 1933
                October 16-17, 1936
                November 2, 1940
Harry S Truman – April 7-8, 1945
George H.W. Bush – late 1940s#
HARRY S TRUMAN – June 13, 1947
                October 8, 1948
Herbert Hoover - October 10-11, 1951
HARRY S TRUMAN - October 9-10, 1952
Dwight D. Eisenhower – October 23, 1952
John F. Kennedy – April 30, 1953
Richard M. Nixon – October 16-17, 1956
John F. Kennedy – May 21-22, 1959
Richard M. Nixon – May 18, 1960
John F. Kennedy – September 28, 1960
Richard M. Nixon – October 17-18, 1960
Harry S Truman – March 25-26, 1962
JOHN F. KENNEDY – October 14, 1962
LYNDON B. JOHNSON – October 17, 1964
                August 19, 1966
Richard M. Nixon – October 7-8, 1968
Gerald R. Ford – May 10, 1974
Jmaes E. (Jimmy) Carter – November 20, 1975
                September 30, 1976
GERALD R. FORD – October 30-31, 1976
Ronald Reagan – 1977/1978##
JAMES E. CARTER – October 28, 1978#
Ronald Reagan – October 6, 1979
                March 25, 1980#

APPENDIX

September 10-11, 1980
Gerald R. Ford – Septmber 26, 1980#
JAMES E. CARTER – October 1, 1980###
RONALD REAGAN – September 12, 1984
George W. Bush - March or April 1988##
George H.W. Bush – April 13, 1988
James E. Carter – May 5, 1989#
William J. (Bill) Clinton – March 21, 1992
Donald J. Trump – June 7, 1992
William J. Clinton - August 23, 1992
James E. Carter – July 11, 1996###
WILLIAM J. CLINTON – October 3,6, 1996
January 20, 1999
George H.W. Bush – September 29, 1999#
George W. Bush – October 3-4, 1999
George W. Bush – March 3-4, 2000#
William J. Clinton – November 2, 2001
April 10, 2002
GEORGE W. BUSH – April 20, 2004
William J. Clinton – December 14, 2005
May 31, 2006
October 1, 2006
August 27, 2007
January 20, 2008
December 10, 2008
BARRACK OBAMA – May 13, 2010
August 22, 2013#
William J. Clinton – April 5, 2016#
April 18, 2016
Donald J. Trump – April 18, 2016

★ probable visit, not specifically documented; ★★ stop at Black Rock harbor, did not come ashore; ★★★ visit as both future and former president
Erie County, did not visit city of Buffalo; ## specific dates not determined
Niagara Falls only

ENDNOTES

CHAPTER 1

1. buffalo.ah.com.
2. Joncaire's settlement was approximately at what is now Ganson Street and South Michigan Avenue. A historical plaque is attached to an out-building of the General Mills plant in the area.
3. Frank H. Severance, *An Old Frontier of France* (New York: Dodd Mead and Co., 1917), 35.
4. Ibid.
5. Ibid., 36-7.
6. Ibid., 37.
7. Ibid., 38.
8. Peter L. Bernstein, *Wedding of the Waters* (New York: W.W. Norton, 2005), 23-4.
9. Ibid., 124-5.
10. Robert M. Owens, *Mr. Jefferson's Hammer* (Norman: University of Oklahoma Press, 2007), 14.
11. The house no longer stands. It was demolished in stages between 1835 and 1951. A commemorative site showing archeological remnants of the house is now open to the public.
12. Charles H. Todd, Benjamin Drake and James H. Perkins, *Sketches of the Civil and Military Service of William Henry Harrison* (Cincinnati: J.A. and U.P. James, 1847), 106-9.
13. William Cutter, editor, *Genealogical and Family History of Central New York, Vol. 2* (New York: Lewis Historical Publishing Co., 1912), 551.
14. Porter would later serve as U.S. secretary of war in 1828-1829.
15. *Buffalo Gazette,* November 2, 1813.
16. *A Narrative Tour of Observation Made During the Summer of 1817 by James Monroe...* (Philadelphia: S.A. Mitchell and Ames, 1818), vii.

17. Ibid., viii; Kathy Warnes, "President James Monroe Inspects Downriver to Detroit,": accessed through definitelydownriver.blogspot.com.
18. *Buffalo Gazette,* July 29, 1817.
19. Ibid., August 12 and September 9, 1817.
20. *Buffalo Commercial Advertiser,* September 2, 1835.
21. Ibid., September 9, 1835.
22. niagarafallsinfo.com.
23. "Site of the Peter Buell Porter House," accessed through niagarafallsundergroundrailroad.org.
24. geni.com
25. Samuel P. Orth, *A History of Cleveland, Vol. I* (Chicago: S.J. Clarke, 1910), 40-1, 94, 97.
26. dmna.state.ny/forts.
27. niagaraparks.com.
28. Also called Patriot's War or Patriots' War.
29. Major J. Wilson, *The Presidency of Martin Van Buren* (Lawrence Kans.: University Press of Kansas, 1984), 157.
30. Robert W. Coakley, *The Role of Federal Military Forces in Domestic Disputes, 1789-1878* (Washington, D.C.: U.S. Government Printing Office, 1988), 112-6.
31. Lance Kasparian, *Ansley Wilcox House – Historic Structure Report* (Lowell. Mass.: U.S. Department of Interior, 2006), 6.
32. Holmes Alexander, *The American Talleyrand: The Career and Contemporaries of Martin Van Buren* (New York: Harper and Brothers, 1935), 359.
33. *Buffalo Commercial Advertiser,* September 5, 1839.
34. nps.gov/thri/buffalobarracks.
35. *Buffalo Commercial Advertiser,* September 3, 1849.
36. Kasparian, 25.
37. Buffalo Historical Society, *Publications, Vol. 8* (Buffalo Historical Society, 1905), 472.
38. K. Jack Bauer, *Zachary Taylor: Soldier, Planter* (Baton Rouge: Louisiana State University Press, 1993). 96-7; Holman Hamilton, *Zachary Taylor, Soldier of the Republic* (Indianapolis: Bobbs-Merrill, 1941), 142.
39. A. Wesley Johns, *The Man Who Shot McKinley* (New York: A.S. Barnes and Co., 1972), 135.
40. buffalonet.org.
41. Bruce V. Sones, *Brigadier General Jefferson C. Davis: Civil War General* (Pickle Partners Publishing, 2014).

42. *Buffalo Gazette,* June 23, 1843; Lyle E. Nelson, *John Tyler: A Rare Career* (New York: Nova Science Publishers, 2008), 86.
43. Robert Seager II, *And Tyler Too* (New York: McGraw-Hill, 1963), 357.

CHAPTER 2

1. Robert J. Rayback, *Millard Fillmore: Biography of a President* (Buffalo: Henry Stewart, 1959), 23.
2. Rayback, 108; Robert J. Scarry, *Millard Fillmore* (Jefferson, N.C.: McFarland and Co., 2001), 37; Frank H. Severance, *Publications of the Buffalo Historical Society, Vol. 24* (Buffalo: Buffalo Historical Society, 1920), 1, 135.
3. *The Diaries of John Quincy Adams,* entry of July 26, 1843, accessed through masshist.org.
4. Court House Park was the original name of today's Lafayette Square in downtown Buffalo. Where the Central Library entrance way plaza exists today was the old Erie County Court House, built in 1818 and which served as such till 1876. The park was renamed Lafayette Square in 1879 and the Soldiers and Sailors Monument was erected in 1884.
5. *Buffalo Commercial Advertiser,* July 27, 1843.
6. Ibid.
7. *Adams Diaries,* July 26, 1843.
8. Ibid., July 27, 1843.
9. Ibid., October 29, 1843.
10. Ibid., October 30, 1843.
11. Paul Finkelman, *Millard Fillmore* (New York: Henry Holt and Co., 2011), 22.
12. Rayback, 159.
13. *Buffalo Daily Republic,* May 16, 1851.
14. Ibid., May 17, 1851.
15. *Buffalo Commercial Advertiser,* May 17, 1851.
16. Ibid.
17. The Mansion House was a four-story hotel on the southeast corner of Main and Exchange Streets, fronting on Main and across from Buffalo's Liberty Pole, a giant flagpole of some 150 feet tall displaying the Stars and Stripes. An elevated section of the New York State Thruway now occupies the site of the hotel.
18. Millard Fillmore Papers, from the collection at the Buffalo History Museum, Fillmore letter to Daniel Webster dated October 23, 1850.

19. *Buffalo Courier,* April 14, 1853.
20. Scarry, 279-80.
21. Ibid., 309.

CHAPTER 3

1. A fugitive slave law had existed in the United States since 1793.
2. Reinhard O. Johnson, *The Liberty Party, 1840-1848* (Baton Rouge: Louisiana State University Press, 2009), 14.
3. The Church stood at the corner of Main and East Buffalo Streets and was replaced by the present brick structure in 1865, now called United Church of Warsaw.
4. Jeffrey C. Mason and Harry S. Douglass, *Alive in the Spirit Since 1813: The Arcade United Church of Christ, Congregational* (Interlaken, N.Y.: Heart of the Lakes Publishing, 1990), 67.
5. According to the Mason book, the original church building was moved, converted to a feed store and destroyed by fire in 1924. The current, second church building dates from 1877. It occupies the same spot as the original and still functions today as the Arcade United Church of Christ, Congregational at Main and Church Streets.
6. Theodore C. Smith, *The Liberty and Free Soil Parties of the Northwest* (New York: Russell and Russell, 1967), 38.
7. Douglas M. Strong, *Perfectionist Politics: Abolitionism and the Religious Tensions of American Democracy* (Syracuse University Press, 1999), 129, 181-2.
8. Temperance houses were inns where alcoholic beverages were not served. Being partial to prohibition of alcohol, Liberty Party members would likely have favored staying overnight at such an establishment, rather than at a hotel or inn where such drinks were available.
9. *Signal of Liberty,* May 8, 1843.
10. Ibid., July 3, 1843.
11. Smith, Theodore C., 69-70.
12. Jonathan H. Earle, *Jacksonian Anti-Slavery and the Politics of Free Soil, 1824-1854* (Chapel Hill: University of North Carolina Press, 2004), 158.
13. John Mayfield, *Rehearsal for Republicanism* (Port Washington, N.Y.: Kennikat Press, 1980), 90-1.
14. *Buffalo Daily Courier,* October 23, 1847.
15. Earle, 159.

16. *Buffalo Daily Courier,* October 22, 1847; *Buffalo Morning Express,* October 22, 1847.
17. Earle, 13-4.
18. *Buffalo Commercial Advertiser,* June 15, 1848.
19. *Buffalo Daily Courier,* June 14, 1848.
20. Merton M. Wilmers, *History of the Niagara Frontier* (Chicago: S.J. Clarke, 1931), 416.
21. Oliver Dyer, *Phonographic Report of the Proceedings of the National Free Soil Convention at Buffalo, N.Y., August 9th and 10th, 1848* (Buffalo: G.H. Derby and Co., 1848), 23.
22. *Buffalo Daily Republic,* August 11, 1848.
23. Depending on the source, the exact numbers can vary.
24. Dyer, 17.

CHAPTER 4

1. *Washington Republic,* September 6, 1849.
2. *Toronto Globe,* September 6, 1849.
3. *Washington Republic,* September 6, 1849.
4. The Paris Peace Treaty of September 3, 1783 established the Niagara Frontier border between British Canada and the United States as the middle of the Niagara River.
5. Bauer, 270.

CHAPTER 5

1. John Fagant, *The Best of the Bargain: Lincoln in Western New York* (Bloomington, Ind.: AuthorHouse, 2010), 1.
2. The Cataract House was a four to five story hotel that stood right along the rapids across from Goat Island, just south of the bridge to Goat Island. It burned down in 1945. The site was covered by the Robert Moses Parkway, which has since been closed down, and the area is slowly being converted to parkland.
3. Fagant, 9.
4. Ibid., 29-31.
5. *Buffalo Daily Courier,* February 18, 1861.
6. The American Hotel was a five-story structure rebuilt in 1851 after a fire had burned down its predecessor of the same name. It stood on the west side of Main Street between Eagle and Court Streets, where the north end of Main Place Mall now stands.

7. The church was built in 1833. It was converted to offices in 1880, a third floor was added and its facade extended. It still stands today and is known as the Title Guaranty Building.
8. St James Hall was located at the southwest corner of Washington and Eagle Streets. It was an exhibition, lecture and stage hall. It was destroyed by fire in 1887. The site was later occupied by the Iroquois Hotel, since demolished, and is now part of the M&T Plaza on Main Street.
9. *Buffalo Daily Courier,* February 19, 1861.
10. *New York Times,* September 2, 1895.
11. *Buffalo Daily Courier,* October 29, 1861.
12. *Buffalo Commercial Advertiser,* July 7, 1863.
13. Ibid., July 8, 1863.
14. *Buffalo Daily Courier,* July 8, 1863.
15. *Buffalo Evening News Scrapbook of 1922.*
16. Dorothy M. Kunhardt and Philip B. Kunhardt Jr., *Twenty Days* (New York: Castle Books, 1965), 219.
17. Martin S. Nowak, *The White House in Mourning* (Jefferson, N.C.: McFarland and Co., 2010), 80.
18. Coakley, 290.
19. John W. Percy, *Buffalo-Niagara Connections* (Buffalo: Western New York Heritage Press, n.d., 205.
20. *Buffalo Commercial Advertiser,* June 2, 1866.
21. Coakley, 291; Percy, 206-7.
22. Percy, 207.
23. Alyn Brodsky, *Grover Cleveland: A Study in Character* (New York: Truman Talley Books, 2000), 29-30.
24. Eric Foner, *Reconstruction: America's Unfinished Revolution, 1863-1877* (New York: Perennial, 2002), 264.
25. *Buffalo Daily Courier,* September 3,4, 1866.
26. *Buffalo Express,* September 3, 1866.
27. A site now occupied by a parking ramp.
28. Hans Trefousse, *Andrew Johnson: A Biography* (New York: W.W. Norton, 1999), 264.
29. *Buffalo Commercial Advertiser,* September 3, 1866.
30. *Buffalo Daily Courier,* September 4, 1866.
31. *Buffalo Express,* September 4, 1866.

32. *Buffalo Commercial Advertiser*, March 12, 1874.

33. Ibid., March 11, 1874.

34. Ibid.

35. Ibid., August 12, 1881; Buffalo Express, August 12, 1881.

36. *Buffalo Daily Courier*, August 16, 1875.

37. Sherman Jewett's house was at 256 Delaware Avenue, a site now occupied by the northern portion of the Delaware North Company headquarters.

38. *Buffalo Express*, October 29, 1880.

39. The Tifft House was a five-story hotel located at 491 Main Street just north of Lafayette Square. It was demolished in 1902 and replaced by the old Hengerer's Department Store, which was later converted into the current Lafayette Court office building.

40. *Buffalo Daily Courier*, October 29, 1880.

41. The original Genesee Hotel was torn down in 1922. The site is now occupied by the Hyatt Regency Hotel.

42. The first name is pronounced EE-lee, to rhyme with the word "freely."

43. Arthur C. Parker, *The Life of General Ely S. Parker* (Buffalo: Buffalo Historical Society), 77-8.

44. American Indians were not granted American citizenship until 1924.

45. Parker, 130-5.

CHAPTER 6

1. William Dorsheimer and William U. Hensel, *Life and Services of Honorable Grover Cleveland* (Philadelphia: Hubbard Press, 1884), 24; Allan Nevins, *Grover Cleveland: A Study in Courage* (New York: Dodd Mead and Co., 1947), 17, 28.

2. Nevins, *Grover Cleveland*, 65-6.

3. Ibid., 55, 65-7, 72, 75.

4. Ibid., 67

5. Ibid., 37.

6. Charles H. Armitage, *Grover Cleveland as Buffalo Knew Him* (Buffalo: Buffalo Evening News, 1926), 16. According to Armitage, Millard Fillmore had an office in a building connected to the Weed Block, where Cleveland had his office, and that as a young lawyer Cleveland was acquainted with the former president.

7. Nevins, *Grover Cleveland*, 66.

8. Allan Nevins, editor, *The Letters of Grover Cleveland, 1850-1908* (Boston: Houghton

Mifflin, 1938), 245.
9. Nevins, *Grover Cleveland,* 213; John G. Milburn, "Grover Cleveland as Seen by Three Friends," *Scribner's,* April 1927, 344-8.
10. Michael Zwelling, "Sheriff, Mayor, President, Jailbird?" *Buffalo Magazine,* 16-19, imprint of *The Buffalo News,* November 6, 2005.
11. Nevins, *Grover Cleveland,* 83.
12. Reverend George H. Ball, a Baptist minister from Buffalo who was a leader in spreading anti-Cleveland rhetoric regarding the Halpin Affair during the 1884 campaign.
13. Nevins, *Letters,* Cleveland letter dated November 13, 1884, 47-8.
14. Ibid., Cleveland letter dated December 5, 1884, 50-1.
15. Nevins, *Grover Cleveland,* 192.
16. Nevins, *Letters,* Cleveland letter dated December 31, 1884, 53-4.
17. Armitage, 240-1.
18. Ibid., Cleveland letter of July 23, 1885, 235.
19. Robert M. McElroy, *Grover Cleveland, the Man and Statesman, Vol. I* (New York: Harper and Brothers, 1923), Cleveland letter of August 6, 1885, 137-9.
20. Nevins, *Letters,* Cleveland letter dated May 20, 1889, 207.
21. *Buffalo Commercial Advertiser,* November 3, 1885.
22. *Buffalo Express,* May 12, 1891.
23. Ibid.
24. The Buffalo Club, one of whose founders was Millard Fillmore, still meets in this same mansion, but the building has been greatly expanded. It was here that the cabinet members, when in Buffalo after the shooting of President McKinley in Buffalo in 1901, made their headquarters.
25. *Buffalo Commercial Advertiser,* May 13, 1891.
26. Nevins, *Letters,* 254.
27. *Buffalo Commercial Advertiser,* May 13, 1891.
28. Nevins, *Letters,* 254-5.
29. *Buffalo Courier,* October 10, 1903.
30. William C. Davis, *Jefferson Davis, the Man and His Hour* (Baton Rouge: Louisiana State University Press, 1991), 658; Adam Mayers, *Dixie and the Dominion* (Tonawanda, N.Y.: Dundern Press, 2003), 19-20.
31. George Cleveland remarks on July 21, 2014 at celebration of Frances Folsom Cleveland's 150th birthday at Buffalo, New York, as noted by the author.
32. Armitage, 272-8.

CHAPTER 7

1. Rutherford B. Hayes, edited by Charles R. Williams, *The Diary and Letters of Rutherford B. Hayes, Vol. I-IV* (Columbus, Ohio: Ohio State Archeological and Historical Society, 1922), Vol. I, 1.
2. Ibid., 110-1.
3. Ibid., 210.
4. Ibid., 453.
5. Ibid., Vol. III, 152.
6. Ibid., Vol IV, 160.
7. Ibid., 338.
8. Ibid., 339.
9. Corydon E. Fuller, *Reminiscences of James A. Garfield* (Cincinnati: Standard Publishing, 1887), 99-100.
10. James A. Garfield, edited by Harry J. Brown and Frederick D. Williams, *The Diary of James A. Garfileld, Vol. I-IV, 1848-1881* (Ann Arbor: Michigan State University Press, 1967), Vol. I, 257-8.
11. Ibid., 258.
12. Fuller, 235-8.
13. *Garfield Diary, Vol. I,* 316-7.
14. Ibid., 362.
15. Ibid., 452.
16. The home was demolished and replaced by an office building in the early twentieth century, and it has been converted into apartments, address 777 Main Street.
17. *Garfield Diary, Vol. III,* 506.
18. *Buffalo Express,* November 4, 1876.
19. *Garfield Diary, Vol. III,* 506.
20. Ibid., Vol. IV, 99.
21. Ibid., 100-1.
22. Ibid., 101.
23. Ibid., 284.
24. Ibid., 289.
25. trainwweb.org.
26. *Buffalo Courier,* August 4, 1880; Buffalo Express, August 4, 1880.
27. *Garfield Diary, Vol. IV,* 438.

28. Harry J. Sievers, *Benjamin Harrison: Hoosier Statesman* (New York: University Publishers, 1959), 34.
29. George F. Howe, *Chester A. Arthur: A Quarter Century of Machine Politics* (New York: Dodd Mead and Co., 1934), 7; Thomas C. Reeves, *Gentleman Boss: The Life of Chester Alan Arthur* (New York: Alfred A. Knopf, 1975), 6-8.
30. Information from Norma Spencer, Wyoming County Historian, November 2014.
31. Information from Steve Gates, Town of York Historian, November 2014; Howe and Reeves contend the Arthurs lived in York from only 1837 to 1839.
32. William J. Ireland, *Through the Ivory Gate* (Edinburgh, Scotland: Bell and Bradfute, 1889), 168-9.
33. *Buffalo Courier,* September 17, 1887.
34. H.H. Alexander and Edward D. Easton, stenographers, *Report of the Proceedings in the Case of the United States vs. Charles J. Guiteau* (Washington. D.C.: U.S. Government Printing Office, 1882), Vol. I, 569-70.
35. Ibid., 570.
36. *Buffalo Courier,* July 5, 1877.
37. *Buffalo Commercial Advertiser,* September 19, 1877; *Buffalo Express,* September 19, 1877.
38. *Buffalo Courier,* July 5, 1881.
39. *Transactions of the Oneida Historical Society at Utica* (Utica, New York: Oneida Historical Society, 1889), 107; Buffalo Courier, July 9, 1881; freepages.genealogy.rootsweb.
40. Craughwell, 134, 201-2.
41. Per niagaracounty.com/parks, the remains of the old Bennett homestead are located in what is today Royalton River Park on Gasport Road in Gasport, New York. According to *Best Day Hikes Buffalo* by Randi Minetor, it stands just before the spur trail to the falls on the edge of the ravine.
42. Jill Norgren, "Belva Lockwood: Blazing the Trail for Women in Law," *Prologue,* Spring 2005, vol. 37, no. 1, accessed through archives.gov.
43. *Buffalo Courier,* October 26, 1894.
44. Ibid.

CHAPTER 8

1. Library of Congress statistics.
2. *Buffalo Courier,* August 25, 1897. It was reported that the route the carriages took

up Prospect Avenue was a change made from the original Delaware Avenue route because the Delaware residents had been criticized for their insufficient display of American flags and other patriotic decorations in the days prior to the GAR convention.
3. The Niagara Hotel was located on the southwest corner of Porter Avenue and Seventh Street. The site is now occupied by a small restaurant.
4. *Buffalo Courier,* August 25, 1897.
5. The Ellicott Club was a Buffalo businessmen's club founded in 1895. It vacated the clubrooms in the Ellicott Square Building in the early 1920s and its members contributed to a new building at 69 Delaware Avenue. The organization transformed into the Buffalo Athletic Club and is now operating as a branch of L.A. Fitness at that Delaware Avenue location.
6. The building still stands on Delaware at the corner of West Tupper Street, but is no longer used as a church. It is used as a concert hall and is known as Babeville.
7. *Buffalo Commercial Advertiser,* August 25, 1897.
8. A site now occupied by a parking lot and a small brick building.
9. *Buffalo Commercial Advertiser,* August 25, 1897.
10. Buffalo Board of Education, *Sixth Annual Report of the Board of School Examiners for 1897* (Buffalo: Haas and Kelley, 1897).
11. *Buffalo Commercial Advertiser,* August 26, 1897.
12. *Buffalo Express,* May 21, 1901.
13. Now a parking lot.
14. Johns, 70.
15. As explained in Chapter Four, President Zachary Taylor had crossed into Canada on the original suspension bridge in 1849.
16. Johns, 81-2; *Buffalo Express,* September 7, 1901.
17. Johns, 42.
18. Walter Channing, "The Mental Status of Czolgosz, the Assassin of President McKinley," *American Journal of Insanity,* October 1902, 23-46.
19. Johns, 43.
20. Channing.
21. Nowak, 124-5.
22. The old police headquarters was located at the northwest corner of Seneca and Franklin. Torn down in 1937, the site is today a small pocket park where a police memorial is located.

23. 810 West Ferry is today occupied by tennis courts of the eleven story 800 West Ferry Apartments.
24. Kasparian, 62.
25. Ibid., 12.
26. The same First Presbyterian Church building still stands today at that location.
27. Now known as Old County Hall.
28. Kohlsaat, H.H., *From McKinley to Harding: Personal Recollections of Our Presidents* (New York, Charles Scribner's Sons, 1923), 96-7. Kohlsaat was a businessman and confidant of Theodore Roosevelt. Woodrow Wilson liked to vacation at Rosseau Falls.
29. Grover Cleveland, "His Eulogy of McKinley," accessed through bartleby.com.

CHAPTER 9

1. Kevin P. Gaughan, "Roosevelt in Buffalo," *ArtVoice,* September 13, 2001, p. 8-13.
2. *Buffalo Express,* November 19, 1883.
3. That structure was demolished and the site is now home to offices of Computer Task Group.
4. theodore-roosevelt.com.
5. The Twentieth Century Club is a women's social club that still operates in the same location.
6. *Buffalo Express,* October 26, 1898.
7. Ibid.
8. Ibid., May 16, 1899.
9. The Saturn Club since 1922 has had its clubrooms at 977 Delaware. 417 Delaware is now a parking lot at the southeast corner of Edward Street.
10. The Arsenal was built in 1858 to house National Guard units and included a huge indoor drilling space. In 1909 it was converted into the Broadway Auditorium and was used for conventions and sporting events. The city of Buffalo took it over in 1947 and after a fire destroyed part of the structure, it became the Broadway Garage in 1952, at which time it was extensively renovated. Today, it bears little resemblance to the original castle-like building outwardly, but much of the interior walls and foundation have survived from the old Arsenal.
11. The address is now a parking lot.
12. Chauncey J. Hamlin was the son of Cicero Hamlin, after whom Buffalo's Hamlin Park neighborhood is named. Chauncey was a lawyer and a driving force behind

the Museum of Science. One of his grandsons is the actor Harry Hamlin. Chauncey owned a farm estate in Snyder (Amherst), New York on Harlem Road. He sold the farm to Park School, which still operates its campus at the site at 4625 Harlem Road. Two buildings from the original farm still exist, including the mansion. It is presumed that Mr. Roosevelt spent the night of June 10-11 in the mansion house. The mansion is now called Hamlin Hall.

13. Since demolished, this was part of the DL&W terminal complex at the foot of Main Street. The train shed still stands and is used as a barn for Buffalo Metro Rail cars.
14. *Buffalo Express,* November 2, 1908.
15. *Buffalo Express,* March 19, 1910.
16. Two years later, Captain Butt would perish at sea during the sinking of the Titanic.
17. The Pierce-Arrow automobile was built by Buffalo's Pierce-Arrow Motor Car Company. All Pierce-Arrows were made in Buffalo. In 1909 President Taft had ordered two Pierce-Arrows to serve as official White House vehicles. Presidents from Taft to Franklin D. Roosevelt used Pierce-Arrows as official presidential automobiles.
18. *Buffalo Commercial Advertiser,* April 30, 1910.
19. The Chamber of Commerce Building was demolished in 1986. The Bank of Buffalo was torn down in 1989. The site of both buildings is now occupied by a parking lot.
20. The University Club was a social organization made up of graduates of the prestigious universities of America. Its building still stands and is now the Bellasara apartment building.
21. *Buffalo Commercial Advertiser,* May 2, 1910.
22. This is not the building currently known as the Statler Building. The old Statler Hotel was located at the southwest corner of Swan and Washington and began operating in 1908. The name was changed to the Buffalo Hotel in 1923 when owner Ellsworth Statler opened his new hotel on Niagara Square. The Buffalo Hotel closed in 1967 and was torn down the following year. The land remained vacant until the main entrance of the current baseball stadium was built over it in the late 1980s.
23. *Buffalo Evening News,* January 22, 1915.
24. The Consistory was located next to the Scottish Rite Cathedral. Both buildings are gone, replaced by the Federal Reserve Bank, whose building was converted into the headquarters of the New Era Cap Company.
25. The building, at 256 South Elmwood, still stands and is now Hutchinson Central Technical High School, the author's alma mater.
26. *Buffalo Courier,* January 5, 1917.

27. It may be hard to believe, but for much of the twentieth century, campaigning in earnest for the presidency traditionally began on Labor Day. Primary elections were few. So, prospective candidates did limited public campaigning for the nomination itself, which was largely determined by party bosses at a national convention. The general public had little input into the nomination process.
28. The Broezel Hotel was located near the old Exchange Street Railroad Station. When the station was closed in 1929, business steadily declined and the hotel was closed in 1935. The building was eventually demolished and the site is now occupied by an I-90 exit ramp.
29. Braun's Park, also called Braun's Grove, was a four acre privately owned park in a largely German American neighborhood. It was located on the north side of Genesee directly east of Floss Avenue. Its grounds included pavilions, a guest house and a dance hall. In 1964 the land was sold to a grocery chain and a supermarket and parking lot were built on it. A popular German restaurant also stood on the site for many years. Those buildings are now occupied by other businesses.
30. This was Kenmore's old village hall, demolished in 1936. On the same site, where Delaware Avenue and Delaware Road divide, now stands Kenmore's current village hall.
31. *Buffalo Courier,* September 3, 1912.
32. *Buffalo Express,* November 2, 1916.
33. Ibid.
34. *Buffalo Evening News,* November 2, 1916.
35. *Buffalo Express,* November 2, 1916.
36. presidency.ucsb.edu.
37. Dom Polski means "Polish Home" in English. It was a social center that served the Polish American community. People attended plays, heard speakers and held celebrations and parties there. The building still stands and is now known as the Lt. Col. Matt Urban Human Services Center.
38. *Buffalo Express,* October 22, 1920.
39. *Buffalo Evening News,* January 8, 1921.
40. *Buffalo Express,* January 9, 1921.
41. Ibid.
42. The home still stands but is used as an office building.
43. *Buffalo Express,* July 12, 1922.
44. Ibid.

CHAPTER 10

1. Jean E. Smith, *FDR* (New York: Random House, 2007), 58.
2. Ibid., 59-60n.
3. *Buffalo Courier,* February 24, 1911.
4. *Buffalo Express,* February 4, 1912.
5. Ibid., October 21, 1928.
6. *Buffalo Courier Express,* July 14, 1929.
7. The building still stands and is known as the Walter J. Mahoney State Office Building.
8. *Buffalo Evening News,* August 27, 1930.
9. *Buffalo Courier Express,* October 21, 1930.
10. *Buffalo Evening News,* July 2, 1932.
11. Ibid., October 19, 1932.
12. Ibid.
13. Ironically, Donovan, a World War I hero and respected Buffalo attorney, would eventually earn the respect of Roosevelt as World War II neared. FDR appointed him to increasingly important positions on intelligence gathering. During the war, he organized the Office of Strategic Services (OSS) spy agency, which played an important role in the U.S. war effort and was the forerunner of today's Central Intelligence Agency (CIA).
14. presidency.ucsb.edu.
15. Hyde Park was named for Charles B. Hyde, a Niagara Falls businessman who left funds to the city to develop a park. Though it bears the same name as FDR's home town, that other Hyde Park was named for a colonial governor of New York. The stadium that the president dedicated was demolished in 1998, and a replacement was built and is known as Sal Maglie Stadium.
16. That building still stands today and serves as the city of Buffalo's police and fire headquarters.
17. *Buffalo Courier Express,* October 18, 1936.
18. The front part of the site is now a parking lot and large home/hardware store. Directly behind the store, a large portion of the old plant remains intact, but vacant.
19. The office building of the complex is now the Charter School for Applied Technologies. The old aircraft plant now houses various industrial businesses.

ENDNOTES

20. *Buffalo Courier Express,* November 3, 1940.
21. Ibid.
22. Harry S Truman, "Memorandum Regarding Relations with the Pendergast Machine," January 10, 1952, accessed through teachingamericanhistory.org.
23. The Buffalo Hotel at Swan and Washington was the old Statler Hotel, renamed when the new Statler opened on Niagara Square in 1923.
24. *Buffalo Courier Express,* October 9, 1948.
25. Recently known as Forbes Theater in the Buffalo Christian Center. The building was bought by a developer with plans to incorporate it into a new building project.
26. Offerman Stadium was the city's baseball park. It was demolished in 1962.
27. Memorial Auditorium was a sports and concert arena located at Upper Terrace and Main Street near the Thruway overpass. It was demolished in 2009 and the site is now part of Buffalo's waterfront entertainment area.
28. *Buffalo Courier Express,* October 24, 1952.
29. Ibid., October 11, 1951.
30. From its inception in 1926 the airport, located north of Genesee Street and east of Cayuga, was known as Buffalo Municipal Airport. The name was changed to Greater Buffalo International Airport in 1959, and to Buffalo Niagara International Airport in 1997. Hereafter in this book, the term "Buffalo airport" refers to this facility, the main airport serving the Buffalo area.
31. *Buffalo Courier Express,* October 17, 1956.
32. The Statler had become part of the Hilton hotel chain.
33. Kennedy was wrong. Cleveland was forty-seven years old when he first entered the White House.
34. *Buffalo Courier Express,* May 19, 1960.
35. Ibid., September 29, 1960.
36. The hotel at Buffalo Avenue and Fourth Street went through several changes, was abandoned in 2009 and demolished shortly afterward.
37. *Buffalo Courier Express,* September 29, 1960.
38. Ibid.
39. Ibid.
40. This building, at 761 Fillmore Avenue, still stands and is currently used as a Baptist church.
41. *Buffalo Courier Express,* October 18, 1960.

ENDNOTES

CHAPTER 11

1. The Niagara Falls Air Force Base shared, and still does share, runways with the civilian Niagara Falls airport located to its south.
2. *Buffalo Courier Express,* October 15, 1962.
3. presidency.ucsb,edu.
4. The Western Electric plant was the former Curtiss Aeroplane plant that President Roosevelt had visited in 1940. It now houses various industrial businesses.
5. *Buffalo Courier Express,* November 1, 1976.
6. Now Rust Belt Bar and Grill.
7. *Buffalo News,* September 12, 1984.
8. Decorators' Show House pamphlet from the *Buffalo News* and Junior League of Buffalo, 2013; "Junior League Decorator's Show House," accessed through puttingitallonthetable.com.
9. Email interview with Thomas A. Loughran, January 25, 2016.
10. There were two articles of impeachment. One charged Clinton with providing perjured, false, and misleading testimony to a grand jury concerning a sexual harassment suit against him. The other charged him with obstruction of justice in the same case. The U.S. Senate failed to remove President Clinton from office. Though never tried for perjury or obstruction of justice in a court of law, his Arkansas law license was suspended and he was barred from practicing before the U.S. Supreme Court. He never reapplied for reinstatement in either case.

CHAPTER 12

1. *Buffalo News,* April 21, 2004.
2. The Flight 3407 disaster occurred on February 12, 2009. The small propeller plane went into a stall and crashed into a house in Clarence. A total of fifty persons were killed and the crash was blamed on pilot error.

BIBLIOGRAPHY

BOOKS

Alexander, H.H. *The Life of Guiteau and the Official History of the Most Exciting Case on Record*. Philadelphia: National Publishing Co., 1882.

Alexander, H.H. and Edward D. Easton, stenographers. *Report of the Proceedings in the Case of the United States vs. Charles J. Guiteau*. Washington, D.C.: U.S. Government Printing Office, 1882.

Alexander, Holmes. *The American Talleyrand: The Career and Contemporaries of Martin Van Buren*. New York: Harper and Brothers, 1935.

Armitage, Charles H. *Grover Cleveland as Buffalo Knew Him*. Buffalo: Buffalo Evening News, 1926.

Axelrod, Alan. *A Savage Empire*. New York: Thomas Dunne Books, 2011.

Bauer, K. Jack. *Zachary Taylor: Soldier, Planter*. Baton Rouge: Louisiana State University Press, 1993.

Bernstein, Peter L. *Wedding of the Waters*. New York: W.W. Norton, 2005.

Bingham, Robert W., editor. *Niagara Frontier Miscellany*. Buffalo: Buffalo and Erie County Historical Society, 1947.

Binkley, Wilfred E. *American Political Parties*. New York: Alfred A. Knopf, 1963.

Boulard, Gary. *The Swing Around the Circle*. Bloomington, Ind.: iUniverse, 2008.

Brands, H.W. *Traitor to His Class*. New York: Doubleday, 2008.

Brodsky, Alyn. *Grover Cleveland: A Study in Character*. New York: Truman Talley Books, 2000.

Buffalo Board of Education. *Sixth Annual Report of the Board of School Examiners for 1897*. Buffalo: Haas and Kelley, 1897.

Coakley, Robert W. *The Role of Federal Military Forces in Domestic Disorders, 1789-1878*. Washington, D.C.: U.S. Government Printing Office, 1988.

Cole, David B. *Martin Van Buren and the American Political System*. Princeton: Princeton University Press, 1984.

Craughwell, Thomas J. *Stealing Lincoln's Body*. Cambridge, Mass.: Belknap Press, 2009.

Curtis, James C. *The Fox at Bay: Martin Van Buren and the Presidency, 1837-1841*. Lexington, Ky.: University of Kentucky Press, 1970.

Cutter, William, editor. *Genealogical and Family History of Central New York, Vol. 2*. New York: Lewis Historical Publishing Co., 1912.

Davis, Kenneth S. *FDR: The Beckoning of Destiny*. New York: G.P. Putnam's Sons, 1972.

Davis, William C. *Jefferson Davis, the Man and His Hour*. Baton Rouge: Louisiana State University Press, 1999.

Donovan, Robert J. *The Assassins*. New York: Popular Library, 1964.

Dorsheimer, William and William U. Hensel. *Life and Services of Honorable Grover Cleveland*. Philadelphia: Hubbard Press, 1884.

Douglas, Harry S. *Arcade, N.Y., Progress With a Past: 1807-1957*. Arcade, N.Y.: Arcade Sesquicentennial and Historical Society, 1957.

Dumond, Dwight L. *Antislavery Origins of the Civil War in the United States*. Ann Arbor: University of Michigan Press, 1939.

Dyer, Oliver. *Phonographic Report of the Proceedings of the National Free Soil Convention at Buffalo, N.Y., August 9th and 10th, 1848*. Buffalo: G.H. Derby and Co., 1848.

Earle, Jonathan H. *Jacksonian Anti-Slavery and the Politics of Free Soil, 1824-1854*. Chapel Hill: University of North Carolina Press, 2004.

Emerson, George D., editor. *The Perry's Victory Centenary – Report of the Perry's Victory Centennial Commission, State of New York*. Albany, N.Y.: J.P. Lyon Company, Printers, 1916.

Fagant, John. *The Best of the Bargain: Lincoln in Western New York*. Bloomington, Ind.: AuthorHouse, 2010.

Finkelman, Paul. *Millard Fillmore*. New York: Henry Holt and Co., 2011.

Foner, Eric. *Reconstruction: America's Unfinished Revolution, 1863-1877*. New York: Perennial, 2002.

Fuller, Corydon E. *Reminiscences of James A. Garfield.* Cincinnati: Standard Publishing, 1887.

Garfield, James A., edited by Harry J. Brown and Frederick D. Williams. *The Diary of James A. Garfield, Vol. I-IV, 1848-1881.* Ann Arbor: Michigan State University Press, 1967.

Gould, Lewis L., editor. *American First Ladies.* New York: Routledge, Taylor and Francis Group. 2001.

Griffis, William E. *Millard Fillmore.* Ithaca, N.Y.: Andrus and Church, 1915.

Hamilton, Holman. *Zachary Taylor, Soldier of the Republic.* Indianapolis: Boobs-Merrill, 1941.

Hayes, Rutherford B., edited by Charles R. Williams. *The Diary and Letters of Rutherford B. Hayes, Vol. I-IV.* Columbus, Ohio: Ohio State Archeological and Historical Society, 1922.

Hosack, David. *Memoir of DeWitt Clinton.* New York: J. Seymour, 1829.

Howe, George F. *Chester A. Arthur, a Quarter Century of Machine Politics.* New York: Dodd, Mead and Co., 1934.

Ireland, William W. *Through the Ivory Gate.* Edinburgh, Scotland: Bell and Bradfute. 1889.

Johns, A. Wesley. *The Man Who Shot McKinley.* New York: A S. Barnes and Company, 1970.

Johnson, Reinhard O. *The Liberty Party, 1840-1848.* Baton Rouge, Louisiana State University Press, 2009.

Kane, Joseph N. *Facts About the Presidents.* New York: The H.W. Wilson Co., 1993.

Kasparian, Lance. *Ansley Wilcox House – Historic Structure Report.* Lowell, Mass.: U.S. Department of Interior, 2006.

Kohlsaat, H.H. *From McKinley to Harding: Personal Recollections of Our Presidents.* New York: Charles Scribner's Sons, 1923.

Kunhardt, Dorothy M. and Philip B. Kunhardt Jr. *Twenty Days.* New York: Castle Books, 1965.

Lachman, Charles. *A Secret Life: The Sex, Lies and Scandals of President Grover Cleveland.* New York: Skyhorse Publishing, 2011.

The Liberal Club of Buffalo, 1892-93. Buffalo: Matthews-Northrup Co., 1893.

Lynch, Dennis T. *An Epoch and a Man: Martin Van Buren and His Times.* New York: Horace Liveright, 1929.

Mason, Jeffrey C. and Harry S, Douglass. *Alive in the Spirit Since 1813: The Arcade United Church of Christ, Congregational.* Interlaken, N.Y. Heart of the Lakes Publishing, 1990.

Mayfield, John. *Rehearsal for Republicanism.* Port Washington, N.Y.: Kennikat Press, 1980.

Mayers, Adam. *Dixie and the Dominion.* Tonawanda, N.Y.: Dundern Press, 2003.

McElroy, Robert M. *Grover Cleveland, the Man and Statesman, Vol. I.* New York: Harper and Brothers, 1923.

Miners, Earl S., editor. *Lincoln Day by Day: A Chronology, 1809-1865.* Washington, D.C.: Lincoln Sesquicentennial Commission, 1960.

Minetor, Randi. *Best Day Hikes Buffalo.* Guilford, Ct.: Globe Pequot Press. 2010.

A Narrative of a Tour of Observation Made During the Summer of 1817 by James Monroe, President of the United States, Through the Northeast and Northwest Departments of the Union. Philadelphia: S.A. Mitchell and Ames, 1818.

Nelson, Lyle E. *John Tyler: A Rare Career.* New York: Nova Science Publishers, New York, 2008.

Nevins, Allan. *Grover Cleveland: A Study in Courage.* New York: Dodd, Mead and Co., 1947.

Nevins, Allan, editor. *The Letters of Grover Cleveland, 1850-1908.* Boston: Houghton Mifflin, 1938.

Niven, John. *Martin Van Buren: The Romantic Age of American Politics.* New York: Oxford University Press, 1983.

Norgren, Jill. *Belva Lockwood: The Woman Who Would Be President.* New York: New York University Press, 2007.

Nowak, Martin S. *The White House in Mourning.* Jefferson, N.C.: McFarland and Co., 2010.

Orth, Samuel P. *A History of Cleveland, Vol. I.* Chicago: S.J. Clarke, 1910.

Owens, Robert M. *Mr. Jefferson's Hammer.* Norman: U. of Oklahoma Press, 2007.

Parker, Arthur C. *The Life of General Ely S. Parker.* Buffalo: Buffalo Historical Society, 1919.

Pederson, William D., editor. *A Companion to FDR.* Malden, Mass.: Wiley-Blackwell, 2011.

Percy, John. *Kenmore, New York.* Charleston, S.C.: Arcadia Publications, 1999.

Percy, John W. *Buffalo-Niagara Connections.* Buffalo: Western New York Heritage Press, n.d.

Ratner, Lorman. *Antimasonry: The Crusade and the Party.* Englewood Cliffs, N.J.: Prentice-Hall, 1969.

Rayback, Robert J. *Millard Fillmore: Biography of a President.* Buffalo: Henry Stuart, 1959.

Reeves, Thomas C. *Gentleman Boss, The Life of Chester Alan Arthur.* New York: Alfred A. Knopf, 1975.

Richardson, Darcy G. *Others: Third-Party Politics.* New York: iUniverse, 2004.

Rizzo, Michael F. *Through the Mayors' Eyes.* Morrisville, N.C.: Lulu Enterprises, 2005.

Scarry, Robert J. *Millard Fillmore.* Jefferson, N.C.: McFarland and Co., 2001.

Schlesinger, Arthur M. Jr. *History of U.S. Political Parties, Vol. I: 1789-1860, from Factions to Parties.* New York: Chelsea House, 1977.

Seager, Robert II. *And Tyler Too.* New York: McGraw-Hill, 1963.

Searcher, Victor. *The Farewell to Lincoln.* Nashville: Abingdon Press, 1965.

Severance, Frank H. *An Old Frontier of France.* New York: Dodd, Mead and Co., 1917.

Severance, Frank H. *Publications of the Buffalo Historical Society, Vol. 24.* Buffalo: Buffalo Historical Society, 1920.

Sievers, Harry J. *Benjamin Harrison, Hoosier Statesman.* New York: University Publishers, 1959.

Smith, Gerritt. *Proceedings of the National Liberty Convention Held at Buffalo, N.Y. June 14 and 15, 1848.* Utica, N.Y.: S.W. Green, 1848.

Smith H. Perry, editor. *A History of the City of Buffalo and Erie County, Vol. I.* Syracuse: D. Mason and Co., 1884.

Smith, Jean E. *FDR.* New York: Random House, 2007.

Smith, Theodore C. *The Liberty and Free Soil Parties in the Northwest.* New York: Russell and Russell, 1967.

Sones, Bruce V. *Brigadier General Jefferson C. Davis: Civil War General.* Pickle Partner Publishers, 2014.

Stevens, Kenneth R. *Border: The Caroline and McLeod Affairs...* Tuscaloosa: University of Alabama press, 1989.

Strong, Douglas M. *Perfectionist Politics; Abolitionism and the Religious Tensions of American Democracy.* Syracuse: Syracuse University Press, 1999.

Taylor, Tim. *The Book of Presidents.* New York: Arno Press, 1972.

Todd, Charles S., Benjamin Drake and James H. Perkins. *Sketches of the Civil and Military Services of William Henry Harrison.* Cincinnati: J.A. and U.P. James, 1847.

Transactions of the Oneida Historical Society at Utica. Utica, N.Y.: Oneida Historical Society, 1889.

Trefousse, Hans. *Andrew Johnson: A Biography.* New York: W.W. Norton, 1999.

Trimble, I.P., editor. *The Proceedings of the United States Anti-Masonic Convention.* Philadelphia: 1830.

Vaughn, William P. *The Antimasonic Party in the United States 1826-1843.*
Lexington, Ky.: University Press of Kentucky, 1983.

Wilentz, Sean. *The Rise of American Democracy.* New York: W.W. Norton and Co., 2005.

Wilmers, Merton M. *History of the Niagara Frontier, Vol I.* Chicago: S.J. Clarke, 1931.

Wilson, Major J. *The Presidency of Martin Van Buren.* Lawrence: University
Press of Kansas, 1984.

PERIODICALS

Cleveland, Grover. "His Eulogy of McKinley," accessed through bartleby.com.

Channing, Walter, "Mental Status of Czolgosz, Assassin of President McKinley," *American Journal of Insanity,* October 1902, pp. 23-46.

"Chaubert de Joncaire de Clausonne, Daniel-Marie," in *Dictionary of Canadian Biography,* accessed through biographi.ca.

Cook, Roy. "Brigadier General U.S. Army, Ely S. Parker, Seneca," accessed through americanindiansource.com.

Crocker, Kathleen A. "Account of President Grant's Visit," accessed through roberthjackson.org.

Gaughan, Keven P. "Roosevelt in Buffalo," *Art Voice,* September 13, 2001.

Gee, Denise Jewell. "Old Chimney in Falls Can't Stand Alone," *The Buffalo*
   News, January 18, 2015.

Grant, Harvey. "Did You Know That…," accessed through warsawhistory.org.

Jandura, Greg. "Buffalo's Towering Temple of Transportation." accessed through trainweb.org.

Jandura, Greg. "The Pan-American Exposition 1901," accessed through trainweb.org.

"Liberty Party," accessed through en.wikisource.org.

"The Liberty Party," accessed through alexpeak.com.

Milburn, John G. "Grover Cleveland as Seen by Three Friends," *Scribner's,* April 1927, pp. 344-8.

National Park Service. "Historic American Building Survey, Ansley Wilcox House," September 1973, accessed through lcweb2.loc.gov.

Norgren. Jill. "Belva Lockwood: Blazing the Trail for Women in Law," *Prologue Magazine,* Spring 2005, vol. 37, no. 1, accessed through archives.gov.

"Site of the Peter Buell Porter House," accessed through niagarafallsundergroundrailroad.org.

Truman, Harry S. "Memorandum Regarding Relations with the Pendergast Machine," January 10, 1952, accessed through teachingamericanhistory.org.

Warnes, Kathy. "President James Monroe Inspects Downriver to Detroit," accessed through definitelydownriver.blogspot.com.

White, Truman C., editor. "Milburn, John G.," in *Our Country and Its People, Boston History Vol. 2,* p.33, 1898.

Zwelling, Michael. "Sheriff, Mayor, President, Jailbird?" *Buffalo Magazine,* pp.16-19, imprint of *The Buffalo News,* November 6, 2005.

BIBLIOGRAPHY

NEWSPAPERS

Buffalo Commercial
Buffalo Commercial Advertiser
Buffalo Courier
Buffalo Courier Express
Buffalo Courier and Republic
Buffalo Daily Courier
Buffalo Daily Republic
Buffalo Evening New
Buffalo Evening Post
Buffalo Express
Buffalo Gazette
Buffalo Morning Express
Buffalo News
Buffalo Patriot and Journal
Buffalo Weekly Republic
Daily National Intelligencer
Los Angeles Herald
New York Daily Tribune
New York Herald
New York Times
Signal of Liberty
Toronto Globe
Troy Daily Whig
Washington Daily Union
Washington Republic

INTERNET SOURCES

army.barracks.buffalonet.org
bechsed.nylearn.org
books.google.com
buffaloah.com
buffalocentralterminal.org

BIBLIOGRAPHY

buffalonews.com
buffaloresearch.com
chroniclingamerica.loc.gov
cnn.com
dmna.state.ny.us/forts
fdrlibrary.marist.edu
findagrave.com
fultonhistory.com
genforum.genealogy.com
geni.com/people
globalsecurity.com
historicstructures.com
imaginaryjewishhomelands.wordpress.com
inaugural.senate.gov
jamesgumellchronicles.com
libraryofcongress.gov
maps.google.com
masshist.org
myoakwoodcemetery.com
niagaracounty.com/parks
niagarafallsinfo.com
niagarafrontier.com
niagaraparks.com
nps.gov
presidency.ucsb.edu
suvcw.org/banner/1897parade
theodorerooseveltcenter.org
theodore-roosevelt.com
trainweb.org
trsite.org
ushistory.org
wikipedia.org
wnyheritagepress.org

BIBLIOGRAPHY

PERSONAL AND EMAIL INTERVIEWS

Cichon, Steve. Email exchange, May 2016.

Cole, Heather, curator of Theodore Roosevelt Collection at Houghton Library, Harvard University. Email exchange, May 2016.

Gaughan, Kevin P. Email exchange and telephone conversation, May 2016.

Gates, Steve, town of York, N.Y. historian. Email exchange, November 2014.

Loughran, Thomas A. Email interview, January 25, 2016.

Spencer, Norma, Wyoming County, N.Y. historian. Email exchange, November 2014.

MANUSCRIPTS

A.C. Bullitt letter dated September 5, 1849 to Orlando Brown, from the Orlando Brown Papers at the Kentucky Historical Society.

The Diaries of John Quincy Adams, accessed through masshist.org.

Millard Fillmore Papers, from the collection at the Buffalo History Museum.

Letter from John M. Clayton to Zachary Taylor dated August 29, 1849, from the John M. Clayton Papers at the Library of Congress.

INDEX

Adams, John, 5, 7
Adams, John Quincy
  in Buffalo as former president, 31-32
  Erie Canal and, 6
  Millard Fillmore and, 30-32
  in Niagara Falls, 31
  Peter B. Porter and, 14
Allen, Lewis F., 15, 29, 101-3, 116
American Party, 41-42
Anti-Masonic Party, 26-28, 41
Arcade, N.Y., 46-48
Arthur, Chester A.
  in Perry, 137
  in York, 137

Barnburners, 54, 56, 63
Batavia, N.Y., 27-28, 31, 39, 73, 77, 106, 185, 222, 268
Birney, James, 46-47, 50
Bissell, Wilson S., 109-117, 120-24, 147, 159, 174
Black Rock, 11-12, 14-15, 19-20, 22, 65-66, 80, 102, 181
Booth, John Wilkes, 73-76
Broadway Arsenal, 180, 183-84, 186, 198, 201-05, 208, 218-19
Broadway Auditorium, *see* Broadway Arsenal
Brown, Byron, 277, 279, 280-84
Buchanan, James, 14, 41, 42
Buffalo Barracks, 16-24, 166-67
Buffalo Club, 151-152, 165, 177, 191, 194, 211, 239-40, 259
Bush, George H.W.
  in Buffalo
    as former president, 273
    as vice president, 268-69
Bush, George W.
  in Buffalo
    to campaign for father, 269
    to campaign for presidency, 273-74
    as president, 276-77
  John G. Roberts and, 277

Canisius College, 247, 271
Carter, James E. (Jimmy)
  in Buffalo to campaign for presidency, 259-60
  in Buffalo area
    as former president, 269-70
    as president, 261-63
  in Niagara Falls, 262-63, 269-70
Cass, Lewis, 32, 54-56, 60, 62
Central High School, 174, 200, 220
Chase, Salmon P., 50, 52, 54, 57, 61-62
Chautauqua Institution, 93-94, 137, 180, 216, 219, 225-26, 271
Chisholm, Shirley, 258
Cleaveland, Moses, 15
Cleveland, France Folsom, 107, 109, 111-12, 125
Cleveland, Grover, 101-25
  arrest rumor, 107
  Beaver Island and, 105
  Buffalo visit
    to attend Bissell funeral, 121-24
    between terms, 115-21
    as president, 112-14
    as young boy, 101-2
  death and funeral of, 124-25
  defends Fenians, 81
  description of, 104, 105
  early life, 101-2
  estrangement from Buffalo, 109-12, 124
  Fillmore funeral and, 88-89
  Frances Folsom (wife) and, 107, 109, 111-12
  Halpin Affair, 108-9, 124
  John G. Milburn and, 106, 121-24, 214
  Lewis Allen and, 15, 101-3, 116
  at Lincoln funeral, 77
  Millard Fillmore and, 88-89, 105-6
  McKinley assassination comments, 165, 172
  moves to Buffalo, 101-2
  Niagara Falls State Park and, 15-16
  opposed by Belva Ann Lockwood, 141
  Oscar Folsom and, 107
  referred to by JFK, 242, 244
  Varina H. Davis (Mrs. Jefferson Davis) and, 122

INDEX

Clinton, Hillary R., 271-73, 278, 281-82
Clinton, William J. (Bill)
  in Buffalo
    to campaign for presidency, 270-71
    as former president, 275-79
    as president, 271-73, 281-82
  in Chautauqua, 271
Collins, Christopher, 283
Conscience Whigs, 54, 63
Convention Hall, *see* Elmwood Music Hall
Coolidge, Calvin, 206, 210-12
Court House Park, 20, 30, 36-38, 49, 56-64
Custer, George Armstrong, 82, 84
Czolgosz, Leon, 161-65

Davis, Jefferson C. (Union General), 23
Davis, Jefferson F. (Confederate President)
  at Niagara-on-the-Lake, 123
  not likely in Buffalo, 23
  widow in Buffalo, 122-23
Davis, Varina H. (Mrs. Jefferson Davis), 122-23
Donelson, Andrew Jackson, 42
Donovan, William J., 209, 211, 224
Douglass, Frederick, 55, 57, 60
D'Youville College, 136, 266-67

East Aurora, N.Y., 25-26, 28, 39, 268
Eisenhower, Dwight D., 237-39
Ellicott Club, 147-49, 155, 178, 183, 195, 199, 211-12, 216
Ellicott Square Building, 147-49, 155, 178, 183, 195, 199, 211-12, 216, 268, 279
Elmwood Music Hall, 182, 184-87, 192, 210, 221, 223-24
Erie Canal, 5, 14, 26, 46, 48, 101, 178
Fenian Invasion, 78-81
Fillmore, Abigail, 25-26, 40
Fillmore, Caroline McIntosh, 42, 92
Fillmore, Millard, 22, 25-43
  American Party and, 41-42
  Anti-Masonic Party and, 26-28
  Grover Cleveland and, 88-89, 105-6
  in Congress, 22, 28-29
  death of, 86-92
  death of Abigail Powers Fillmore (Mrs. Millard Fillmore), 40
  description of, 26
  early life, 25-26
  first Buffalo visit, 26
  as former president, 39-43
  Free Soil Party and, 62-63
  J.Q. Adams and, 30-32
  Lincoln funeral and, 77
  marriage to second wife, 42
  meets Buchanan in London, 41
  meets Lincoln in Albany, 70
  meets Van Buren in London, 41
  moves to Buffalo, 26, 28
  moves to East Aurora, 25-26
  opposition to Jackson, 28
  as president in Buffalo, 35-39
  slavery and, 34, 39-40, 43
  succeeds to the presidency, 34
  as vice president, 33-34
  welcomes J.Q. Adams to Buffalo, 30-31
  welcomes A. Johnson to Buffalo, 84-85
  welcomes Lincoln to Buffalo, 72-73
  welcomes Taylor to Niagara Falls, 34, 66
Fillmore, Millard Powers (son), 86, 89, 106
Folsom, Frances, *see* Cleveland, Frances Folsom
Folsom, Oscar, 88, 107
Forest Lawn Cemetery, 4, 40, 91-92, 100, 124, 258
Ford, Gerald R.
  in Buffalo
    as president, 260-61
    as vice president, 258-59
  in Buffalo area as former president, 269
Fort Niagara, 1, 3, 12, 16, 27, 123, 203
Fort Porter, 22, 23, 80, 82, 145, 146, 166, 179, 191
Fort Schlosser, 16-17
Free Soil Party, 32-33, 51, 54-64

319

INDEX

Garfield, James A.
 in Buffalo before presidency, 129-36
 campaigns in Buffalo with Harrison and McKinley, 134-36
 in Chautauqua, 137
 in Niagara Falls, 129-33
Goldwater, Barry, 240, 254-56
Grand Island, N.Y., 17, 30, 105, 220, 227, 251, 254
Granger, Erastus, 6
Grant, Ulysses S.
 in Buffalo
  before presidency, 78, 80-85
  as former president, 95-98
  as president, 94-95
 in Chautauqua, 93-94
 Fenians and, 78-81
 in Niagara Falls, 82
 Ely S. Parker and, 98-100
 statement on Fillmore death, 87
Griffin, James, 262, 266-67
Guiteau, Charles J., 138-40
Guiteau, Julius, 140

Hale, John P.. 53, 55, 61
Hall, Nathan F., 28, 30, 35, 38-39, 92
Harding, Warren G., 206-9, 217-18
Harrison, Benjamin
 Buffalo visit probable before presidency, 137
 campaigns in Buffalo with Garfield and McKinley, 134-36
 in Niagara Falls, 137
Harrison, William Henry, 6-11, 29
 in Buffalo during War of 1812, 10-11
 Liberty Party distrust of, 46
 Robert Morris-Buffalo connection and, 7-8, 15
 and Samuel Wilkeson, 9-10
Haven, Solomon G., 28, 91-92
Hayes, Rutherford B.
 in Buffalo
  before presidency, 126-28
  as former president, 128-29
 in Niagara Falls, 127-28
Hazel, John R., 142, 168, 176, 178, 211
Hoover, Herbert
 in Buffalo
  as commerce secretary, 212
  as former president, 239-40
  to promote European relief, 206-7, 209-10
 in Niagara Falls, 212-13
Humphrey, Hubert, 240, 255, 258
Hutchinson Central Technical High School, 248
Hutchinson High School, 193-94

Jackson, Andrew, 27, 42
Jackson, Robert H., 231
Jefferson, Thomas, 7
 Erie Canal and, 5
 Erastus Granger and, 6
Johnson, Andrew
 in Buffalo as president, 78, 82-86
 in Niagara Falls, 82
 invited to Fillmore funeral, 87
 welcomed by Fillmore, 82-85
Johnson, Lyndon B., 253-57
Joncaire, Daniel, 1-2
Joncaire, Philippe Thomas, 2, 3

Kemp, Jack F., 257, 258-60, 263-67, 271-72
Kennedy, John F., 240
 in Buffalo
  before presidency, 240-42
  campaigns for presidency, 243-46
  as president, 250-53
 in Niagara Falls, 243-44, 250
 reference to Cleveland, 242, 244
Kennedy, Robert F., 253, 257
Know-Nothings, see American Party
Lafayette Hotel, 196-98, 207, 210, 215, 218-19, 221-22, 242
Lafayette Square, 199, 217, 230, 237
Liberty League, 52, 55
Liberty Party, 44-54, 58, 63-64
Lincoln, Abraham
 in Buffalo before presidency, 70-73
 Buffalo visit canceled in 1860, 71
 Millard Fillmore and, 70, 72-73
 funeral in Buffalo, 77-78
 in Niagara Falls, 71
 St. James Hall and, 73, 77
Lockwood, Belva Ann, 140-42

320

INDEX

Madison, James, 6
Mahany, Rowland B., 206
McKinley, William
  in Buffalo
    to campaign for tariff, 142-44
    campaigns with Harrison and Garfield, 134-36
    death and funeral of, 167-72
    at GAR Encampment, 145-53
    at Milburn house, 122, 158-61, 164, 167-69
    at Pan-American Exposition, 156-64
    shooting of, 161-64
    Cleveland comments on assassination of, 165, 172
    John R. Hazel and, 142, 168
    in Niagara Falls, 151-52, 161
    postpones visit to Pan-Am, 157
Memorial Auditorium, 103, 237-39, 241, 245-47, 257-58, 269
Milburn home, 106-7, 122, 124, 153, 155, 158-61, 164-65, 214
Milburn, John, 106-7, 117, 121-24, 153-56, 158, 160, 174, 194, 214
Miller, William E., 239, 250, 255-56, 283
Monroe, James
  in Buffalo as president, 11-13, 21
  Erie Canal and, 6
  at Fort Niagara, 12
  in Niagara Falls, 12
Morris, Robert, 7-8, 15
Music Hall (Main St.), 116-17, 120, 142-44, 176-77, 184
National Liberty Party, 55-56
Niagara Falls, N.Y., 3, 12, 14-16, 22, 31, 34, 71, 82, 127-33, 137, 151-52, 155-56, 161, 163, 177-81, 183, 192, 217, 219, 221, 226-27, 243-44, 247, 250, 254, 262-63, 269-70
Niagara Square, 83-84, 89, 170, 174, 200, 220, 227-31, 251-56, 259
Nixon, Richard, 240
  in Buffalo
    campaigns for presidency, 246-47, 257-58
    as vice president, 241, 242-43

Obama, Barrack, 279-80

Pan-American Exposition, 142, 145, 151-64, 171-72, 179, 214
Parker, Ely S., 98-100
Patriot War, 16-19, 29
Perez, Thomas E., 280, 283
Perry, N.Y., 48, 137, 180
Perry, Oliver Hazard, 8-11
Poinsett Barracks, *see* Buffalo Barracks
Polk, James K., 32, 51, 99
Porter, Augustus, 12, 14-16
Porter, Peter Buell, 10, 12-16, 31, 82, 102

Reagan, Ronald
  in Buffalo
    before presidency, 263-64
    as president, 266-67
Red Jacket, 15, 99-100
Roberts, John G., 277
Rogers, Sherman S., 106, 134-36, 174, 175, 181
Roosevelt, Franklin D.
  in Buffalo
    at airport (Cheektowaga), 222-23
    to campaign for governor, 218-22
    dedicates new federal building, 227-28
    early visits, 215-17
    as governor, 219, 223
    lays cornerstone for state building, 220
    as president, 224-31
    as presidential candidate, 223
    as vice presidential candidate, 217-18
  in Chautauqua, 216, 219, 225-26
  William J. Donovan and, 224
  Robert H. Jackson and, 231
  John G. Milburn and, 214
  in Niagara Falls, 217, 219, 226-27
Roosevelt, Theodore, 67
  in Buffalo
    campaigns for governor, 175
    campaigns for vice presidency, 181-82
    first formal visit, 173
    first known visit, 173
    as former president, 183-85

321

as governor, 178-83
at Milburn house, 122, 153, 155, 167
McKinley funeral and, 169-71
oath of office taken, 168-69, 190
and Pan-American Exposition, 153-56
as president, 168-71
returns as president after McKinley death, 168
rushes to city after McKinley shooting, 165
as vice president, 153-56, 165-67
as NYC police commissioner, 174-75
at Wilcox house, 156, 165, 168
Woodrow Wilson and, 171
in Chautauqua, 180
at Cleveland funeral, 124
John G. Milburn and, 122, 153-56
in Niagara Falls, 155-56, 177-80, 183
not first president to leave country, 67-69
at Olcott Beach, 179
and Woodrow Wilson, 171, 195, 198

St. James Hall, 73, 77, 131, 132, 134
Schlosser's Landing, 18, 30, 66
Scott, Winfield, 19, 39, 80
Smith, Gerritt, 55-56, 63
State University of NY at Buffalo, *see* University of Buffalo
Statler Hilton Hotel, *see* Statler Hotel at Niagara Square
Statler Hotel at Niagara Square, 220, 223, 232-33, 235, 237-43, 247-48, 258, 260-61

Taft, William Howard
in Buffalo
to campaign for presidency, 185-87
as former president, 192-94
as president, 188-92
Taylor, Zachary, 32-34, 54, 62, 65-69
at Black Rock harbor, 65-66
Buffalo visit probable before presidency, 22-23
Canada visit, 66-69

in Niagara Falls, 22-23, 66-69
welcomed by Fillmore, 66
Tilden, Samuel J., 57
Tonawanda and North Tonawanda, 82, 177, 181, 217, 229, 239-40, 243, 251
Truman, Harry S
in Buffalo
as former president, 247-49
as Missouri judge, 232
as president, 233-38
as vice president, 232-33
Trump, Donald J., 282
Tyler, John, 29
Buffalo trip as president canceled, 23-24
Buffalo visit probable as former president, 24
in Niagara Falls, 24

University of Buffalo, 211, 269-70, 273, 275-76, 278, 280
Urban, George, 108, 175, 177, 181

Van Buren, John, 55-57
Van Buren, Martin, 29, 33
in Buffalo
as president, 20-22
as vice president, 13
Free Soil Party and, 54, 60-62
Liberty Party distrust of, 46
meets Fillmore in London, 41
Patriot War and, 18-19

Warsaw, N.Y., 46, 48
Washington, George, 1-3, 7, 27
Buffalo, closest approach to by, 3
Erie Canal and, 5
Niagara Frontier intelligence by, 3
Williams, America, 3-4, 23
Whitman, Walt, 57
Wilcox, Ansley, 119, 165-67, 169, 178, 180-81, 184, 186-87, 190, 211
Wilcox house, 166-67, 170-71, 190, 192
Wilkeson, Samuel, 9-10
Wilson, Woodrow
in Buffalo
to campaign for presidency, 194-98

after McKinley assassination, 171
as president, 199-205
Rowland B. Mahany and, 206
Worth, William, 22

York, N.Y., 137

ABOUT THE AUTHOR

Martin S. Nowak is a native of Buffalo and a long-time resident of Western New York. He has researched the history of the presidents of the United States for many years, and has previously authored *The White House In Mourning*, which detailed the deaths and funerals of the presidents who have died while in office. He has also written history-themed articles for various publications and is a member of the American Historical Association and the Association for a Buffalo Presidential Center.

www.ingramcontent.com/pod-product-compliance
Lightning Source LLC
Chambersburg PA
CBHW050547160426
43199CB00015B/2570